© 2016 Quarto Publishing Group USA Inc.
Original text and illustrations © Ogden Publications

First published in 2016 by Voyageur Press, an imprint of
Quarto Publishing Group USA Inc., 400 First Avenue North, Suite 400,
Minneapolis, MN 55401 USA. Telephone: (612) 344-8100 Fax: (612) 344-8692

quartoknows.com
Visit our blogs at quartoknows.com

Voyageur Press titles are also available at discounts in bulk quantity for industrial or sales-promotional use.
For details contact the Special Sales Manager at Quarto Publishing Group USA Inc.,
400 First Avenue North, Suite 400, Minneapolis, MN 55401 USA.

10 9 8 7 6 5 4 3

ISBN: 978-0-7603-4985-4

Library of Congress Cataloging-in-Publication Data

Title: The Mother Earth news almanac / by the staff of Mother Earth news.
Description: Minneapolis, MN, USA : Voyageur Press, an imprint of Quarto
Publishing Group USA Inc., 2016. | Includes bibliographical references and index.
Identifiers: LCCN 2015037640 | ISBN 9780760349854 (sc : alk. paper)
Subjects: LCSH: Home economics--Handbooks, manuals, etc. | Sustainable
living--Handbooks, manuals, etc. | Organic gardenign--Handbooks, manuals,
etc. | Survival--Handbooks, manuals, etc.
Classification: LCC TX162.2 M685 2016 | DDC 640--dc23
LC record available at http://lccn.loc.gov/2015037640

Acquiring Editor: Thom O'Hearn
Project Manager: Caitlin Fultz
Art Director: Cindy Samargia Laun
Cover Designer: Ann McCampbell
Book Design and Layout: Diana Boger

Printed in the United States of America

MOTHER EARTH NEWS ALMANAC

A GUIDE THROUGH THE SEASONS

New Edition!

By the Staff of MOTHER EARTH NEWS

VOYAGEUR
PRESS

This book is dedicated to Mr. and Mrs. Richard Shuttleworth,
Mr. and Mrs. Quentin Hendricks, Milton Kirkpatrick, and all the MOTHER EARTH NEWS
subscribers and readers, whose warm support has made so much possible.

CREDITS FROM THE ORIGINAL EDITION

RESEARCH FOR THIS BOOK was done by Bob Arnold, Bob Crudele,
David Jordan, Elizabeth Kandare, Gene Logsdon, Julie Needham, Esther Shuttleworth,
Jane Shuttleworth, John Shuttleworth, Kim Zarney, and David Zavortink.
Copy written and proofread by Kenny Hodges, Julie Needham, Jane Shuttleworth,
Cass Wester, and David Zavortink—with some special assistance from
Gene Logsdon—under the direction of John Shuttleworth.
Index by Cass Wester and David Zavortink.
Fantastical artwork by Kim Zarney.

SPECIAL ACKNOWLEDGMENTS FROM THE ORIGINAL EDITION

Some of the material in this book originally appeared in different form in the
magazine MOTHER EARTH NEWS, published by MOTHER EARTH NEWS, INC., and/or
was used on the syndicated radio program, *News from the MOTHER EARTH NEWS*, distributed
by MOTHER EARTH NEWS, INC. and/or appeared in the syndicated newspaper feature,
"The MOTHER EARTH NEWS," distributed by the Register and Tribune Syndicate, and/or
appeared in *LIFESTYLE! Magazine*, published by MOTHER EARTH NEWS, Inc.

Special thanks to *Organic Gardening* magazine, Rodale Press, Inc., for permission to
reprint the companion-planting information on pages 54–57 of this book, and to Deere
& Co. for permission to reprint farm and planting charts (especially the copyrighted
John Deere Handy Acreage Guide) in the Charts and Tables section of this book.

CONTENTS

FOREWORD . 9

THE PLANET EARTH . 10
ITS PLACE IN SPACE, ITS SEASONS, HOW THEY GOT THAT WAY, AND WHAT WE CAN DO ABOUT IT

SPRING . 12
THE TIME OF AWAKENING

SUMMER . 58
THE TIME OF GROWTH

AUTUMN . 104
THE TIME OF MATURING

WINTER . 152
THE TIME OF REST

CHARTS & TABLES . 192

INDEX . 230

FOREWORD

WHEN JOHN AND JANE Shuttleworth founded MOTHER EARTH NEWS about fifty years ago, little did they imagine that the tiny startup launched from the kitchen table of a summer cottage would grow into one of the most recognized and successful names in magazine publishing.

What started as a simple newsletter—a printed clearinghouse for information on self-reliance, rural living, ecological stewardship, and a decentralized lifestyle—quickly became the holy word for the "Back to the Landers" of the 1970s. The message was clear, and it struck a chord with the growing number of people disillusioned with a broken society: take control of your own lives, live lightly on the planet, and don't put all your faith in government.

In just three years the magazine exploded to include a syndicated radio show and newspaper feature, a sister publication called *Lifestyle!*, a mail-order book business, and a mail-order general store specializing in practical tools and merchandise. People were hungry for information, and the enterprising Shuttleworths struck off on yet another course to help spread the word through book publishing.

Thus was born the MOTHER EARTH NEWS *Almanac*, a compendium of inspiration and old-timey wisdom, made available in print to our readers. Content extracted from the pages of the periodical was blended with a range of new pieces written to guide readers through the exciting world of alternative energy; owner-built homes; and healthy, organic food. The *Almanac* became a bestseller, owing to its casual, conversational tone, its accessible hand-rendered graphics, and its real bargain price.

A familiar adage has it that the more things change, the more they stay the same. From our vantage point nearly five decades later, it's clear that people still seek a richer, more fulfilling life and are still hungry for the tools to make that happen. This new MOTHER EARTH NEWS *Almanac* features many of the timeless topics that made the original edition such a reader favorite. While more things than you'd expect have stayed the same over the years, we have made considered and careful updates throughout. (We've also removed a few topics due to changing times.)

You'll find, presented in the same friendly and approachable style as the original, features that just don't go out of date—money-saving tips, wild food foraging, weather wisdom, organic growing techniques, crafts, kitchen know-how, homestead animal husbandry, sensible home finance, and much more. Like comfort food for the spirit, the *Almanac* will leave you satisfied and have you coming back for more.

Richard Freudenberger
Senior MOTHER EARTH NEWS Editor and
Research Coordinator, 1978–1990

THE
PLANET EARTH

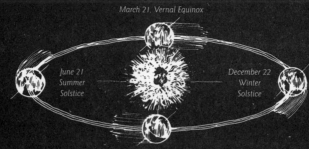

March 21. Vernal Equinox

June 21
Summer
Solstice

December 22
Winter
Solstice

September 23: Autumnal Equinox

ITS PLACE IN SPACE, ITS SEASONS,
HOW THEY GOT THAT WAY, AND
WHAT WE CAN DO ABOUT IT

THE "BLACK VOID OF SPACE"—as we sometimes say—is neither as black nor as empty as popular folklore would indicate. It now seems fairly certain that the detectable universe contains at least one trillion galaxies, each of which is made up of billions of stars. Around each star, in turn, may revolve several planets, many of which have satellites of their own.

It is estimated that a single galaxy, the Milky Way, contains a minimum of 100 billion stars. On the edge of that cluster, nearly 27,000 light years from its center, is our own sun . . . circled by nine known planets.

One of those planets (we call it Earth) revolves—at a distance ranging from about 91,500,000 to 94,500,000 miles—once around the sun every 365 days, 6 hours, and 53 seconds. At the same time, the earth rotates on its own axis (which is tipped at an angle of almost 23½ degrees to the plane of orbit) once each 23 hours, 56 minutes, and 4.09 seconds.

We call every one of the earth's complete circuits of the sun a year—and, if the globe on which we live "sat up straight" (instead of being canted over about 23½ degrees the way it is), every day of every year would be almost exactly the same at any given spot on the planet's surface. As it is, however, that seemingly insignificant little tilt is the major reason that the earth's Northern and Southern Hemispheres enjoy opposing summer-winter and spring-fall seasons.

Thanks to that tilt, you see, the planet's North Pole points the whole 23½ degrees toward the sun only once—on June 21—every year. In the same fashion, the earth's South Pole also points the whole 23½ degrees toward the sun just once—on December 22—each year. And for brief moments twice every orbit—on March 21 and September 23—the globe's slant is directly "crossways" to the sun.

These four specific positions along each circuit that the earth makes around the sun have been precisely plotted. They have also been named. The two instances when one of the planet's poles momentarily points as directly as possible at the sun—in June and December—are both known as a solstice (Latin for "sun stands still"). The positions halfway between—in March and September—when the earth's tilt is exactly sideways to the sun, and day and night are of equal length at all points on the globe's surface, are both called an equinox.

It should be apparent that the Northern Hemisphere receives the maximum possible sunlight on June 21 and the minimum possible solar energy on December 22, whereas the southern half of the planet does just the opposite. It seems logical, then, to expect June 21 to be the warmest day north of the equator and December 22 to be the coldest— and vice versa in the Southern Hemisphere.

Just as the hottest part of the day is never at high noon but a couple of hours later, the earth's atmosphere moderates the heating and cooling of the planet and causes its temperature fluctuations to "lag"—by several weeks. Thus, the four neat dates pinpointed on its orbit around the sun. For this reason, the two equinoxes and two solstices mark the beginnings—rather than the midterms—of each hemisphere's four yearly astronomical periods, called seasons.

APPROXIMATE LENGTH OF THE SEASONS			
Northern Hemisphere	**Southern Hemisphere**	**Length of season**	
		Days	**Hours**
Spring	Autumn	92	20
Summer	Winter	93	14
Autumn	Spring	89	19
Winter	Summer	89	1

It should also be noted that—due to influences exerted by some of the other heavenly bodies mentioned above, due to the slightly flattened shape of the earth itself, and due to some other complicating factors—our planet's orbit is not exactly circular nor is the globe's speed entirely uniform at all points along its path. For these reasons the March 21, June 21, September 23, and December 22 beginning dates of the four seasons for each hemisphere are only averages. Even more interesting is the fact that the length of the seasons vary by as much as four and a half days, as shown in the accompanying table.

All in all, the origins of the seasons are a lot more complex than most of us realize. The forces of the universe seem to be in good hands, however, so we might just as well settle back and enjoy our yearly swings around the sun . . . which is exactly what this almanac is designed to help you do.

SPRING

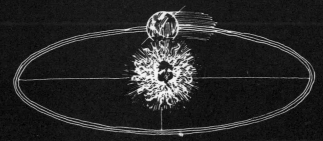

March 21. Vernal Equinox

THE TIME OF AWAKENING

FOR ALL PRACTICAL PURPOSES, spring generally seems to slip into the North Temperate Zone sometime during mid-March. Astronomically speaking, however, the starting date for the whole affair—the vernal (which means "spring") equinox—is March 21. From this date—when the sun seems to circle the globe at the equator—Ole Sol will appear to move further north every day until the summer solstice, when the fiery sphere will seem to swing around the earth at the Tropic of Cancer. Hence the Anglo-Saxon word "spring," which means "rising."

Just the reverse is true in the Southern Hemisphere, of course. There, March 21 marks the autumnal equinox and the beginning of fall. As the days grow longer north of the equator, the nights will correspondingly lengthen for the bottom half of the globe. As the farmers of Nebraska begin plowing, their counterparts in Argentina shall harvest. Baby lambs will be born in Montana at the same time their New Zealand relatives are sent to market. It's a time for the first wild salad in Minnesota and adding the last jar of homemade preserves to a groaning cupboard on a cattle station in Australia. Sail on, sweet universe!

EGGSHELL PLANTERS

SEEDLING

SOIL

EGGSHELL

CUTWORM COLLAR

BOTTOM REMOVED

STYROFOAM SEEDLING CONTAINERS

PEAT CUPS

THE ART OF EARLY PLANTING

As ANY GARDENER KNOWS, sowing plants indoors in late winter or early spring gives the flowers or vegetables a valuable head start (especially in the northern parts of the country where the growing season is none too long). The only trouble is that delicate root systems suffer when seedlings have to be coaxed out of flats or small pots, and—even if a young plant survives the shock of transplanting—its growth is likely to be set back.

The solution, obviously, is to use planting containers that come away from the roots easily, or needn't be removed at all when the seedling is set out—and that's just what smart gardeners do. Everyone has his own favorite method, of course, and here are a few of those ideas to help prime *your* creative juices.

Many folks start their plants in commercially prepared peat cups that simply disintegrate in the soil when the new sprouts are set out. A cheap equivalent of this excellent method is to sow in cardboard egg cartons (one seed to a cup if you're pretty sure most of them will germinate). The box can be cut apart and the little sections put in the earth "as is" at transplanting time, as the paper fiber will soon rot in the damp ground.

The problem with the egg carton method, though, is that you'll have to water the seedlings very often (moisture isn't retained well by soft cardboard) and the containers may start to disintegrate before you want them to. There's an easy way around the difficulty, however: Co-opt the eggshells as well as the box (break the eggs so that you have a good-size end left whole) and plant the seeds in the shells, which you can set in the cartons for convenience. Some gardeners say that you can put

continued on next page

the eggshells in the ground just like peat pots and trust to the growing roots to crack them open, while others prefer to peel away at least part of the container at transplanting time. All who've tried the idea, however, agree that the minerals in the shell are beneficial to the soil.

Along with these disintegrating seed pots, there are a whole slew of easy-release types that can simply be popped off or stripped away without disturbing a seedling at all. One Missouri gardener tells us that he's had excellent results with scrounged Styrofoam cups. He says that the Styrofoam retains moisture well and insulates the seedlings from sudden changes of temperature, besides peeling off easily when it's time to set the plants out. (If he's putting in tomatoes, he cuts the bottoms out of the cups and uses what's left to make each plant a collar against cutworms.)

When it comes right down to it, there's almost no container you can't use for early planting, as long as it's temporarily waterproof and easy to remove. (Cut-down paper milk cartons and yogurt containers come to mind.) It's a satisfying feeling to take a "useless" object and do something important with it. Sort of like starting a new life . . . and what more pleasant recycling project could you ask for?

GRANOLA IS VERY NUTRITIOUS and very easy to bake from scratch. When made from the following recipe, it's also downright delicious!

1. MIX
2 cups rolled oats
2 cups rolled wheat
1½ cups shredded unsweetened coconut
1 cup wheat germ
1 cup chopped nuts
1 cup hulled sunflower seeds
½ cup sesame seeds
½ cup bran
1 cup ground toasted soybeans

2. HEAT
½ cup oil
½ to 1 cup honey (or 1 cup honey)
1 to 2 teaspoons vanilla
3. COMBINE honey-oil mixture with dry ingredients and mix.
4. BAKE on oiled cookie sheets at 375°F for 20 to 30 minutes, stirring more and more frequently as granola becomes toasted and crispy.

Buy the above ingredients from a natural food store, or the organic section of your grocery store, and add to or subtract from the basic formula until you find the exact combination that suits your family or tribe best. As long as your original mixture is seven parts dry to one part wet and you follow all four steps, you can't go wrong!

GREAT TRILLIUM

BLACK MORELS

BRUSH PILE

SPRING PLEASURES

DON'T LET WORK WEASEL you out of an enjoyable spring. If you can't find time to sit down beside a wild-flower and keep it company for a couple of hours, you might as well go someplace and sell life insurance. Reserve one whole day each week (at least) for:

- **HUNTING MOREL MUSHROOMS.** Often called "sponge mushrooms" or "honeycombs," this delicacy grows where you find it, especially under elm, pin oak, cedar, and white ash trees. Get yourself acquainted with a good, ole-time mushroom hunter and have him show you what you're looking for. When you hit it right, you can fill a peck basket with the delicious munchies in minutes. Then again, you may not find any morels at all—which isn't so hard to take either, not with the May woodlands around you.
- **BURNING BRUSH PILES.** Although it's usually called work, this job is soothing to the spirit—don't ask me why. Just go out and set fire to a stack of trimmed tree branches and uprooted scrub growth on a March evening during the first real thaw. Do be sure to conduct the undertaking on a garden or field plot if at all possible—the ashes are rich in lime and potash.
- **RIVER MEDITATION.** This one is guaranteed to be the most effective of all spring replenishers of mind and body . . . and it's probably the easiest too. Just find yourself a private stretch of river or stream on the season's first really warm day, deposit your clothes on a log sticking out into the water, and jump in. Then you climb back on the log and just plain sit there, concentrating on the gentle breeze that is drying you off. Lose yourself in being tranquil.

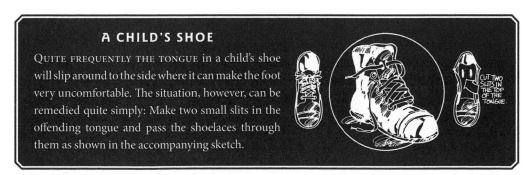

A CHILD'S SHOE

QUITE FREQUENTLY THE TONGUE in a child's shoe will slip around to the side where it can make the foot very uncomfortable. The situation, however, can be remedied quite simply: Make two small slits in the offending tongue and pass the shoelaces through them as shown in the accompanying sketch.

CUT TWO SLITS IN THE TOP OF THE TONGUE.

Wild Foods

DURING ONE SEASON OR ANOTHER, nearly every scrap of the common cattail—found in almost every temperate section of the world—is edible. The plant can be consumed in so many different ways, in fact, that experienced wild-food foragers call it the "supermarket of the swamps."

From earliest spring to latest fall, any stand of cattails should yield you a bucketful of "Cossack asparagus" in minutes. This vegetable is the white, tender, inner portion of the plant's stem. It can be harvested by grabbing the inside leaves of a stalk and pulling as you would leaves from an ear of corn. The stem should break off crisply down inside the outer leaves, exposing a white, celery-like piece of mild-tasting stem that is anywhere from 1 inch to 1 foot long.

Wash it in clean water and chop it up raw for salads. It's also good cooked in stews. Cossack asparagus is at its absolute prime when taken in the spring from plants no more than 2 feet tall.

A little later in the year, the green spikes on top of a stand of cattails can be boiled in salted water and eaten like roasting ears. They're a little dry but, when doused in butter and eaten piping hot, have a definite "corny" taste that is quite satisfying.

Later still (in early and midsummer) cattail pollen can be collected and—if stored in glass jars—kept for months. For a new taste treat, try mixing the bright yellow powder into your next batch of pancakes. Use half the flour called for and use the powder for the other half.

Cattail roots can be pulled up, dried, ground, and used as a starchy flour for baking purposes at any time of the year, and the little potato-like bulbs on the roots are especially good in the spring. Harvest the knobs, boil 'em, and serve 'em with butter, or cook a batch with the next roast you prepare. You're sure to like their nutty-potato flavor.

ANALYZE THE SOIL

How, as a prospective buyer, can you tell if a particular piece of land will produce good crops? Well, the simplest way to make a quick check (assuming the acreage you want is lying fallow) is by looking over nearby gardens and farms that have the same kind of soil. If your potential neighbors are raising noteworthy harvests, chances are good that you can too.

Remember, also, that the best acreage usually raises the neatest farmsteads and most comfortable farmers. Sturdy, well-painted barns and outbuildings tended by cheerful landowners are frequent sights in areas of rich soil—few and far between where the earth is poor.

Of course, when it comes right down to it, you'll probably want to analyze the soil on any piece of land that you're really serious about purchasing. To do that, take maybe a pound of dirt—surface to 5 inches down—from various sections of the acreage you're examining. Each sample should be representative of a

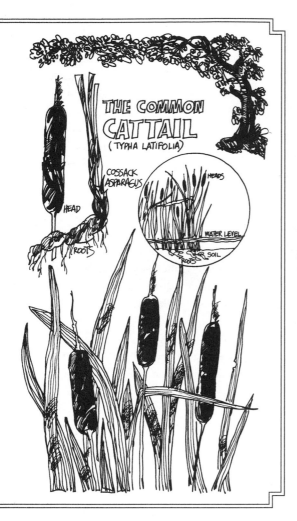

THE COMMON CATTAIL
(TYPHA LATIFOLIA)

COSSACK ASPARAGUS

HEAD

ROOTS

HEADS

WATER LEVEL

ROOTS   SOIL

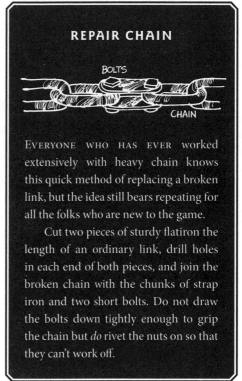

REPAIR CHAIN

BOLTS

CHAIN

EVERYONE WHO HAS EVER worked extensively with heavy chain knows this quick method of replacing a broken link, but the idea still bears repeating for all the folks who are new to the game.

Cut two pieces of sturdy flatiron the length of an ordinary link, drill holes in each end of both pieces, and join the broken chain with the chunks of strap iron and two short bolts. Do not draw the bolts down tightly enough to grip the chain but *do* rivet the nuts on so that they can't work off.

particular area—one from a hill, another from a low spot, and so on—and kept separate, in a clean, sealable bag. A couple of collections per acre are plenty.

Dry the dirt and take it to your county agent or the local extension office. Many universities and colleges have labs that run analyses on such samples, and the extension office will send your collection to one of the labs. The soil will be tested for pH and nutrients, and you'll get recommendations for how to amend it for planting.

CULTIVATE CLAY

DON'T TRY TO PLOW, rototill, hoe, or otherwise cultivate clay soils when the ground is wet, unless you want an assortment of clods so hard that you can use the biggest for bowling balls.

Hold off working such earth until it has dried out enough to become crumbly. Test it by squeezing a little of it as hard as you can in your fist. The ball of dirt so formed should fall apart when gently pushed with your thumb.

FIGHT POLLUTION

. . . WITH A CAMERA

SOMETIMES THE BATTLE FOR a cleaner environment can get downright discouraging. All too often, that is, the fight boils down to lone individuals and shoestring environmental groups squared off against an unbeatable combination of "business as usual" money, lawyers, and political clout. Naturally, in such an uneven match, the big boys who seem to have such a vested interest in making money all too often come out the winner.

It's very important, then, to know that you can arm yourself with a real "equalizer" before you lock horns with any powerful, nonenvironmentally friendly poltroon.

And what, pray tell, is this magic lever? Nothing more than a simple, ordinary, camera. A picture is worth a thousand words, you know, and *protest photography* has been used to save the environment since at least the turn of the century.

A long time ago a fellow named Andrew Putnam Hill built himself a darkroom in (are you ready for this?) a burned-out tree and began documenting the still-unspoiled beauty of California's Big Basin region. Hill's pictures were good—so good, in fact, that they inspired the California legislature to declare Big Basin a state park. Truly, one man plus one camera can move mountains (or, even more difficult, congressmen).

Hill's success has been repeated down through the years by thousands of other environmental activists working on local, state, national, and even international levels. Perhaps the most dramatic of all examples of changing environmental awareness with a single frame of film occurred when our astronauts snapped the first color photograph of the earth from outer space. That haunting image of our tiny, fragile—and exquisitely lovely—planet suspended alone against endless nothing, dramatized the precious nature of Spaceship Earth and kicked off the whole modern environmental movement.

You don't have to orbit the planet with lens to strike a meaningful blow for conservation, however—as a teenager from Fair Oaks, California, proved. Anyone who can intelligently take a picture can use that skill to advantage in the fight to save the environment.

This particular young man became just a little exasperated when his town allowed some slobs to dump junk cars on a plot of land that was earmarked for a city park. So he took a number of photographs of the wrecks and distributed large prints of the pictures (with appropriate publicity) to the Chamber of Commerce officials at their next meeting. You can guess the rest.

Think about it. What would happen if you managed to feature your region's biggest polluters in full, living sewage and belching smokestack detail on the front page of the local newspaper?

As Ansel Adams said, "The environment is only as safe as people—knowing about what is happening—want it to be." With a camera and a little practice, you can help make sure that folks *do* know what is happening.

GERMINATION TEMPERATURES

SOME OF THE REALLY OLD farming manuals state that corn should be planted when the oak leaves are the size of a squirrel's ear. This surely meant something to great-grandpa, but leaves most modern would-be tillers of the soil wondering just how the hell big a squirrel's audio appendage actually is.

Well, to heck with it, especially since this enlightened age has turned up a far more scientific and sure-fire way of determining when to tuck corn—or any other seed—into the ground.

Stick a soil thermometer about 4 inches into the good earth and take its temperature. If the instrument registers 55°F or less, you're best off forgetting the whole idea of sowing for a few days. Most seeds won't germinate worth a hoot until soil temperatures climb to around 60°F. And, as might be expected, they'll germinate faster at somewhat higher readings if sufficient moisture is present.

MAKE A DIRT CATCHER FOR YOUR DRILL

REMODELING AN OLD HOUSE is a great recycling idea, but it does involve a good many unusual and dirty jobs, such as boring holes in the ceiling for additional wiring, pipes, and more. You can make that particular task a lot more pleasant by rolling up a stiff cardboard funnel and fastening it to the drill bit with a wire guide at the dirt catcher's top and a rubber band at its bottom. It's a simple idea—just the ticket for keeping plaster, dust, and debris out of your eyes and hair.

THE PESKY ANT

HOW'S THAT AGAIN? You just opened the kitchen cupboard and found a whole army of little red ants running all over the honey jar?

Take heart! The sweet tooth that brought the little pests into the house in the first place can also help you get 'em out. Mix a solution of sugar (or honey) and water (the ratio isn't critical), dip sponges in the syrup, squeeze out the excess moisture, and leave these homemade ant traps around where the invaders are thickest. When your lures are swarming with the hungry insects, drop the sponges into a pail of boiling water and start again.

Or, if you don't want to snare the ants, you can try repelling them. Clean the pantry floor and shelves thoroughly (especially that honey jar) and cover the whole area with fine salt. Just leave it there for a while and the little pests will go away.

CONSERVE THE SOIL

An inch of rain puts 27,154 gallons of water on an acre of land. And, if that acre is an already-soaked bare hill, most of the liquid races right on off to create a flood problem for folks living downstream. On its way, that same water takes a goodly amount of soil with it—as much as twenty tons per surface acre after a hard 5-inch downpour!

It's quite evident, then, that soil and water conservation should not be just another government project. It should be *your* project.

Do build ponds to hold rainfall close to its point of impact and do keep your land under a winter cover crop whenever possible. It's also a wise idea to plant rows *around*, rather than up and down, all slopes and—on really steep ground—to alternate strips of grain or other crops with grass. Don't drain every pothole in sight and don't fall-plow ground that is subject to high erosion.

Give your children and grandchildren the most valuable possession on earth—the earth itself in a healthy condition.

"I planted my garden when the moon was in Taurus... and the whole dang thing died!"

I won't say planting by the signs of the moon is a mistake, but it sure takes a lot of faith. My mother's grandpa and his one-eyed cousins, for instance, say to plant potatoes in the dark of the moon. But all my German ancestors, on the other side of the family, hold that that isn't necessarily always the best idea. *Early* potatoes, according to the second set of experts, have to be put in the ground when the horns of our natural satellite are pointed up or else the spuds will grow too deep. Then again, *everybody* knows that taters are traditionally supposed to be planted on Good Friday, which absolutely *never* occurs in the dark of the moon (although, where I live, it sometimes snows on Good Friday). As I said, it takes faith.

Of course, gardening "by the signs" goes a whole lot deeper than just paying attention to the moon. Folklore has it that Cancer, Scorpio, Libra, and Pisces are crackerjack symbols to plant under (especially Scorpio for corn). Gemini isn't bad either, particularly when it comes to vining niceties like cucumbers and melons.

That same folklore, however, claims that Virgo is good for flowers but nothing else. Since most all plants have flowers and can't produce unless those buds blossom, the Virgo bit has always assaulted my credibility even worse than the rest.

What it boils down to is that a fair number of good gardeners still swear by following astrological signs. The rest of us lack faith and just swear, period.

LIFT UP WHEN VESSEL IS FULL

PLUNGER DROPS TO STOP FLOW

A FUNNEL SHUTTER-OFFER

ONE OF LIFE'S MAJOR small frustrations takes place almost every time someone tries to fill a blind container through a funnel and—like as not—runs the can, barrel, or whatever over. A second of life's major small frustrations then follows: when the same individual jerks the funnel away, thereby losing all the liquid that it still contained.

Well, we don't have the answer to the first problem yet, but the simple little funnel shutter-offer shown here will sure solve the second . . . making the score "one frustration down and one to go."

STONE STOPS HORSE FROM WASTING FEED

PLACE A LARGE, SMOOTH stone in the middle of the feed box and your horse will no longer eat so rapidly that he throws his grain out of the container.

MULCH GARDENING

MULCH GARDENING IS A great way to go if you don't go too soon. That is, when you apply mulch too early, you often insulate the cold, wet ground from the warming sun and thereby do little more than "help" your garden off to a slow, stunted start. You're generally better advised, then, to hold off mulching the vegetable patch until hot weather comes.

Except for exceptions, such as strawberries.

Strawberries *like* cool, moist ground and you can mulch the little blighters just as soon as you set 'em out in the spring if you want to. The "old" plants—the ones you put out last year or the year before—will, of course, already be covered with the mulch that protected them through the winter. As soon as they start growing again, rake the covering off their tops (so it won't smother 'em) and down into the middle of the rows for . . . mulch.

PROTECT PLANTS FROM CUTWORMS

YOUNG CABBAGE AND TOMATO plants can be protected from cutworms by cutting both ends out of metal cans or the bottom off a Styrofoam cup and imbedding one of the cylinders about 2 inches deep around the stem of each plant.

A TEMPORARY SCAFFOLD

EVERYBODY NEEDS a good scaffold occasionally, but nobody seems to know a handy way to put one together. Here, then—once and for all—is an extremely simple manner in which an ordinary ladder can be rigged to support one end of a plank. Set up a second ladder in the same way to hold the other end of the board and move the whole assembly as desired.

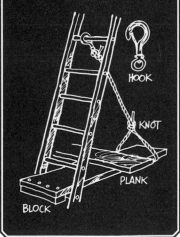

HOOK

KNOT

PLANK

BLOCK

COLUMBINE

You know, one of the nicest things about sustainable living is the fact that we can *all* get in on it. Every day, everyone—from grade-school child to retired grandpa—darn well *can* contribute something meaningful toward preserving our planet's priceless natural environment.

That's an important thought to consider, by the way, as all too often we let ourselves be bamboozled into believing that the so-called "action" is taking place somewhere else. This is not true at all. When it comes to the environment, we *are* the action.

Every decision you make today—whether you'll drive the car instead of walk; or burn the newspaper rather than recycle it; or throw away the garbage instead of starting a compost pile—directly affects the environment of your neighborhood, your town, your nation, and *your* planet. Not just now, but from this point on. That's a big responsibility.

Sure, sure . . . it may *seem* small and unimportant to turn off the lights every time you're the last one out of a room, but there's more than *300 million people* living in this country now. If each one of us turns out the lights that aren't being used, well, that figures out to a lot of hydroelectric power, nuclear generators, and strip mining of coal that we *won't* have to worry about every year. And *that* is a very good thing for the planet.

Of course, there's another side to this coin that's just as important: It's the fact that if everyone in your family DOES keep all the lights and appliances firmly switched OFF when they're not in use, you're going to be pleasantly surprised right in the pocketbook when your next electric bill comes around. Because it's

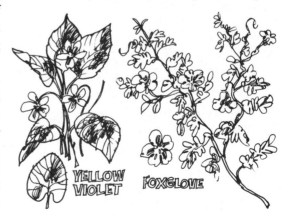

YELLOW VIOLET   FOXGLOVE

HOW TO SCALD MILK

It's extremely difficult to keep milk from burning and sticking to the bottom of the pan when boiling or scalding the liquid as some recipes require . . . unless you first put a small amount of water into the pot and heat it to boiling before adding the milk.

going to be a couple more dollars *less* than it otherwise would have been.

Green living, then, doesn't cost—it PAYS . . . both in the short and the long run. That's a powerful idea and you can put it to work right now, a hundred times a day.

Consider your transportation, for example: If you MUST drive a car, you can drastically lessen its impact on the environment by combining errands whenever possible. One trip is better than three, in other words. Leaving the gas guzzler at home and using public transit, of course, is better yet. And walking or riding a bike, whenever possible, is best of all. That last idea—by the way—simultaneously cuts air pollution, leaves more dollars in your pocket, *and* solves the infuriating problem of finding a parking space!

It takes twelve trees to make one ton of paper, and every family in America squanders several tons of that commodity each year. You can help reverse the trend and—again—cut *your* living expenses by substituting a rag or sponge in the kitchen and cloth handkerchiefs and napkins for paper tissues and towels. Recycle and share with friends the magazines and newspapers you do read and cancel your subscriptions to those you don't. When you go shopping, refuse all plastic sacks and extra wrappings that you don't really need but save and reuse the ones you do carry home—or bring your own recyclable bags.

You'll find that you both consume and pollute less if you buy clothes and shoes of better quality, and then take care of them so they last longer. Forget the insane fashion trends. Buy what YOU like and then live with it long enough to really enjoy it. Life is much more satisfying that way and your clothes will actually cost you a lot less.

The idea, of course, is that nobody's asking you to scrimp and suffer in the name of the environment. On the contrary: By consuming thoughtfully and conscientiously, instead of blindly and wastefully—you can both take a little pressure off the planet AND noticeably raise your standard of living. The air you breathe, the water you drink, the food you eat will be less polluted; your surroundings will be more pleasant; and you'll spend fewer dollars in the process.

Sustainable living doesn't cost—it PAYS.

ENLARGE A ROOM

SOME ROOMS IN HOUSES and apartments are so small that they're almost worthless. Occasionally, however, a cramped kitchen or other room can be "enlarged" enough to relieve an intolerable situation . . . by merely changing the hinges on a door so that it swings out instead of in.

PURPLE MARTINS

PURPLE MARTINS ARE AMONG the most effective natural insect controls known, and North Americans have long had an affinity for these handsome birds. Resourceful Native Americans were already attracting martins with nesting sites made from hollowed-out gourds when the first white settlers arrived on the continent, and the European immigrants soon adopted the practice. Today, specially constructed, multicompartment purple martin houses are familiar fixtures in many farming communities.

Martins are the largest members of the swallow family and feed exclusively on airborne bugs—if it doesn't fly, they don't recognize it as food. On a daily basis, these birds consume close to their own body weight in food, and a four-ounce purple martin could—conceivably—eat 14,000 mosquitoes in one twenty-four-hour period. These efficient insect catchers do not limit themselves to such an exclusive diet, however. Although martins *do* devour more than their share of mosquitoes every day, they also feast on flies, beetles, moths, and many other airborne pests at the same time.

Before European settlers changed eastern North America from a heavily forested wilderness to neatly manicured farms and cities, the purple martin often nested in dead trees and hollow stumps. As such habitat was cleared, the population of this valuable bird declined until it reached an all-time low—probably sometime in the early 1960s. Thanks, though, to (1) a renewed interest in natural pest controls and (2) some dramatically improved martin house designs, the giant swallow's numbers are once again increasing at a satisfying rate.

Purple martins are gregarious, nest in colonies, and are easily attracted to areas with even large human populations. If you live east of the Rockies and your town or farm has an insect problem it could well pay you to put up several houses for these birds.

BUILD A MARTIN HOUSE

ALTHOUGH WE NOW KNOW that they are far from ideal living quarters, gourds are commonly used as purple martin houses in the South. If you'd like to try this traditional design, get some bottle gourds (or grow your own), let them dry, and cut a single opening (about 2⅛ to 2½ inches in diameter) in the side of each. Shake out the seeds and bore a smaller hole (large enough for the insertion of a wire) through the narrow end of every dried shell just under the stem.

Next find a good, stout pole long enough and heavy enough to be firmly set in the earth to support crosspieces at least 8 feet above the ground. Add more arms higher up the pole if possible—the sky's the limit for purple martins—then wire the gourds securely to the horizontal supports and wait for your new tenants.

As nice and traditional as gourd houses may be, though, they're hard to clean, and baby martins have been known to die from lack of ventilation in such apartments. Sooner or later—if you become a real, sure-enough purple martin enthusiast—you'll probably want to build or buy one of the compartment houses that experience and research have proven to be superior to the gourd designs.

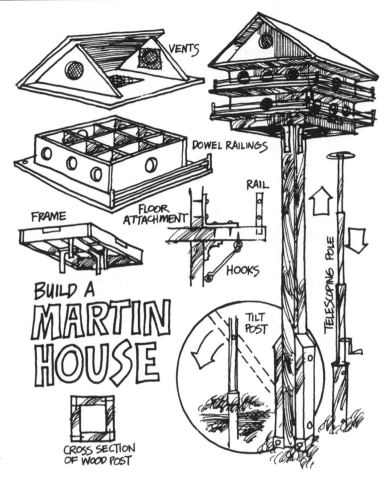

VENTS

DOWEL RAILINGS

RAIL

FRAME

FLOOR
ATTACHMENT

HOOKS

BUILD A
**MARTIN
HOUSE**

TILT
POST

TELESCOPING POLE

CROSS SECTION
OF WOOD POST

Each room in a martin complex should be about 6 inches square and have its own 2⅛-inch entrance hole. A 2-foot-square house, divided into nine cubes (with the floor cut out of the center section to turn it into an air shaft), makes an eight-compartment martin domicile that is practical and easy to build. The sides or roof of the structure should be removable for handiest cleaning and eviction of unwanted occupants. Wood is fine for such a house and, surprisingly, aluminum (which is impervious to mites and other bird parasites) is even better.

Purple martins winter in Brazil and begin appearing in Florida in late January. By April the birds have arrived in the northern states and Canada. You should figure on having your martin quarters set up well before the swallows are due in your area. Remember to place the house or houses at least 8 feet off the ground on a metal pole or wooden support equipped with a metal guard (to keep predators from climbing to the nests).

If your living quarters are to their liking, chances are good that some martins will move right in the very first spring. If they don't, however, don't be disappointed. It may take as long as three or four

continued on next page

years before your colony is established, but once it's a going operation, the swallows will return season after season after season.

English sparrows and starlings often try to take over martin houses, and you may have to remove such birds' nests from your swallow quarters on a regular basis until they get the idea that they aren't wanted. You'll also find it easier to reserve your martin house for martins if you close the structure or take it down for the winter.

Yes, there's a little bit of labor involved in attracting and maintaining a colony of purple martins but, at the rate of 14,000 mosquitoes a day, the little insect catchers will more than repay you for your trouble.

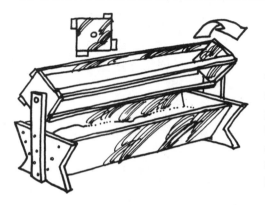

A CHICKEN FEEDER

CHICKENS DEARLY LOVE TO roost on anything available, including their feeding pans, which, in the process, become filled with droppings if not overturned. Either way, the result is wasteful. You can put an end to such shenanigans in your flock by attaching a reel—somewhat like the one shown here—to your homemade chicken feeding troughs.

TRIM A TREE LIMB

To PREVENT A LIMB from peeling down the side of a tree as it's removed, saw partway through the branch from the underside first. Make your upward cut close to the trunk and about one-third of the way through. Then start a second cut on top of the limb about ½ inch farther from the trunk than the first cut. When you have sawed down almost to the undercut, the limb will break away cleanly.

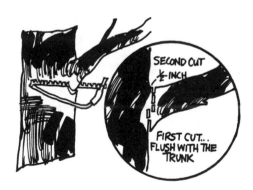

SECOND CUT ½-INCH

FIRST CUT... FLUSH WITH THE TRUNK

JENNY WRENS

JENNY WRENS ARE ONE of the nicest little birds to have around the backyard or homestead and many people build special small birdhouses (with an opening the size of a quarter) for them. Unfortunately, a great number of these folks are disappointed when wrens refuse to occupy the houses in question. Why? Because the builders mistakenly installed a perch at the entrance of each little home.

Wrens land directly in the entrance of their houses and have no need for a perch. Other birds that attack wrens, such as sparrows, find the perches to be convenient bases from which to launch their harassment. Thus, the little wrens have learned to stay away from houses that are so equipped.

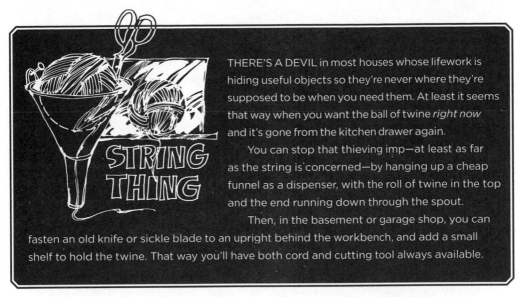

STRING THING

THERE'S A DEVIL in most houses whose lifework is hiding useful objects so they're never where they're supposed to be when you need them. At least it seems that way when you want the ball of twine *right now* and it's gone from the kitchen drawer again.

You can stop that thieving imp—at least as far as the string is concerned—by hanging up a cheap funnel as a dispenser, with the roll of twine in the top and the end running down through the spout.

Then, in the basement or garage shop, you can fasten an old knife or sickle blade to an upright behind the workbench, and add a small shelf to hold the twine. That way you'll have both cord and cutting tool always available.

RECYCLE MILK CARTONS

IF YOU MUST BUY them, save and recycle those waxed, cardboard milk or juice cartons into at least a few of the hundreds of uses that have been found for them.

The containers can be cut down into small flats and planted with seeds. Fill a couple with sand and carry them in your car trunk—you can then use their dispenser spouts to shake grit under your car's wheels the next time you're stuck in snow or on ice.

Cut the top off a carton and use it for a paint bucket. Freeze ice in several and carry them in an insulated chest on your next long cross-country trip: as the ice melts, you'll have a constant supply of cold drinking water. Use the containers as molds for giant candles. Wash 'em and let the kids build castles and fortresses, and garages and homes from the sturdy cartons the next time they play. Seal one, turn it on its side, glue on four spool legs and a set of paper ears, paint on a face, cut a slot in the back, and you've got a homemade piggy bank.

Let your imagination run free and you'll soon be able to recycle every carton at least once before you throw it away.

AMAZING FACTS ABOUT ONIONS, RADISHES, AND GARLIC

ONE PERSISTENT BIT OF folklore—which stretches back to at least the time the pyramids were built—concerns the medicinal properties of radishes, onions, and garlic. It's strange, then, that it never seemed to occur to anyone in the scientific establishment to seriously investigate the curative properties of these common plants.

Every day, however, it seems scientists are letting us know about their "aha" moments as they discover that the stuff that grows around us can cure what ails us. . . . Radish seeds contain a substance that possesses a mild antibiotic action against staphylococcus, streptococcus, pneumococcus, and coliform organisms. This discovery inspired other scientists to do further research and it wasn't long before something called *alliin* was isolated from onions, garlic, and leeks. Experiments soon showed that alliin formed a strong antibacterial substance (named *allicin*) when mixed with enzymes from the same vegetables.

Well, sir. That's good news because allicin has proven to be an effective agent against the bacteria responsible for fungus infections of the skin and wounds, typhoid, paratyphoid, and cholera. What's more, the antibiotic property of onions, leeks, and garlic is pretty potent (one milligram of allicin has about the same effectiveness as twenty-five units of penicillin).

Them ole folk medicine advocates just might have been on to something!

Interestingly enough, further tests have shown that allicin—this natural antibiotic from the onion family—does no harm to the "good" bacteria that our bodies need. The benign bugs so important to robust health—and which penicillin slaughters right along with the bad bacteria—actually thrive on allicin. Chalk one up for down-home medicine!

And wait, there's more! Research shows that onions contain "something" that increases the enzyme action needed to split up fibrin (the cause of blood clots). This would appear to be a substantial scientific basis for the old peasant practice of feeding onions and garlic to horses that develop clots in their legs. The idea might even work on people, for that matter.

And, who knows? It now seems only a question of time before some researcher somewhere either proves or disproves the old folk belief that a teaspoon of chopped garlic, taken twice a day with water, will relieve the pain and swelling of arthritis (with, it's claimed, no disagreeable odor on the breath).

Still and all, it does appear doubtful that modern science will ever unbend long enough to investigate another medieval claim: that garlic hung in every window and doorway is a sure-fire repellent for werewolves . . . and the occasional vampire.

GRILL STEAKS OVER SAWDUST

THE NEXT TIME YOU'RE working with untreated hickory or cherry wood in your home workshop, save the "manufactured" sawdust. Soak a handful in water and spread it across the charcoal in your outdoor grill just before you throw on those slices of steak. The smoke from the particles of wood will add a notable flavor to the meat.

PRUNE THAT GRAPEVINE

THOSE INTRICATE GRAPEVINE PRUNING diagrams in the gardening books look great until, that is, you try to make your own arbor shape up the same way and come out feeling like a one-armed diver cornered by a Siamese octopus.

Well, don't let it discourage you. If truth be known, you can prune and train a grapevine any ole way you please if you know one simple fact: Grapes fruit from—and only from—buds on the wood of the previous summer's growth. All you have to do to any good, strong vine, then, is leave about sixty buds—any sixty on the bearing wood—and whack off the rest. Those buds should produce about 150 medium-size bunches of grapes.

And by the way, don't fertilize grapes too heavily. A little nitrogen goes a long, long way with them.

BUILD A COLD FRAME

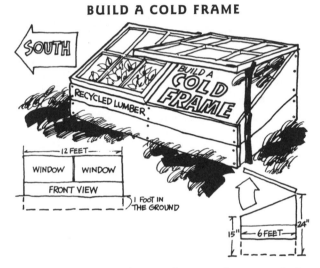

WITH A COLD FRAME you can start plants early, grow them out of season, and raise garden fare that ordinarily does not thrive in your climate. Place the frame so that it faces south with protection to the north and windy sides (but not under dripping eaves). Drain it well. Two old window sashes, hinged to open on warm days (hold maximum inside temperature to 80°F), make an ideal top. For easiest working reaches, keep frame 6×12 feet or smaller. Fill with good, rich loam and plant thickly.

You can start plants that like a cool beginning to their lives and unfussy ones like lettuce and radishes in your cold frame. It can also be used as a transition place to help harden young plants before final placement in the garden.

Some people use their cold frames for storage bins for root vegetables. Just remove a foot or so of soil before putting the lower layer of straw in for these vegetables. Cover well inside and out and invert a bushel basket over the latch to make the bin accessible under snow or when everything freezes up.

PROTECT YOUR AXE HANDLE

WRAP AN AXE HANDLE with fine wire for the first 3 inches back from the axe head and it will last many times as long before splitting.

THE OWNER-BUILT HOME

IF YOU'VE EVER FELT that a new home costs too much these days and you've vaguely wondered whether it's really possible to save money by constructing your own, it's time you were introduced to the ideas of a fellow named Ken Kern.

Ken Kern was an architect who lived in California and—back in 1948—began collecting information on low-cost house construction. Ken claimed that almost any average family could custom-build a lavish home designed just for them without ever being tied down to a 20- or 30-year mortgage.

One of the ways you can realize this miracle, according to Ken Kern, is by designing and planning your own house. After all, *no one* knows exactly what you want better than *you* do . . . so why should you pay an architect for a service you probably don't really need? Remember now, the man making this statement *was* an architect . . . so that was a rather unusual idea for him to be throwing around.

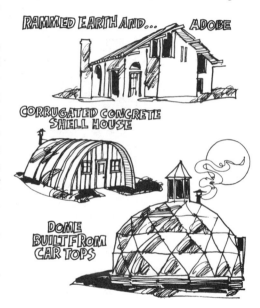

Kern also said that you should do your own building whenever possible. I *know* that's a good idea because I've built or helped build a number of houses and barns and saved several thousand dollars in labor and contractor's fees on each one.

Now, if the idea of building your own home scares you . . . it probably shouldn't. Even the best master carpenter was all thumbs the first time he picked up a hammer and—chances are—if you work slowly and carefully in the beginning, you'll gain speed as you go along and the finished job will be good enough to make you very proud indeed.

You can save another good-sized chunk of money and—incidentally—build a much

WRAP PACKAGES WITH DAMP STRING

DAMPEN STRING BEFORE USING it to tie packages. The string then will not slip during the work and—as it dries—it will shrink itself tighter than you could possibly have pulled it.

BRIGHTEN ALUMINUM POTS AND PANS

ALTHOUGH MANY PEOPLE FEEL that cooking in aluminum utensils is an unhealthful practice, other folks follow the practice daily. If you're one of the latter and you find your aluminum pots and pans becoming badly discolored, you may brighten the utensils quite easily by boiling apple parings in them for a short time.

more attractive house in the bargain if you use native materials whenever possible. All those "new improved" plastic panels and processed insulating materials are poor substitutes for rock and earth and concrete and timber anyway . . . and besides, which would you *really* rather live in?

Naturally, if you do much of the work on your home yourself and you build that house largely of natural materials, you can take advantage of yet another of Ken's money-saving ideas: "pay as you go." Did you know that the interest alone on a 30-year mortgage can easily add up to more than the worth of the house the mortgage finances? That's a lot of dollars you can keep right in your pocket instead.

Ken Kern had a great many more ideas all designed to help you build your own house for a ridiculously small amount of money . . . but he certainly didn't stop there. Not at all. Kern also thoroughly researched solar heat, wind power, regional climates and just about every other possible factor that can affect and influence the design, placement, construction, comfort and livability of a dwelling.

Ken Kern, in short, dug up enough information about low-cost do-it-yourself housing to write a *book* on the subject, and luckily for you and for me, he did exactly that. The book is titled, appropriately enough, *The Owner-Built Home*, and it's packed with everything you need to know to design, build and live in your own custom dream house for less money than you've ever thought possible.

Now this is not an ordinary book. *The Owner-Built Home* contains trade secrets and construction ideas from other countries that even your best local architect and contractor don't know. This is the Real Thing, and there's no other book like it in the world. I'm certain that *The Owner-Built Home* can save anyone, anywhere, thousands of dollars on a new house.

SET METAL POSTS IN CONCRETE

A metal post or pipe will "hold" much better when embedded in concrete if a few holes are drilled through the portion that is to be encased so that the wet mix can set *through*, as well as around, the walls of the upright. Then, of course, if you stick a couple of spike nails or metal rods through those holes before pouring the concrete, that pipe or post will *really* become "growed fast" when the cement sets up.

EGG WHITE MAKES CREAM WHIP

The next time your whipping cream refuses to whip, try adding an egg white to the liquid.

PROTECT A SHOP SWITCH

A SCREEN DOOR HANDLE placed over a shop switch will prevent anyone from bumping into that switch and accidentally turning it on or off.

EARLY PLANTING TIPS

IF YOU TRY TO beat everyone in the neighborhood in the game of "Who Can Raise the First Ear of Corn" (or tomato or whatever), the score over a five-year period will generally add up to: You 1, Them 4. To make matters even worse (on those years when you hustle seeds into the ground so early that cold weather, bugs, or both actually kill or severely injure your crops and you have to plant all over again), you're really losing some of those innings *twice*.

Better you should wait until all danger of frost, cold, and wet weather has passed in your area before attempting to nestle those little packets of life into the ground. And if you just plain can't resist planting *something* the first time you see a bluebird, take a vacation instead. When you get back—two weeks later—conditions should be about right for sowing those seeds in safety.

REJUVENATE CANE SEATS WITH VINEGAR

CANE CHAIR SEATS THAT have sagged may be rejuvenated by sponging them with a hot, fifty-fifty solution of vinegar and water, and then placing the chairs in the sun to dry.

GLYCERIN KEEPS GLASS FROM FOGGING

IF YOU BUY A small bottle of glycerin at the local pharmacy and apply a thin coating of the liquid to both sides of your car's windshield, you'll prevent moisture—and the frost that often follows—from forming on the glass.

SWEEP A PATH
FOR YOUR HAND TRUCK

HAND TRUCKS ARE GREAT . . . except that those little bitty wheels on their bottoms sure can get hung up on the smallest bits of gravel and other obstructions. At least one smart operator has cured that problem, however, by attaching a doubled piece of old fabric belting directly in front of each roller on his truck. The loops—suspended so that they rub the floor firmly as the carrier is pushed—"sweep" a clear path for the wheels that follow.

APPLE KEEPS
BAKED GOODS MOIST

AN APPLE, CUT IN half and put inside an airtight container with bread or cake, will keep the bakery goods moist and flavorful for days.

BOIL BLACK WALNUTS
TO SAVE WHOLE KERNELS

BLACK WALNUT KERNELS WILL come out in much larger pieces if the nuts are soaked in boiling water for forty minutes before they're cracked.

HOW TO PATCH
GRAIN SACKS

GRAIN SACKS MAY BE readily patched by turning the bags inside out, smearing a thick flour-and-water paste around each hole, covering the area with a patch, and pressing with a hot iron until the glue is dry. The bag may then be turned back the right way and used.

SAVE CHICKENS
FROM DROWNING

CHICKENS AND WILD BIRDS seem to have a positive genius for drowning themselves in cattle, horse, and other large watering tanks during dry weather. If you float a small board in such a container, however, the fowls will be able to climb up on the wood and save themselves.

MAKE MINT
PINCUSHIONS

CLUMPS OF OLD-FASHIONED, SWEET-SMELLING mint grow on almost every midwestern farm (and a good number of city lots). Gather this free-for-the-picking bounty and store it in a clean muslin sack hidden among your clothes. Then—for Christmas gifts—sew up some small silk pincushions and stuff them with the dried, aromatic leaves.

RULES FOR SAFE
TRACTOR OPERATION

Compiled by the National Safety Council's Agricultural Division, the National Educational Center for Agricultural Safety.

1. Safety first. ALWAYS, **ALWAYS** adhere to safe work practices.
2. Be well rested and physically and mentally alert when operating your tractor. Lack of sleep, stress, certain medications, alcohol, and drugs can impair your ability to be safe. Also, take breaks.
3. Review all safety information in your operator's manual and on every warning decal on your tractor.
4. Use the seatbelts . . . use the seatbelts.
5. Install a Rollover Protective Structure (ROPS).
6. Always inspect your tractor for any hazards before using it and fix them before heading out.
7. Turn off all equipment, shut off the engine, remove the key, and wait for all parts to stop moving before leaving your tractor.
8. Never permit persons other than the driver to ride on tractor when it is in operation.
9. Make sure no one is in the area of tractor operation.

REMEMBER: A CAREFUL OPERATOR ALWAYS IS THE BEST INSURANCE AGAINST AN ACCIDENT!

ANCHOR RUG WITH JAR RINGS

FRUIT JAR RUBBERS SEWED on each corner of a small rug will prevent the floor covering from slipping underfoot.

SAVE SEWING SCRAPS

HANG A PAPER BAG on the side of your sewing machine and toss in all scraps of material and thread as you work. You'll save much time cleaning up later and the bits and pieces of cloth make good filling for small throw pillows.

CHILLED CANDLES BURN LONGER

DECORATIVE CANDLES GENERALLY KEEP their shape better and burn much longer when chilled thoroughly in the refrigerator before use.

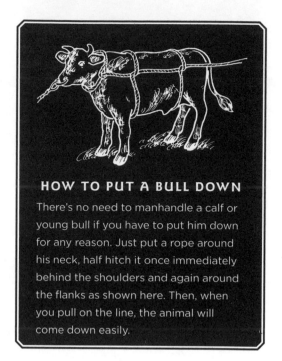

HOW TO PUT A BULL DOWN

There's no need to manhandle a calf or young bull if you have to put him down for any reason. Just put a rope around his neck, half hitch it once immediately behind the shoulders and again around the flanks as shown here. Then, when you pull on the line, the animal will come down easily.

BANANA STEMS ATTRACT INSECT PESTS

OLD-TIMERS CLAIM THAT A few banana stems hung up in the poultry house will attract lice and make it easier to eradicate the pests. The stems will also attract ants wherever they've proved bothersome.

CUT STRAWBERRY RUNNERS

STRAWBERRIES ARE GREAT FAVORITES of many backyard gardeners—until it comes time to cut runners from the plants. If you take an old galvanized bucket, however, trim out its bottom, sharpen the edge all the way around, fasten a board across the top for a handle, and chuck the improvised tool right down over each plant . . . you'll zip off all its runners at once.

PUT YOUR WOOD LOT ON A PAYING BASIS

FARM TRADITION OF A past (and wiser) day kept sacred the practice of preserving one-tenth of the ole homestead in woodland. That was more than just a tithe to nature too. Grandpa saw in his wood lot a new barn or house, if the present one burned. He also saw heat for winter, squirrels for the table, tongues for wagons, handles for tools, and posts for fences.

Granddad's vision should be your vision. Manage your wood lot by cutting out cheap weed trees and allowing white oak, hickory, black walnut, yellow poplar, hard maple, black cherry, and white ash to grow. When a tree begins to die out in the top, harvest it. Younger seedlings and saplings will grow up to take its place. A forest of hardwoods is a savings account with an interest rate no banker can match.

TRACTOR FRONT-END LOADERS ARE HANDY

IF YOU PLAN TO buy a tractor, be sure it's one that you can put a hydraulic forklift on. That's a front-end loader or manure scoop, in farm lingo. All new tractors can be so equipped; on some older models, however, you might have a problem. Your implement dealer will know.

Until you've worked on a farm with and without a front-end loader, you won't appreciate this tool's advantages. I've used one to do everything from jacking up a sagging barn roof to lifting cars out of snow-drifts to building pond dams.

BUTCHERING IS BETTER THAN BUYING

HERE'S A STORY TOO true to be an Aesop fable, although it has a moral anyway: Joe was a small farmer, very much in debt. He was, in fact, on the brink of disaster. But he did have ten hogs ready for market. "Going to save one out for your own family use?" I asked. "Oh no, I can't afford to. Need all ten for the mortgage payment," said Joe.

"Your family likes pork and eats a lot of it, right, Joe?"

"Sure."

"Where you get it?"

"At the store."

By selling the hog to meet his payment, Joe was tossing money smack-dab in the furnace. Even though he made money by selling his hog, it would have cost him less to feed his family had he butchered it for the meat and the lard. At the local grocery store, the cost for pork loins, roasts, ribs, and chops add up fast.

WRENCH MAKES
HANDLE FOR BUCKET

You can take a lot of the "ouch" out of a bucket's wire handle by using an open-end wrench as a temporary handle as shown in the accompanying illustration.

A MODIFIED PAINT CAN

Punch several holes in the bottom of the groove that runs around the top of a paint can. Each time you wipe the brush on the container's edge, the excess paint will run back *into* the bucket, rather than down its side.

FAST AND EASY COMPOST

Some organic gardeners make much to-dos about their secret formulas for producing compost. Generally, the carefully guarded recipes in question involve special "activators" and the backbreaking turning and stirring on a regular schedule of tons of decomposing matter.

Balderdash! Compost is nothing but decayed plant and animal material that is spread on a garden in place of chemical fertilizers and growth stimulators. It's the simplest and most natural thing in the world and—left to its own devices—*makes itself* in woods and untended fields every year. The best you can, or should, hope to do is assemble an optimum set of ingredients for a royally rich batch of natural fertilizer, throw 'em all together, and let Mother Nature do the rest.

The more variety in your compost pile, all the better. Grass clippings, kitchen trimmings, leftovers, coffee grounds, wood ashes, weeds, straw, spoiled hay, hair cuttings, and scraps of old cotton or woolen fabrics all fit into

a humus heap just fine. Spent hops from a brewery and seaweed pulled in from the ocean add to any natural fertilizer pile as do rabbit, goat, cow, poultry, pig, sheep, horse, and other manures. A special tip: Many big city stables and racetracks gladly give horse manure away free to anyone who'll haul it off.

Additional composting candidates include leaves, cornstalks, tomato vines, twigs, branches, and sawdust. It's only logical, however, to shred such tough or bulky matter for best results. You'll also find your heap of humus decomposes more rapidly if you leave whole bones, grease, animal fat, and chunks of meat out entirely. They'll all break down eventually, of course, but the idea here is to produce finished natural fertilizer in the shortest possible time.

HOMEMADE CONE SHADES PLANT

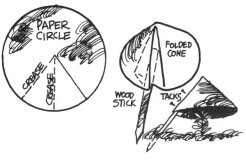

Cut a circle of heavy paper and mark a triangle from center to edge as shown in the illustration. Fold line A over to meet line B creasing the paper at A and C. Tack or staple the resulting cone through its folded part to a flat stick. The support may then be stuck into the ground to hold the hood in position over a newly set plant. The cone can be raised as the plant becomes accustomed to the sun and, if desired, the point of the device may be cut off to provide ventilation through its top.

LAYERS

CONTINUE UP TO
5 FEET
SEAWEED
GRASS
GARBAGE
LEAVES
LIMESTONE
PINE NEEDLES
MANURE
LEAVES
SPRINKLING OF
ROCK POWDER
GARBAGE
MANURE
GREEN MATTER
BARE SOIL
LOOSENED TO EXPOSE THE
SOIL BACTERIA

OK. Pace off a 5x5 foot square in an out-of-the-way sunny corner of your property and spade up the soil to expose the bacteria that live there. Then start forking one 6-inch layer of organic material on top of another until the stack is about 5 feet tall. The order and mixing of the ingredients is not important, but you should water each tier as you lay it down. A sprinkling of ground limestone, rock phosphate, or potash rock on every layer will improve the quality of the finished fertilizer and is much advised.

Cover the completed pile with a sheet of black plastic and anchor the tarp around the bottom with bricks or rocks. The plastic will hold the moisture in, protect the nutrients in the heap from rain, and speed the composting process by absorbing the sun's heat.

Now go away and forget your experiment for five or ten days. When you come back, the decomposing humus should be registering between 130°F and 160°F. That's good. If it *isn't* heating, it needs more nitrogen (manure, blood meal, or bone meal). Add more ground limestone if the pile smells.

You may want to turn the heap after two or three weeks, just to check its progress. If the center of the stack has not completely broken down at that time, add some nitrogen. Splash more water into the pile if it seems dry. Restack the material "inside out" (so that the top and sides become the center) and re-cover with the black plastic.

Use this "quickie" technique for making compost and you'll have rich, crumbly mulch three months after setting a stack of humus to work in any but the coldest weather. Compost started in the dead of winter and covered with the plastic may well freeze solid and not start to digest itself at all until spring. Don't worry about it. Once the heap thaws, it'll decompose fastest of all.

WORMS THRIVE ON CARDBOARD

IF YOU'D LIKE TO raise fishworms but have been stymied by lack of compost, cornmeal, vegetable matter, or manure to feed the little critters, try this:

Fill the worm box with pieces of corrugated cardboard. Wet the chunks of scrap down good, let 'em stand for a couple of days, and then put the worms in on top. The wigglers will burrow right down into the moist corrugations and live on the *glue* that's in the material. Keep an inch of damp peat moss on top of the cardboard to hold the moisture in and the little fellers in the box will thrive as long as there's any stickum left to eat.

Since you can get broken-down cardboard for nothing and then sell worms to fishermen for plenty, someone should latch onto this idea in a hurry and use it to fatten their bank account.

HEELING IN PLANTS

ANY DAY NOW YOU'LL be getting that shipment of strawberry plants you ordered from the nursery around the end of winter. You'll be delighted to see your future strawberry bed, of course, whenever it arrives. The supplier, however, ships to suit his work schedule, not yours, so there's a good chance that your plants will turn up at a time when you can't possibly get around to setting them out for a couple of days.

No problem. The young strawberries will await your convenience if you use the method called "heeling in" (which just means storing newly arrived plants in a shallow trench). Here's how to do it:

If the plant roots are very dry, put 'em to soak for a few hours. Meanwhile, dig a *V*-shaped trench deep enough to let the root systems of your young strawberry plants spread out below ground level while the crowns remain above the surface. Then set the new arrivals in the ditch, leaning against one side of the *V* and far enough apart so their roots won't get tangled together. Fill in your temporary storage space with earth and press the soil down firmly. Your plants should be perfectly comfortable in this shelter until you have their final location ready for them.

If the strawberry plants' roots were all dried out when they arrived, it's a good idea to leave the newcomers heeled in until they get a new start on life. If you do, though, you'll need to be especially careful not to damage the fresh growth when you remove the plants from the trench.

CLEAN YOUR GRINDSTONE

A GRINDSTONE CAN BECOME so badly coated with dirt and flecks of steel that it's almost worthless. Such accumulations can be removed with little effort, however, by holding a piece of ice against the wheel while it is turned slowly.

BOLT REPAIRS WATER TANK

FOR A QUICK AND highly satisfactory repair of a leaking metal water tank, put a bolt with a good-size leather washer both inside and out through the hole to be fixed and screw a nut on tightly.

RELIEF FROM HEADACHES!

WE'VE ALL BEEN TOLD often enough by advertisements "What to Do When Headache Strikes." Almost always, the remedy we're urged to reach for turns out to be aspirin, or one of its many variations. Now, aspirin really is a very effective pain reliever and most of us have been happy to use it at some time or other. There's no doubt, though, that aspirin *is* hard on the stomach. If we can get rid of headache with nontoxic methods, then, it's probably preferable to do so.

Here's a homeopathic headache remedy that you can try out on the next friend or relation who complains of the ailment: Have the patient sit down. If you're right-handed, place your right hand at the base of the person's skull and your left on his forehead. (Southpaws reverse the hand position.) Now leave your hands there quietly for thirty seconds to three minutes.

It helps if you and the sufferer close your eyes and imagine a weak electric current passing through the head and sorting out the messed-up circuitry in there. The theory is that—because the hands are very slightly polarized—something of the kind really does happen. Could be. All we know is that the cure *does* seem to work more often than not, even if neither patient nor healer thinks it will. Tension headaches will stay healed; migraines may return after being relieved for a while.

VINEGAR SWEETENS JUG

IT'S STILL QUITE COMMON to carry water into backcountry or remote work sites in jugs and it's just as common to find such jugs musty inside when they've been capped and stored for any length of time. You can eliminate that unpleasantness altogether if you'll put a tablespoon of vinegar into each such container before capping and storing it away for the winter or whatever.

PROTECT PITCHFORK AND SHOVEL HANDLES

RUB THE HANDLES OF pitchforks and shovels once in a while with a rag dipped in linseed oil and you'll find the shafts both last longer and are much more pleasant to use.

HOW TO FRY EGGS

AN AMAZING NUMBER OF cooks (both male and female) seem content to serve tough, slippery, indigestible fried eggs that appear to be little short of vulcanized. Apparently the secret of light, tender, morning eggs *is* still a secret: cook them sloooowly. High temperatures congeal and toughen the whites of eggs, and hen fruit should always be fried at a leisurely pace.

HOW TO BRAND TOOLS

MARK YOUR IRON TOOLS for easy identification by covering a spot on each one with beeswax or hard tallow. Then scratch your name or initials through the coating with a nail or ice pick, pour nitric acid into the groove, and let it stand for a short time. When the acid and wax are removed, the "brand" should be quite visible.

COSMETICS FROM THE KITCHEN

MANY PEOPLE WHO'VE TRIED it report that ordinary cornmeal is a superlative skin cleanser, especially when the complexion is tired and looks it. Lather your hands with mild soap, sprinkle the meal into the suds, and gently but thoroughly scrub your face and neck with the mixture. The slightly abrasive action will remove dead tissue, clean the pores, and leave the skin fresh and revitalized.

Mayonnaise—of all things—is another good skin cleanser, particularly for sensitive complexions or those that have been overexposed to the sun, wind, or cold. The light vegetable oil it holds penetrates more quickly and deeply than the heavy petroleum oils in most commercial skin creams. In addition, the egg yolk contained by the mayonnaise is a rich source of vitamin A (essential for proper skin nourishment), and the vinegar in the dressing provides acidity, which is useful in maintaining an ideal pH balance on the surface of the body.

An egg white—slightly beaten, generously applied, and allowed to dry—is a very fine skin toner and tightener. Apply the mask, let it dry, and then put on another coat. Lie down without a pillow and with your feet elevated. Used tea bags (saved in the refrigerator), cucumber slices, chunks of raw potato, or cotton pads soaked in witch hazel may be placed over the closed eyelids at the same time. After twenty or thirty minutes, rinse off the egg white and rub on a film of almond oil, avocado oil, or fresh cream to offset the mask's drying effect.

Honey—applied alone and at room temperature after moistening your face with water—is another good skin mask. It works even better if slightly warmed and mixed with nonfat powdered milk, cream, or egg white.

Avocados are 25 percent oil and that oil, in turn, contains eleven vitamins and seventeen minerals, which just has to be good for the complexion. Cut one of the fruit in half, remove the seed, scoop the golden-green pulp into a bowl, and mash it into a lumpless cream (adding a little water if necessary). Smooth the preparation over your face and freshly shampooed hair, and massage it well into the scalp. Then rub the inside of the avocado peel

WOOD ASHES SEAL CRACK IN STOVE

YOU CAN SEAL CRACKS in a woodstove with this simple old-time homemade cement: Put about a cupful of wood ashes in an old can, add about half a cup of salt, and slowly stir in enough water to make a stiff paste. Plaster the broken places in the metal with this mixture. Then build a fire and bake the sealer hard. Your repair job will last quite well if you don't bump the mended spots.

over your elbows, feet, hands, and other problem dry spots. Wait one half hour and shower the goo away. Amazingly, it won't cling or stick . . . and the treatment should give your hair noticeably more body than even the most expensive commercial preparations.

After cleaning the face, people with average or dry skin generally find it beneficial to apply a light application of cucumber, strawberry, bell pepper, grape, or cabbage juice. Those with oily complexions and enlarged pores may prefer the astringent juice of the grapefruit.

Nothing lubricates a complexion like fresh cream. It seeps readily into the pores, nourishes the skin, and leaves it remarkably soft and velvety.

Hippocrates advised the ladies of ancient Athens to moisten their hands and legs in the morning, rub them lightly with honey, and—later—rinse the honey away with clear water. The treatment was supposed to relieve unattractive redness, roughness, and chapping—and it still does.

A soothing lotion for the legs and hands can be made by covering a large handful of green lettuce leaves, pine needles, or cucumber slices with water and simmering them in a covered glass or stainless steel saucepan for half an hour. Strain the liquid into a clean jar and add enough benzoin—a drop at a time—to produce a milky appearance.

Cosmetic vinegar is a great skin pacifier, relieves dryness and itching, and restores a natural acid mantle (which is removed by cleaning) to the complexion. It's nothing but cider vinegar with its acrid scent disguised by aromatic plants or the petals of fragrant flowers. Put a cup of lavender, lemon verbena, violet, honeysuckle, mint, carnation, or geranium leaves or petals into a pint of boiling water in a glass or stainless steel saucepan. Simmer for two minutes. Add a cup of cider vinegar, pour the liquid into a clean jar, and tightly seal the container with a lid. Open the jar after two weeks and strain the solution through a piece of clean cloth. Added to the final rinse after a shampoo, this soothing lotion will remove any remaining soap film that dulls the luster of the hair and causes it to tangle. Patted on with a piece of cotton or soft cloth, it will also relieve sunburn.

EGGS TELL HEALTH OF HEN

DID YOU KNOW THAT you can tell a lot about a laying hen's diet—and the nutritional value of her eggs—from the color of the yolk? The product of the modern "egg factory"—the kind of egg the supermarket sells—has a pale yellow center. The hen, however, who's lucky enough to live on a small family farm where she gets plenty of green stuff to eat will present her owners with eggs that have brilliant orange yolks, rich in vitamin A.

PUT WAX ON CHAIR LEGS

THE NEXT TIME YOU wax a linoleum floor, wax the bottoms of your rockers and chair legs too. It'll prevent a lot of unsightly marks from forming on your shiny masterpiece.

RECYCLE A BARN

THAT TUMBLEDOWN OLD BARN on the piece of property you want to buy could be a blessing in disguise. Being dilapidated, the structure will certainly not add to the asking price and may actually detract from it. But (to yourself) calculate how many feet of good two-by-fours, two-by-sixes, four-by-fours, and so forth, you can rescue from the building for your own new house or barn. Then visit your local lumberyard and find out how much it would cost you to buy that many boards and beams new!

Examine old timbers and siding by scratching away slivers with a pocketknife. If the inside shows up a nice chocolate brown, the wood is black walnut. And seasoned black walnut is worth its weight in . . . well, copper anyway. I know of one farm with several old barns where *all* the beams are walnut. The place is a blooming treasure house. No, I'm not telling—not even the owner.

ETCH METAL WITH VINEGAR

RUB OVER GALVANIZED METAL first with a rag dipped in vinegar and you'll find that paint will adhere much more tightly to the surface.

LIME THAT SOIL

MOST SOILS NEED LIME—at least 1,000 pounds per acre once every five years (twice that amount is fine, especially for grasses and legumes).

Early spring is the best time to apply the dressing to lawns or hay crops, and fall—before the ground is frozen—runs a close second. Forget the idea entirely after the ground is frozen; any lime or fertilizer spread on a field then is more liable to wash away than soak in during thaws.

Do NOT plow lime under on land that's being planted to crops. If you have to plow something down, do it to the manure you spread on the fields and then just broadcast your lime across the broken surface. Leave it there or, at most, disc or harrow it into only the top layer of dirt. Lime sinks (leaches) into plowed ground fast enough on its own.

WHITEN KITCHEN CUTTING BOARDS

DISCOLORED BREAD AND MEAT boards may be whitened by rubbing them with lemon rinds turned inside out and then washing the wood in warm water.

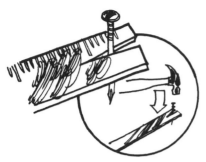

NAIL ABOVE YOUR REACH

IF YOU'VE EVER TRIED to install a nail or other drive-in fastener higher than you can reach, you know the meaning of frustration: the hammer adds 8 inches to your driving arm, but there just ain't no way you can hold that nail up there where you want it.

But there is a way! Saw a short slit just a little narrower than the shank of the fasteners you're using into the end of a yardstick or other light piece of wood, stick in one of the nails, and you're in business. Once the fastener is started, pull down on the holder to free it and hammer the piece of hardware flush.

VINEGAR MAKES PLASTER CURE MORE SLOWLY

MIX A HALF TEASPOON of vinegar into each quart of plaster you use on your next repair job, and the "mud" will take longer to set up, thereby giving you just that much more working time.

ADD SALT TO CEMENT

ADD ONE OR TWO pounds of salt to each sack of cement when you mix concrete in cold weather and the finished work will not freeze nor dry too rapidly.

HOT NAILS PROTECT PLASTER

IF YOU'LL HEAT A nail hot enough so that you have to handle it with pliers, you'll find that it can be driven into a wall with much less danger of cracking the plaster.

BLOTTER PROTECTS SEWING MACHINE

SEW THROUGH A BLOTTER once or twice after oiling the sewing machine. The action will absorb surplus lubricating fluid that might otherwise stain the next fabric placed under the needle.

HOW TO CARRY PLYWOOD

GET YOURSELF A PIECE of clothesline or similar rope about 18 feet long and tie its ends together to form a big closed loop. Hook the loop around two corners of a sheet of plywood (or any other large, flat piece or pieces of material), tuck the items in question under your arm, grasp the middle of the doubled "handle," and you'll be able to maneuver the otherwise ungainly load with ease.

WILD IN THE CITY

A TREMENDOUS NUMBER OF folks are discovering the delights of foraging and eating wild foods . . . even in the city.

The city? Right. Contrary to popular belief, most of the really valuable, nutritious, and tasty wild plants grow best NOT in the deep woods, but on cleared land close to, and even inside, the boundaries of our population centers.

If you find that hard to believe, just consider the example set by Cathy and Sleepy out in Kansas City. Once their eyes were opened to the possibilities, the Johnsons found they could both enjoy a great deal of healthful outdoor exercise and stretch their food budget a country mile by foraging an amazing variety of free food right inside their town's city limits.

Cathy says, "Our foraging begins just outside the back door with the dandelions in our yard. In the spring they supply us with early greens for salads. We also steam the leaves and serve them with a little vinegar and lots of butter, salt, and pepper. Later, in the summer when the lawn is covered with pretty yellow blossoms, we pick hundreds of the flower heads and make them into wine with which to celebrate the following Christmas. During the fall we dig some dandelion plants and pot them in the basement for blanched, mild salad leaves all winter. We even add roasted, ground dandelion roots to our coffee to make it go farther.

"Our untidy lawn is also filled with plantain, which is good in salads, good for potherbs, good for the nerves, and good as a soothing poultice . . . and—around the yard edges—we gather the tart, lemony-flavored wood sorrel that really perks up a salad or glass of iced tea."

A hundred feet further from their Kansas City home, Sleepy and Cathy forage milkweed pods in season (boiled in three changes of water to remove the bitter "milk," they're delicious) and poke. Young poke leaves and shoots, they have found, can be eaten as summer greens, or frozen for use all winter. The plant's roots can also be blanched—or forced—in the basement right along with the potted dandelions, and then the shoots (NOT the roots, which are poisonous) cooked like asparagus.

"Behind our house," Cathy says, "an elderberry shoot has somehow taken root and flourished. Bonanza! Elderberry flowers (or elder blow, as some folks call the pretty white froth) are excellent in pancakes or fritters and the berries are good dried and eaten like raisins. We spread ours on newspapers in the attic and store 'em in airtight jars for use in

cakes, muffins, puddings, and elderberry-apple pie (somehow the taste of the fruit is improved by the drying process). When we want enough elder blow to stock the cellar with fine, light-yellow wine, we harvest the blossoms down along an old streetcar track here in town."

One of their favorite city edibles is the big, orange day lily that sometimes escapes the flower patch and grows wild on its own. Cathy and Sleepy relish the plant's crisp, pale-green young leaves just as they sprout and often eat their fill of unopened buds and just-opened flowers later in the summer. The buds are steamed and served with butter, salt, and pepper, while the newly bloomed flowers become a real treat when dipped in batter and fried.

Another handy weed that flourishes in town and country alike is the blue-flowered chicory. Cathy and Sleepy find acres of this relative of the dandelion growing alongside a railroad that passes right through the heart of Kansas City, and they eat the plant's young leaves as greens. They also dig chicory roots, roast them in the oven over low heat until they're brown, and then grind them for coffee.

Naturally, Sleepy and Cathy have discovered more Queen Anne's lace—or wild carrots—than they know what to do with. The darn stuff seems to grow EVERYWHERE. If you get the plant early before it turns tough, its root smells and tastes and cooks just like a carrot . . . and it should because that's exactly what it is. The leaves of Queen Anne's lace make a good diuretic tea, and the seeds are great for flavoring soups and stews or sprinkled on homemade bread.

Only a block or so from the place Sleepy works, they have found a stretch of ground loaded with curly dock and wild mustard (both delicious spring greens). Another great spring potherb or salad addition that sprouts almost everywhere (even through driveway cracks) is lamb's-quarters, and Cathy especially likes the tender-tip leaves of the plant in cream-cheese-on-homemade-sourdough-bread sandwiches.

Chickweed, wild onions, May apples, pawpaws, persimmons, crab apples, butternuts, Jerusalem artichokes, mint, red clover, walnuts . . . the list of wild edibles Cathy and Sleepy forage in Kansas City goes on and on. And there's no reason you can't equal or exceed their success.

One word of caution, however, might be in order before you rush out to start supplementing your trips to the grocery store with wild-food-harvesting excursions: use common sense and avoid gathering any volunteer fare that might be contaminated. Of course, this warning shouldn't unnecessarily frighten you: the same restrictions now apply to virtually any edible—wild or domestic—from any corner of the world. Maybe it even balances out: The city's foraged foods might be exposed to a lot of air pollution, but to few or none of the herbicides, pesticides, and chemical fertilizers that are spread over the nonorganic vegetables now on sale in your local supermarket.

So, if you're looking for some healthful outdoor exercise, a chance to beat the food budget just a little, and experience some new-taste treats, invest in a good foraging book and go to it.

BREAKFAST BREAD

ONE OF MOTHER EARTH NEWS'S friends, Edwin R. Pugsley, would like to pass along the following recipe. It's for Breakfast Bread and it goes like this:

2 cups buttermilk
½ cup honey
¼ cup molasses
2 teaspoons soda
1 teaspoon salt
1½ cups of whole-wheat flour
½ cup of wheat germ
1 cup white flour
¼ cup raisins (optional)

Mix together the buttermilk, honey, molasses, soda, and salt in a large bowl. Then, in another bowl, combine the whole-wheat and white flours and the wheat germ and add that blend to the buttermilk mixture. Stir in the raisins and pour the batter into a 9x5x3 loaf pan. Preheat your oven to 400°F, then reduce the temperature to 350°F. Slide in the pan and bake the bread for one hour. Turn the loaf out, inverted, on a rack to cool. Wait one day before slicing and toasting this breakfast bread.

A THRIVING TREE FULL of apples or other fruit is a heartwarming sight, unless the weight of the crop threatens to break an overloaded branch. You can support that groaning bough by cutting a sturdy pole a few inches longer than the height of the limb and nailing a short length of old tire to its top end. Force the bottom of the prop into the ground directly below the branch, wrap the rubber cradle around the bough, and tie the wrapping firmly in place. This improvised sling won't chafe the tree but it *will* help the burdened limb bear up until picking time.

VIOLETS MAKE A VITAMIN-RICH SALAD

SPRING IS SALAD TIME and after a winter of dried, salted, or stored root vegetables, it's no wonder that the early settlers fell rejoicing on the first edible green shoots that poked their heads out of the ground. Come to think of it, lack of fresh vegetables and fruits over the long cold months probably had a lot to do with the weakness, tiredness, and low resistance that traditionally went with early spring.

SAFEGUARD TOOLS WITH RUBBER TUBING

JUST A FEW ODD bits of rubber in the right places can make your carpentry jobs safer, more pleasant, and more efficient.

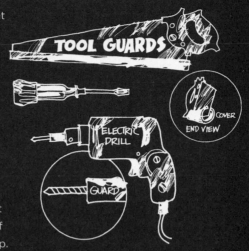

For example, until you get around to building a holder for your saws (see page 103), you can protect the saw teeth—and any human skin that happens to brush against them—by splitting open lengths of old garden hose and fitting them over the tools' cutting edges.

Another rubber guard can save you a blistered hand when you have to put in a lot of screws: Fit a crutch tip over the handle of your screwdriver for a firm, comfortable grip.

Finally, here's a trick to keep your power drill from biting deeper than you want when you're trying to punch a hole just so deep and no deeper. Find a scrap of rubber or plastic tubing that will slip over the drill bit you're going to use. Then cut off a piece that—once slipped onto the bit—will press against the drill's chuck and stop you when the hole has been opened to the desired depth.

Even though we're not as vitamin starved as our forefathers when the early greens come up, the spring salad bowl is still a treat to look forward to. And for an added ingredient that will boost the nutritional value of your dish more than anything else you can find, keep your eyes open for wild violets while you're on your way to the early lettuce patch. The leaves are unbelievably rich in vitamins C and A, so shred them into your salad and celebrate the end of winter with a fine—and pretty—spring tonic.

CHARRED DRIFTWOOD IS DECORATIVE

No BEACHCOMBER SHOULD PASS up a fascinating chunk of driftwood just because it's charred instead of silver-gray from weathering. If you chip away the burned surface and sand the rest of the charcoal off the hard wood inside, you'll reveal a subtly curved shape and a rich dark grain that takes on a polish when rubbed. You'll get covered with powdered charcoal, of course, but the result is worth the trouble.

Once you've seen what charred wood looks like underneath, you may want to reproduce the effect for decorative purposes by using a blowtorch to lightly burn a wooden object you've made . . . and then rubbing the piece till it shines.

SPROUT A GARDEN

Ordinary seeds, grains, and legumes (packed full of natural fats and starches) are quite wholesome, but *sprouted* seeds, grains, and legumes (bursting with vitamins, simple sugars, and proteins) are even more nutritious.

Who knew, for example, soybean shoots and oranges would have something in common? Ungerminated soybean seeds don't show any inkling of having any relationship to oranges. Add water and time, and . . . eureka! One-half cup of soybean shoots—tested for vitamin C, when sprouted 72 hours later—contained as much of the vitamin as *six glasses* of orange juice.

Similar incredible vitamin content have been recorded for other sprouts: oats sprouted five days had 500 percent more B6, 600 percent more folic acid, 10 percent more B1 and 1,350 percent more B2 than ungerminated oats.

It should be noted, of course, that such vitamin increases are not always a straight-line thing. Vitamin B1—for instance—runs up and down like a yo-yo in soybeans as they sprout. The general trend, however, is always spectacularly *up* and germinated seeds are an excellent source of vitamins A, B complex, C, D, E, G, K—even U—and minerals such as calcium, magnesium, phosphorus, chlorine, potassium, and sodium. All in natural forms that the body can readily assimilate.

BUT DO SPROUTS TASTE GOOD?

Not every sprout will suit every taste but, in general, folks who like fresh green salads and raw vegetables will enjoy a goodly number of the little shoots. And the people who don't . . . well, there are a great many ways to serve the sprouts so that their natural flavor is completely disguised.

To be more specific, almost anyone should like a few raw alfalfa sprouts mixed into a salad, but a lot of folks find that germinated soybeans have a little too much "raw" taste to be served the same way. The same soybean shoots, however, become magically delicious with only the slightest (about one to two minutes) steaming.

Sprouted wheat goes well on cereal and is excellent in home-baked bread; rye shoots add a mouthwatering wild rice taste when sprinkled into soups just before serving; and sprouted peas are fantastic if lightly steamed and served with a pat of butter melting down through them.

Which is to say that there's almost as much variety in the taste of sprouts as there is in "traditional" vegetables. Give 'em an honest try and you're sure to find at least half a dozen "kinds" of shoots and a couple of hundred sprout recipes that suit you to a T. Almost any organic, vegan, or vegetarian cookbook features a great number of ideas for using the little critters, starting with raw salads and ending with "pick-me-up" beverages made by blending the germinated seeds with various combinations of fruit juices, nuts, and honey. The possibilities are truly endless.

SPROUTING CONTAINERS

There are a great number of complicated and expensive sprouting containers on the market but none really seem to work any better than a common, ordinary, one-pint or one-quart large-mouthed canning jar. Most folks who use such a sprouter simply dump in the seeds, stretch a piece of cheesecloth over the top, and secure the fabric with a rubber band. Others prefer to cut a circle of wire mesh and clamp it to the jar top with a screw-on canning ring. Either way, the idea is to allow convenient and thorough flushing of the germinating seeds every four to six hours as they develop.

No matter what kind of sprouter you try, bear in mind that your little garden will thrive best in a warm, dark, moist—but *not wet*—environment. It's also a good idea to reserve your germination container exclusively for raising shoots (to help prevent tainting them).

HOW AND WHAT TO SPROUT

Almost any seed, grain, or legume can be successfully sprouted, although most devotees of the art think that alfalfa, mung beans, lentils, peas, and the cereal grasses—wheat, oats, barley, and rye—give the best results. Unhulled sesame and sunflower, radish, mustard, red clover, fenugreek, corn, lima beans, pinto beans, kidney beans, chick peas, cress, millet, and nearly any other seed you can think of will work. You should *never*, however, eat potato sprouts (the plant is a member of the poisonous nightshade family).

Select clean, whole seeds that have not been chemically treated in any way. Wash the grain or whatever thoroughly, pick out any chaff or cracked hulls, and check the seeds for fertility (if they're sterile, they'll float).

Place a tablespoon of alfalfa seeds (or four or five tablespoons of beans) in a pint jar and soak them overnight in triple their volume of water. This soaking should be done in a dark place (such as a kitchen cabinet) and the water should be warm (70 to 80°F) and free of chlorine or fluorine (which can sterilize the tender embryo). The smaller seeds—alfalfa, clover, and so forth—will sprout without this overnight soak, but doing so won't hurt them.

Pour the water off the next morning and save it to add to fruit juices or use as stock (it's loaded with water-soluble vitamins and minerals). The seeds will have doubled in size and should be rinsed carefully to prevent mold.

Leave the swelling little packets of life in their jar after rinsing, cap the container with either cloth or screen wire as described earlier, invert the jar at a 45 degree angle in a big bowl, and set your sprouter back in the cupboard.

The last two steps are very important. Germinating seeds will sour and rot if left standing in water, so by tipping the sprouter upside down at the specified angle, you'll always be certain the developing shoots drain well after each rinsing. Similarly, since sunlight toughens the miniplants, you'll ensure yourself the tenderest and tastiest harvest by growing your garden in total or near darkness.

continued on next page

Keep the cupboard vegetable patch warm (room temperature to 90°F) and try to flush some fresh water into and out of the jar every four to six hours. No need to follow a slavish schedule on this maintenance, however, if you're out of the house or apartment all day. A quick rinse twice every twenty-four hours (once in the morning and once at night) works almost as well.

In three to six days, depending on temperature and seed variety, your sprouts will again have doubled or tripled in volume and turned themselves into both tasty and nourishing victuals. The greater number of shoots are at peak vitamin potency sixty to eighty hours after germinating, but personal preferences in taste, texture, and appearance may persuade you to let yours grow longer.

Soybeans, peas, and alfalfa are about right when their sprouts are 2 to 3 inches long. Grain shoots should be eaten when much shorter—about the length of the kernel itself—or they're somewhat bitter. Sunflower sprouts also develop a rather unpleasant tang when they exceed the length of the seeds from which they develop. The lentil sprout is best when about an inch long, while shoots from the mild-flavored mung bean (the mainstay of Chinese cooking) may be allowed to reach a length of 3 or 4 inches before harvest.

By the way, some people fastidiously pluck the hull from each sprout before serving but that's a waste of time and good nutrition—eat the whole shebang!

OLD BEDSTEAD MAKES BIKE RACK

THERE ARE AN AWFUL lot of old bedsteads that are scrapped in this country at the same time that bicycling is being enjoyed by young and old alike. Wonderful! An ideal recycling situation has been set up.

What you do, see, is you take the headpiece off one of those antiquated iron bed frames and you remove the casters and embed the legs of the assembly in cement and presto! You've got yourself a bicycle rack that's every bit as good as an expensive store-bought model.

HOMEMADE ICE CREAM

GOOD HOMEMADE ICE CREAM is kind of runny, melts fast, has a rough graininess . . . and is so much better than most store-bought versions of the dessert that, in comparison, words fail me.

If you've ever tried to make your own and it turned out tasting pasty and slippery, you're using the wrong recipe. Try this one:

4 eggs	1 cup heavy cream
2 ½ cups sugar	2 tablespoons vanilla
6 cups milk	½ teaspoon salt
3 cups light cream	

Beat the eggs until they're light, then add the sugar gradually. Continue to beat the mixture until it thickens. Add the remaining ingredients and mix thoroughly.

For chocolate ice cream, add as much chocolate syrup as you like and cut the vanilla to one tablespoon (and forget entirely all the recipes that call for "cooking a custard").

Once you have the above mix prepared, pour it into the old handcranked ice cream freezer, pack ice and salt around the sides of the bucket, grab the handle, and start turning. As soon as the dessert thickens so much that you can hardly turn the crank, cover the freezing unit with a heavy layer of old burlap sacks and newspaper, and let the whole rig set for twenty minutes while the ice cream inside "ages." Then pull out the container of frozen dessert, pry off its lid, and dig in!

STIR-FRY LEFTOVERS

WHEN THE MONEY AND the food are both getting low—or it looks like you'll have to feed some extra people on short notice—it's handy to know that you can turn your leftovers into an "instant" stir-fry dish. How you make the dish depends on what you have around, but you can start by chopping a couple of onions and cooking them gently in a little oil (don't brown them). Cut up and add any crisp vegetables you can get your hands on (celery, peppers, cabbage, green beans, or sprouts to name a few) and throw them in with the onions along with small pieces of whatever leftover meat there is (or a can of tuna or some raw hamburger). Add a cup of boiling water and a teaspoon of salt, cover the pan, and steam until the vegetables are hot but still crunchy. Thicken with a tablespoon of cornstarch mixed with cold water and a couple of tablespoons of soy sauce. Serve with rice.

GROW BEGONIAS IN A STUMP

IF THERE'S AN OLD rotting stump in your front yard, you might like to scoop out some of the decayed wood at the top, add a little rich soil and put in some begonia plants. They seem to flourish in this kind of container and will grow and flower with a vigor that will surprise you.

HOW TO MAKE KITES

SPRING IS KITE TIME, and here's how to make three different models. The bow kite shown below, of course, is the old standby and is very simple to construct. The drawing, as they say, is self-explanatory. Ash, pine, spruce, or other lightweight wood should be used for the crosspieces, and any lightweight, sturdy paper will make a suitable cover. The frame will be strongest if the strips of wood are lashed rather than notched where they cross.

The French war kite illustrated on the opposite page is somewhat more complicated in design, but each individual step of construction is no more difficult than a corresponding step in the fabrication of the bow kite. Just remember that the area of the wing surfaces must be smaller than the covered area of the triangle (to prevent diving) and the covering on the lower triangle should be about ½ inch wider than the covering on the upper one (for correct balance). The paper should bag slightly, rather than being stretched too tightly, and you'll find it easier to cover the triangles first and the wings last.

Somewhere between the bow and French war kites in complexity is the box kite. Again, the paper covering the lower section should be about ½ inch wider than that on the upper and the paper should not quite be drawn tight. Note: The truss strings on both the box and French war kites and the reinforcing string run around the edges of all pieces of paper.

Pay particular attention to the detail on the French war kite showing the way in which the tips of the major framing members of all three kites are notched to accept the string that runs along the outside of each section of paper covering. You'll note that each tip should be reinforced with a few wraps of thread or string (which is held in place with glue) to prevent the sticks from splitting.

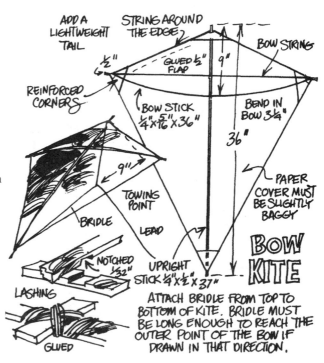

ADD A LIGHTWEIGHT TAIL

STRING AROUND THE EDGE

BOW STRING

½"

GLUED ½" FLAP

9"

REINFORCED CORNERS

BOW STICK ¼" X 5/16" X 36"

BEND IN BOW 3¼"

36"

PAPER COVER MUST BE SLIGHTLY BAGGY

9"

TOWING POINT

BRIDLE

LEAD

NOTCHED 1/32"

UPRIGHT STICK ¼" X ½" X 37"

BOW KITE

LASHING

GLUED

ATTACH BRIDLE FROM TOP TO BOTTOM OF KITE. BRIDLE MUST BE LONG ENOUGH TO REACH THE OUTER POINT OF THE BOW IF DRAWN IN THAT DIRECTION.

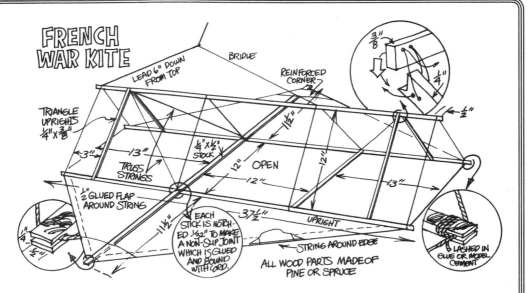

You should also know that any of these kites can be scaled either up or down from the sizes shown in the drawings—all the way from tiny models 12 inches tall to giants that measure 6 feet or more in height—as long as you hold the proportions constant and scale the weight of the construction materials accordingly (thread, balsa strips, and tissue paper for the little ones; and 150-pound twine, ½-inch-square spruce sticks, and a heavy kraft-paper covering for the monsters).

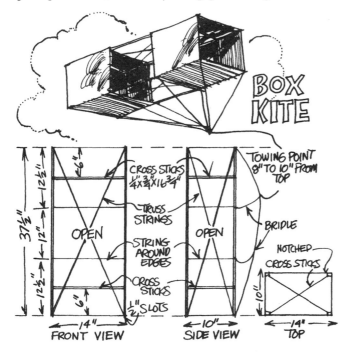

SPECIAL NOTE:
The information for this piece was largely taken from a classic issue of *Popular Mechanics*, a magazine that gives great advice on woodworking projects, tools, and other household projects.

A COMPANIONATE HERBAL FOR THE ORGANIC GARDEN

A LIST OF HERBS, THEIR COMPANIONS, THEIR USES,
INCLUDING SOME BENEFICIAL WEEDS AND FLOWERS

Reprinted Courtesy of Organic Gardening and Farming

HERB	COMPANIONS AND EFFECTS
Basil	Companion to tomatoes; dislikes rue intensely. Improves growth and flavor. Repels flies and mosquitoes.
Beebalm	Companion to tomatoes; improves growth and flavor.
Borage	Companion to tomatoes, squash, and strawberries; deters tomato worm; improves growth and flavor.
Caraway	Plant here and there; loosens soil.
Catnip	Plant in borders; deters flea beetle.
Camomile	Companion to cabbages and onions; improves growth and flavor.
Chervil	Companion to radishes; improves growth and flavor.
Chives	Companion to carrots; improves growth and flavor.
Dead Nettle	Companion to potatoes; deters potato bug; improves growth and flavor.
Dill	Companion to cabbage; dislikes carrots; improves growth and health of cabbage.
Fennel	Plant away from gardens. Most plants dislike it.
Flax	Companion to carrots, potatoes; deters potato bug. Improves growth and flavor.
Garlic	Plant near roses and raspberries; deters Japanese beetle; improves growth and health.
Horseradish	Plant at corners of potato patch to deter potato bug.
Henbit	General insect repellent.
Hyssop	Deters cabbage moth; companion to cabbage and grapes. Keep away from radishes.
Lamb's-Quarters	This edible weed should be allowed to grow in moderate amounts in the garden, especially with corn.

Lemon Balm	Sprinkle throughout garden.
Lovage	Improves flavor and health of plants if planted here and there.
Marigold	The workhorse of the pest deterrents. Plant throughout garden; it discourages Mexican bean beetles, nematodes, and other insects.
Mint	Companion to cabbage and tomatoes; improves health and flavor; deters white cabbage moth.
Marjoram	Here and there in garden; improves flavors.
Mole Plant	Deters moles and mice if planted here and there.
Nasturtium	Companion to radishes, cabbage, and cucurbits; plant under fruit trees. Deters aphids, squash bugs, and striped pumpkin beetles. Improves growth and flavor.
Peppermint	Planted among cabbages, it repels the white cabbage butterfly.
Petunia	Protects beans.
Pigweed	One of the best weeds for pumping nutrients from the subsoil, it is especially beneficial to potatoes, onions, and corn. Keep weeds thinned.
Pot Marigold	Companion to tomatoes, but plant elsewhere in garden too. Deters asparagus beetle, tomato worm, and general garden pests.
Purslane	This edible weed makes good ground cover in the corn.
Rosemary	Companion to cabbage, bean, carrots, and sage; deters cabbage moth, bean beetles, and carrot fly.
Rue	Keep it far away from sweet basil; plant near roses and raspberries; deters Japanese beetle.
Sage	Plant with rosemary, cabbage and carrots; keep away from cucumbers. Deters cabbage moth and carrot fly.
Southernwood	Plant here and there in garden; companion to cabbage; improves growth and flavor; deters cabbage moth.
Sow Thistle	This weed, in moderate amounts, can help tomatoes, onions, and corn.
Summer Savory	Plant with beans and onions; improves growth and flavor. Deters bean beetles.
Tansy	Plant under fruit trees; companion to roses and raspberries. Deters flying insects, Japanese beetles, striped cucumber beetles, squash bugs, ants.
Tarragon	Good throughout garden.
Thyme	Plant here and there in garden; it deters cabbage worm.
Valerian	Good anywhere in garden.
Wild Morning Glory	Allow it to grow in corn.
Wormwood	As a border, it keeps animals from the garden.
Yarrow	Plant along borders, paths, near aromatic herbs; enhances essential oil production.

A LIST OF COMMON GARDEN VEGETABLES, THEIR COMPANIONS, AND THEIR ANTAGONISTS

TOMATO   CHERRY TOMATOES

VEGETABLES	LIKES	DISLIKES
Asparagus	Tomatoes, parsley, basil	*None*
Beans	Potatoes, carrots, cucumbers, cauliflower, cabbage, summer savory, most other vegetables and herbs	*Onions, garlic, gladiolus*
Bush Beans	Potatoes, cucumbers, corn, strawberries, celery, summer savory	*Onions*
Pole Beans	Corn, summer savory	*Onions, beets, kohlrabi, sunflowers*
Beets	Onions, kohlrabi	*Pole beans*
Cabbage Family (cabbage, cauliflower, kale, kohlrabi, broccoli, Brussels sprouts)	Aromatic plants, potatoes, celery, dill, camomile, sage, peppermint, rosemary, beets, onions	*Strawberries, tomatoes, pole beans*
Carrots	Peas, leaf lettuce, chives, onions, leek, rosemary, sage, tomatoes	*Dill*
Celery	Leek, tomatoes, bush beans, cauliflower, cabbage	*None*
Chives	Carrots	*Peas, beans*
Corn	Potatoes, peas, beans, cucumbers, pumpkin, squash	*None*
Cucumbers	Beans, corn, peas, radishes, sunflowers	*Potatoes, aromatic herbs*
Eggplant	Beans	*None*
Leek	Onions, celery, carrots	*None*
Lettuce	Carrots and radishes (lettuce, carrots, and radishes make a strong team grown together), strawberries, cucumbers	*None*
Onions (including garlic)	Beets, strawberries, tomatoes, lettuce, summer savory, camomile (sparsely)	*Peas, beans*

VEGETABLES	LIKES	DISLIKES
Parsley	Tomatoes, asparagus	*None*
Peas	Carrots, turnips, radishes, cucumbers, corn, beans, most vegetables and herbs	*Onions, garlic, gladiolus, potatoes*
Potatoes	Beans, corn, cabbage, horseradish (should be planted at corners of patch), marigold, eggplant (as a lure for Colorado potato beetle)	*Squash, pumpkin, cucumbers, sunflowers, tomatoes, raspberries*
Pumpkin	Corn	*Potatoes*
Radishes	Peas, nasturtium, lettuce, cucumbers	*None*
Soybeans	Grows with anything, helps everything	*None*
Spinach	Strawberries	*None*
Squash	Nasturtium, corn	*None*
Strawberries	Bush beans, spinach, borage, lettuce (as a border)	*Cabbage*
Sunflowers	Cucumbers	*Potatoes*
Tomatoes	Chives, onions, parsley, asparagus, marigold, nasturtium, carrots	*Kohlrabi, potatoes, fennel, cabbage*
Turnips	Peas	*None*

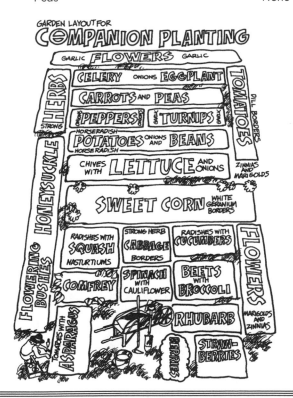

SUMMER

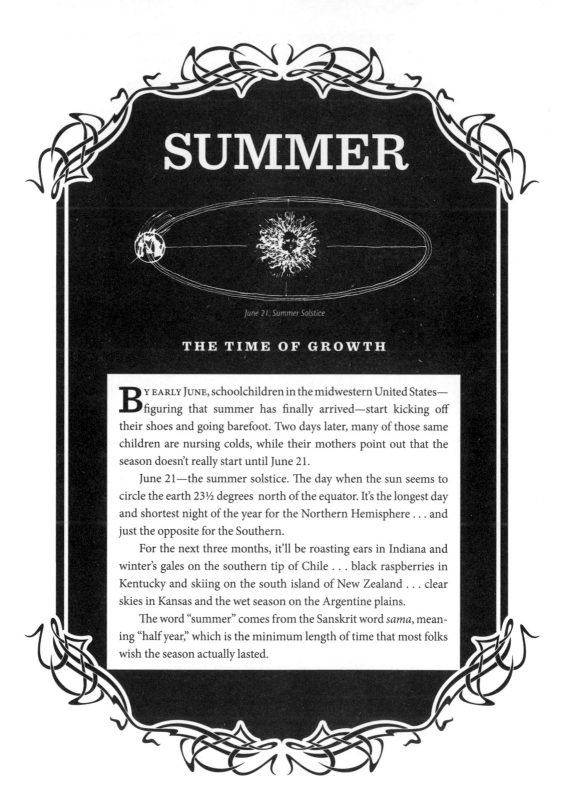

June 21, Summer Solstice

THE TIME OF GROWTH

B Y EARLY JUNE, schoolchildren in the midwestern United States—figuring that summer has finally arrived—start kicking off their shoes and going barefoot. Two days later, many of those same children are nursing colds, while their mothers point out that the season doesn't really start until June 21.

June 21—the summer solstice. The day when the sun seems to circle the earth 23½ degrees north of the equator. It's the longest day and shortest night of the year for the Northern Hemisphere . . . and just the opposite for the Southern.

For the next three months, it'll be roasting ears in Indiana and winter's gales on the southern tip of Chile . . . black raspberries in Kentucky and skiing on the south island of New Zealand . . . clear skies in Kansas and the wet season on the Argentine plains.

The word "summer" comes from the Sanskrit word *sama*, meaning "half year," which is the minimum length of time that most folks wish the season actually lasted.

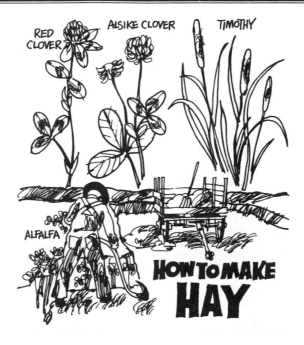

RED CLOVER   ALSIKE CLOVER   TIMOTHY   ALFALFA

HOW TO MAKE HAY

MAKING HAY IS A basic country (survival) art you need to understand if you intend to keep animals. The good subsistence farmer figures he can buy a little grain if he has to, but he won't last long if he must suffer the expense of purchasing hay. *Good* hay is expensive, if you can buy it at all.

Hay is a most blessed crop. Grasses and clovers enrich the soil while they keep it from eroding away. Almost all farm animals can be supported on the dried forage if necessary, and with mineral and protein supplement, it's about all that cows and horses need.

Alfalfa makes the best hay, especially when planted with bromegrass. A mixture of red clover and timothy ranks second in quality. Good alfalfa produces at least five tons of baled hay per acre on three cuttings; red clover about two and a half tons on one harvest. (You can't cut red clover three times like you can alfalfa but, on the other hand, red clover doesn't get alfalfa weevil.)

Hay crops are planted the year before you first harvest them. You can seed grass right on top of the snow in February, or on frozen ground in March, or in the ground in April with a grain drill. The last way is the best, although early broadcasting also gives good results.

Making hay is quite similar to what you do when you mow a lawn; let the clippings dry and then rake them up. If you store the dry grass clippings in your barn for your rabbits, as I do, then you already know what "making hay" is all about.

For real hay crops, you should cut just as the clovers begin to blossom, which is usually in June in the North. You can mow small amounts by hand with a scythe, but a sickle bar mower (available for both small garden and larger farm tractors) is better for the bigger plots.

The name of the haymaking game is to get the stuff dry enough to put in the barn before rain falls. Rain harms cut hay and lots of rain will ruin it. Normally, if you mow on one day, the

continued on next page

hay will be cured enough to store or stack two days later (within twenty-four hours or less, if the weather is hot, dry, and windy).

When the hay is nearly dry, rake it into windrows. On small plots you can do this easily by hand with a pitchfork or a leaf rake; in large fields you need a tractor-drawn side-delivery rake. Old, but usable, equipment of this kind is easy to find and buy in farm country. You can purchase small mechanical rakes for garden tractors too.

Once hay is windrowed and dry, you can bale it, or load it on a wagon or truck "loose" with a pitchfork, or stack it right in the field. Long-stranded hay, carefully stacked in a conical shape, will shed most water and the hay will store reasonably well, except for the outer layer that faces the weather.

How do you tell when the fodder is dry enough to put in the barn? My way works for me, and it may work for you. I take a hank of hay about three fingers thick and twist it as if I were wringing out a dishrag. If the hank separates into two pieces on the third twist, it's about right. If it just wrings like a limp rag, it's still too wet.

A full-grown cow needs about a ton of hay—with grain—to get her through the winter. A ton of good fodder will handle a horse, or four sheep or goats, or forty rabbits. Good green alfalfa hay makes good hog feed. Chickens will appreciate the cured forage in winter, too, if you have nothing else green to give them.

DAMP CLOTH CURES DENTS

By placing a damp cloth over a dent in wooden furniture and then applying a hot iron for a few minutes, you can often make the wood fibers spring back into place.

PUT GRAVEL UNDER OUTDOOR FAUCET

You can keep that outdoor faucet or pump from turning the surrounding area to mud if you dig out a hole beneath the water spout and replace the soil with rocks or gravel.

SOW BIRDSEED FOR YOUR CAT

If your cat nibbles the leaves off your house plants, sow birdseed in a shallow pot and give him his own private supply of greens.

CUT AND SHARPEN a *V* notch into one side of your garden hoe and you'll find it much easier to nip off those tough weeds that seem to delight in growing in tight corners. The *V* won't slip off as you bear down on a particular weed and the edges of the notch—protected as they are from constantly chopping into the ground—will stay sharp an uncommonly long time.

SPEND A SUMMER IN A
FOREST FIRE LOOKOUT

MAKE MONEY AS A FOREST FIRE LOOKOUT

A LOT OF LUCKY folks are moving out of cities to little homesteads where they plan to live happily ever after raising their own food and/or operating a home business. Even more people would like to make the same break, but let's face it, some of us just do not have enough cash to buy—or even make the down payment on—country property. Besides that, it can be kind of scary to go from the city to self-sufficiency on the land all in one jump.

Wouldn't it be nice if there was kind of a halfway step in between? Perhaps something like a job that would get you and your mate out of the city and into some beautiful, remote location without leaving you feeling that you've been suddenly cut off. A job at which you could quickly earn—and save—enough for the down payment on your own place in the country, while being introduced to life on the land.

The job is that of Forest Fire Lookout, and an article by Miss G. Scott, a young lady who's done it, appeared a while back in MOTHER EARTH NEWS. Miss Scott feels that working in a fire lookout tower is an ideal introduction to country living because, as she says, "Although you'll be located on a mountain with only primitive facilities, you'll know that your time there is limited and you'll be in constant radio communication with other lookouts." She also points out that being a forest fire watcher is an honorable job, puts you in the woods during the most pleasant part of the year, gives you a lot of time that is entirely your own, and virtually forces you to save money since, obviously, you won't be tempted to spend much while living 40 or more miles from the nearest town.

If this sounds good, contact the U.S. Forest Service, the Bureau of Land Management, or the National Park Service to ask for a list of the forests that need lookouts, both paid and volunteer. The West Coast, as might be expected, offers the most opportunities since that's where most of the dense woods are. This type of job is dwindling because of the prevalence of automotion, but you may find an opening in a section of the country with national forests or large timber holdings.

SPRING PROTECTS GARBAGE CAN

FASTEN A LONG SCREEN door spring permanently to one handle of your garbage can and bend the loop on the other end into an easily fastened hook. Then, whenever you place the lid on the container, run the spring through the top's handle and secure it to the second handhold on the can. That way, no dog will be able to get the lid off . . . but the trash man can.

SPRING

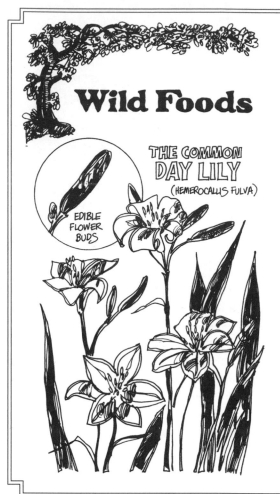

Wild Foods

THE COMMON DAY LILY
(HEMEROCALLIS FULVA)

EDIBLE FLOWER BUDS

WASHER PREVENTS CHAIR LEG FROM CUTTING RUBBER TIP

THE RUBBER TIPS COMMONLY put on kitchen chair and patio furniture legs do a great job of protecting the floor until, that is, the tubular metal within cuts through the tips. You'll never have that problem again if, like some savvy individuals, you buy a small supply of flat washers just large enough to fit over the ends of the furniture legs before the tips are put on. Once in place, the washers absolutely prevent the sharp edge of the tubing from slicing through the rubber guards.

NATURAL MOSQUITO CONTROLS

YOU'LL HAVE FEWER MOSQUITOES around your place (unless you live next to a swamp) if you clean up all possible breeding spots for the little varmints. Note the use of the word "all"—a whole cloud of the pesky vipers can grow to maturity in a half-full bucket of water left behind the barn.

THE DAY LILY, ALTHOUGH not native
to North America, now grows wild throughout most of the continent.
It's eaten far too seldom in this country but is an important food plant in Asia
and can be prepared in a great many tasty, nutritious, and appetizing ways.

Cut the spring's first day lily stalks just above the roots and cook the tender
inner sections of the stems like asparagus (that is, boiled just a few minutes)
and "wash 'em down" with butter. Wow! Talk about good! The stalks can also be
sliced and added to a salad.

Throughout the summer, unopened day lily flowers are tastier than freshly picked spring
green beans if boiled three or four minutes and served with butter and salt. The buds are
even better dipped in a thick egg batter and quickly fried to a golden brown in almost smoking hot fat. Opened flowers can be prepared the same way, but better fix lots of 'em, 'cause
they're delicious.

The flavor of soups and stews can also be enhanced by the same flowers and buds. Just
drop the blooms into the pot during the last minutes of cooking time. No need to enjoy these
"vegetables" only during the summer, either. Dry the blossoms in a warm room, squirrel them
away in glass jars, and add 'em to soups and stews year-round.

In addition to the flowers and stems it offers aboveground, the generous day lily also hides
a treat beneath the surface of the earth. This is the cluster of small (seldom more than an inch
long) tubers that are tightly grouped directly below the plant. The tiny "potatoes" are noticeably at their best when dug in the spring and summer but can be harvested during any season.
Just discard the older, soft bulbs and concentrate on the firm, sweet, crisp younger ones. Eat
'em raw or enjoy their nutty flavor in a salad, boiled, or creamed. The thinning will do the day
lilies good.

When it comes to warding off mosquitoes that are already growed up big enough to bite, smoke still
seems to be as good a repellent as any, and we always carry along the smoldering, soft, rotten wood (punk)
dug out of an old stump or log on our camping, fishing, and boating trips. Light one end of a piece of punk
and it will puff away for hours, holding off about three-quarters of the mosquitoes in the immediate vicinity
all the while. Out of each one hundred of the humming devils, then, that only leaves you twenty-five to slap at.

AN INTERESTING FACT ABOUT MOSQUITOES

IT IS A SCIENTIFIC fact that only the female mosquito bites (she needs a drop of blood before she can breed
or lay her eggs or something). The male does not suck blood at all and, as a matter of fact, he can't. Some
folks, though, swear for a fact that the male of the species *will* point you out to the female whenever she has
trouble finding your tender body in the dark.

CHUCK KEY PREVENTS ELECTRIC DRILL SHOCK

MORE THAN A FEW carpenters—both professional and amateur—
still have use for electric drills. And some have been
hurt by accidentally hitting the switch of the drill
while they changed bits in the machine's chuck. You'll find that such
an accident can never happen to you, though, if you tape the power
tool's chuck key to its electrical cord right down at the plug end. That
way, the drill simply *has* to be disconnected before the key can be used.

THE BIG CHEMICAL MANUFACTURERS would dearly
love to have us believe that insect pests can be con-
trolled only through the use of their poisonous
sprays and dusts. Well, as any organic gardener can
tell you, that's simply not true. You can control and
repel harmful insects in a number of natural ways
including, to name only a few: companion planting,
natural repellents, predator insects, birds, poultry,
reptiles, and small animals.

Take companion planting, for instance. Maybe
you didn't know it, but insects are among the most finicky eaters in the world. Those beetles that
feast on melons and cucumbers can't stomach radishes; the cabbage butterfly is positively repelled
by tomatoes, mint, and rosemary; and potato bugs stay as far as possible from horseradish and flax.

It stands to reason, then, that you can severely limit insect attacks on your garden merely by the
way in which you arrange it. If you alternate a row of green beans with a row of potatoes, for example,
the beans will tend to ward off the Colorado potato beetle and the potatoes will help protect the beans
from the Mexican bean beetle.

Chives will keep aphids away from roses; most
of the aromatic herbs—such as borage, lavender,
sage, parsley, or dill—will repel great numbers
of garden pests; and marigolds seem to protect
almost any garden plant from almost anything!

Now, just as marigolds keep beetles off the
beans, so may a natural marigold *spray* be used
for the same purpose. In fact, any plant or flower
that protects another from pests may be liquefied
and made into a protective spray for the other
plant. The process is simple—you just grind the
whole marigold or whatever into a pulp, dissolve

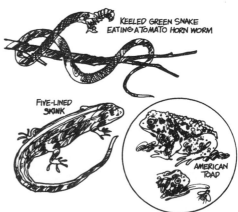

KEELED GREEN SNAKE
EATING A TOMATO HORN WORM

FIVE-LINED
SKINK

AMERICAN
TOAD

FLAVOR APPLE BUTTER WITH RED HOTS

Add a few Red Hots or cinnamon candy drops as you cook up your next batch of homemade apple butter, and the spread will have both a better flavor and color.

HOW TO PEEL A TURNIP

To peel a turnip or other tough-skinned vegetable, score the rind in bands all the way around (like the Tropics of Capricorn and Cancer on the globe) and cut the strips off one at a time.

it in two to three times as much water, strain off the liquid, and use it on the plants you want to protect.

Another good natural spray of an entirely different kind is a mixture of two cups of flour, four ounces of buttermilk, and two and a half gallons of water. It's guaranteed to chase spider mites right out of your apple trees. Milk—either whole, powdered, or diluted—will also control tomato mosaic virus in a greenhouse.

The easiest way to stay ahead of snails and slugs in the garden is to get 'em drunk! They LOVE beer and, if you bury a few saucers flush in the ground and fill 'em with brew in the evening, you'll find those same saucers half full of happily drowned slugs and snails the next morning.

We mustn't forget, either, that some of the insects out there in the garden are our friends and allies. Ladybugs, as you probably know, steadily munch their way through scales, harmful insect eggs and larvae, white flies, and spider mites. The praying mantis relishes lice, flies, grasshoppers, and chinch bugs. Lacewings, wasps, bees, ants, and stinkbugs also lend a hand on the insect pest control detail.

And, of course, the larger "animated bug catchers" more than earn their keep around the vegetable patch. Geese, ducks, chickens, toads, snakes, birds, skunks, and other of our small feathered, scaled, and furry friends will constantly patrol the garden if we only let them.

Beatrice Trum Hunter—in her book, *Gardening without Poisons*—states that a single house wren will feed 500 spiders and caterpillars to its young during one summer afternoon; a swallow can devour 1,000 leafhoppers in twelve hours; a Baltimore oriole can consume 17 hairy caterpillars a minute; and a brown thrasher can eat more than 6,000 insects a day.

Yep, there are many ways of controlling house, yard, and garden insects without once falling back on dangerous pesticides. Your local library or favorite bookseller will have more on safe and simple pest regulators, as well as books on how to garden organically, such as *The Gardener's Bug Book* by Barbara Pleasant.

FOUR FINGERS OF DAYLIGHT

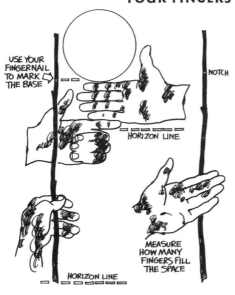

USE YOUR FINGERNAIL TO MARK THE BASE

NOTCH

HORIZON LINE

MEASURE HOW MANY FINGERS FILL THE SPACE

HORIZON LINE

EVENING'S COMING ON AND you're still a long way from camp. Will you make it in before dark? Maybe, maybe not . . . . Here's how to accurately estimate the time till sundown:

Face the setting sun with your arms extended and measure the distance between Ole Sol's base and the horizon in fingers (no thumbs). Each finger counts as fifteen minutes. Four of them, then, equal one hour; four on one hand and two on the other add up to an hour and a half, and so on.

If the space to be measured is greater than all eight fingers, hold a stick at arm's length with its base on the horizon and mark the position of the sun's bottom edge with your fingernail. The number of fingers it takes to fill the distance is your time.

In deep woods or hilly country where it's difficult to judge the horizon, work from an imaginary line at eye level.

A HANDY CLOTHESLINE TIGHTENER

A GOOD PERCENTAGE OF green-living advocates have discovered that the old-timey clothes line will save them lots off their electric and gas bills. Unfortunately, the same people have also learned just how much ornerier a sagging clothesline can be to use than an indoor dryer.

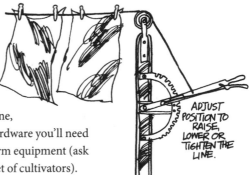

ADJUST POSITION TO RAISE, LOWER OR TIGHTEN THE LINE.

There is a way to tame the most contrary clothesline, though, as the accompanying sketch shows. All the hardware you'll need is available for scrap prices from any dealer in used farm equipment (ask for something like the adjustment lever from an old set of cultivators).

TIP SHOELACE WITH PARAFFIN

THE NEXT TIME THE tip comes off one of your shoelaces, dip the unprotected end of string in melted paraffin and shape it to a point before the wax hardens.

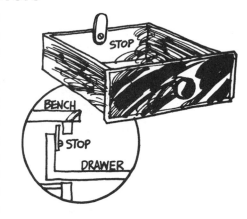

DRAWER STOPS

THERE WILL BE NO more pulling packed drawers all the way out and dumping their contents on the floor if—on that next rainy afternoon—you take the time to add a stop to each sliding ministorage chest.

Screw a small block of wood to the inside or front surface of each drawer's back panel. The little stop should be located, of course, so that it sticks up high enough to hit the inside of the cabinet's front, thereby preventing the sliding box from coming completely out. Be sure to use a screw—rather than nails or glue—to hold the stop in place. That way, you can always reach in and remove the block with a screwdriver whenever you *do* want to take the drawer all the way out of the cabinet.

REFLECT HEADLIGHTS WITH MIRROR

IF YOU'RE EVER CAUGHT along the road at night with a flat tire and no flashlight, have a member of your party stand in front of the car with a mirror and reflect the strong beam of one of the headlights back to where it's needed.

TRY THIS SIMPLE SUBSTITUTION FOR AN EXPENSIVE BAR CLAMP

ANY HALFWAY SELF-SUFFICIENT homeowner enjoys a good, one-day construction project like building a rabbit hutch or fabricating a set of ornate picture frames. The only trouble with both these jobs—and a lot of others—though, is that they involve large frames that somehow must be clamped together for nailing

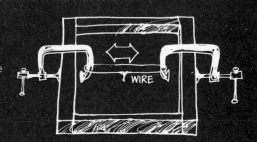

and gluing. And that can be a difficult undertaking in the Average Amateur Workshop because, as we all know, the AAW seldom contains a good, big, husky bar clamp (the tool made especially for the job).

No problem. Whenever you're faced with one or another variation of this situation, simply loop two C-clamps together with wire so that the total span of the makeshift rig is roughly the same as the reach you're trying to cover. As you then slip the assembly over the piece of work in question and screw in the adjustments on the C-clamps, the improvised three-section bar clamp will "pull itself together" and, in turn, pull the project together just as well as any expensive bar clamp.

BUILD YOURSELF A RECYCLED HOUSE . . . AND SAVE A BUNDLE!

WITH THE PRICE OF new housing—and, for that matter, old homes—scaring buyers, it's always nice to find an idea that can help ordinary folks save money on building their own homes. Here at MOTHER EARTH NEWS, we've looked over a lot of do-it-yourself construction ideas—from some as old as adobe to others as new as tiny houses—and, time and again, we've found that the easiest way to save out-of-pocket cash on a new house is also the most obvious.

So obvious, in fact, that most of us tend to overlook the method completely. Which is unfortunate, because the approach we're talking about offers double-barreled benefits. Used correctly, it will (1) allow you to save money and (2) at the same time, do something very nice for the planet.

The secret is *recycling* the materials from old buildings to create your new home. Which, as stated, is so darn obvious that you've probably completely overlooked the idea. More's the pity. There's hardly a town, city, or farming area in North America that doesn't offer a ready supply of free-for-the-hauling building materials to those who know how to go about getting it. You might as well tap this treasure lode as the next fellow . . . and all it takes is a little know-how and a little hard work.

It doesn't matter how lavish or unlavish a house you intend to construct, either—you can still cash in on the recycling or *upcycling* idea. For instance, old barns are loaded with potential housing materials—beams, timbers, and siding can be repurposed into new ceilings, floors, and, yep, "new" siding. Broken-down homes offer doors, windows (sometimes even stained glass), kitchen cabinets, bathroom fixtures, fireplace mantles, and more.

The raw materials are all around you although, as you'll soon learn when you go out looking for them, old buildings have a miraculous way of blending into the background. There's no need to rush off and start dismantling the first structure that's offered to you. Pick only the buildings that are easiest to take down and that will furnish you with the most usable material.

In general, old garages and barns are what you want. Either type of building has almost as much framing and siding, foot for foot, as a house. And yet, neither a barn nor a garage has the tons of plaster or drywall that a house has and which you won't be able to use . . . but which you *will* have to find some way to dispose of.

Stick to one- and two-story wooden frame buildings, at least at first, and don't bother with anything built of bricks—even if you want them. Only a small percentage of salvaged bricks come out usable unless you really know how to take them apart.

Remember too, when talking to its owner about dismantling a structure, that it's always wise to tell him you'll do the job very, very inexpensively . . . but NOT FOR FREE. You're going to have to spend *some* dollars on tools and a truck . . . and even if you already have all the equipment you need, you should still charge *something* for your work. Otherwise, the owner may get the idea that you want the salvaged materials so much that HE should charge YOU for them. Check with your local town hall about permits and or licenses to demolish buildings. There may be a fee as well.

Now comes the fun part. You'll need to buy, rent, or borrow a couple of crowbars, a couple of hydraulic jacks, some heavy rope or cable, a pick, shovel, sledgehammer, hacksaw, enough hammers to go around, a nail-pulling tool called a cat's-paw, a dumpster, and a truck. Round up your friends and relatives and begin.

Use your head, work slowly and carefully, and always put one person in charge of the whole crew whenever several individuals turn out to help. No need for a confused flapping about that could well end with someone getting a roof dropped on them by mistake.

Old copper wiring and roof flashing can be recycled through a scrap dealer for money, and an

ad will usually sell such salvaged items as ceramic or marble tiles, bathtubs, and other fixtures. Chances are you'll want to keep all the lumber and slate or metal roofing you find for use on your own project.

And by the way: If you pay careful attention to the construction details of those old buildings as you take them apart, you're going to know a lot about putting that new house of yours together before you start on it, even if you've never tried your hand at carpentry—or saving several thousand dollars all at once—before.

SUPPORT YOUR TOMATOES

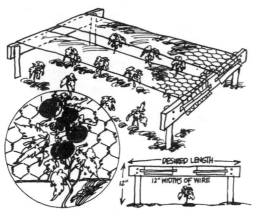

NATURE WORKS IN WISE, wondrous, and—sometimes—seemingly contradictory ways. Experienced gardeners, for instance, know that very late tomato plants bear longer, more, and better when allowed to spraddle out close to the warm, mulched ground where first frosts can't hurt them. The same gardeners have also learned that tomato vines in a summer vegetable patch generally produce better fruit when staked *up off the*

ground away from dampness, mold, and bugs. Smart growers, then, heavily mulch their late tomatoes and let 'em run . . . but take the time to build a trellis for their summer "love fruit" plants to climb.

The accompanying illustration shows one way to keep your July and August tomatoes off the ground (and away from the crickets), while allowing the vines to spread and receive full benefit of the sun.

Set short, sturdy posts in pairs (one on each side of a tomato row) at 8 foot intervals. Cut 1x4 boards to length and nail one across each pair of posts. Then stretch and tack a 12-inch-wide strip of poultry wire from support to support down each side of the row. One caution: Do be sure to leave enough space between the two strips of chicken wire for the tomato plants to grow up through!

A CHIGGER CURE

A SUMMER'S AFTERNOON SPENT picking berries in the woods can be a lot of fun until, that is, the chiggers start to dig in as they sometimes do. Foolish folks, confronted with that situation, often try to pick the little pests out with a needle. A much safer course of action, it is claimed, is to tightly press a piece of adhesive tape over a chigger welt and then pull it away, taking the parasite with it.

HOW TO REMOVE CANNING JAR LIDS

HOME CANNING IS BACK in fashion once again, and—once again—you'll sometimes find a sealed glass jar with a lid that just won't come off. If the container is one of the old-fashioned kind with a separate rubber ring seal, however, it can be opened quite easily. Just take a pair of pliers, grip the ring and pull it out until air is released. The ornery cap will then come right off.

EGG WHITE TAKES OFF CHEWING GUM

CHEWING GUM THAT HAS become attached to washable fabric will generally come right off if softened with egg white and then scrubbed.

VINEGAR SOFTENS PAINT BRUSHES

HARDENED PAINT BRUSHES CAN often be made as good as new by simmering them in boiling vinegar for a few minutes and then washing them in soapy water.

TOOTHPASTE TUBES MAKE GOOD SINKERS

VERY SATISFACTORY FISH LINE weights can be made from old toothpaste tubes. Simply cut the container into strips about an inch long and any width you like. Wrap a chunk or chunks around the line (or the shank of a hook, if you prefer to weight *that*) and crimp. One more bit of waste safely recycled.

Of course, if you brush your teeth with salt and baking soda you won't have any silly old toothpaste tubes around anyway. Then again, some dentists say that salt shouldn't be used for this purpose as it's too abrasive (I brushed with salt for years, not knowing any better, and my teeth are just fine).

As far as I know, however, nobody criticizes the use of baking soda for cleansing the teeth. So you might just as well brush your pearly whites with that powder . . . except for the fact that I have no handy uses for old baking soda boxes . . .

HOW TO CARRY PLYWOOD ON A CAR

AIN'T NOTHING MORE UNWIELDY to tote home on an ordinary sedan-type automobile than a few sheets of plywood. About the only way to get around that proposition with any dignity at all is to take along a couple of old inner tubes and some rope with you to the lumberyard. Inflate the tubes, lay them on the roof of the car, place the plywood on top of the "cushions," and run a couple 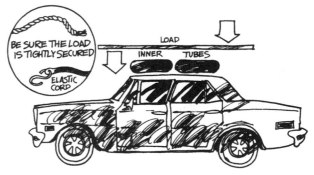 loops of the rope through the car windows and over the whole shebang. Snug the loops down tight and throw an appropriate hitch on 'em (see the knot section of this book). You'll be able to ride home in style with—even—the windows rolled almost clear up.

ROLL AN ORANGE BEFORE YOU SQUEEZE IT

TO GET MORE JUICE out of an orange or lemon, roll the fruit firmly on a hard surface before you squeeze it.

VINEGAR MAKES WINDOWS SPARKLE

FOR A BRILLIANT POLISH, add a little vinegar to the wash water the next time you clean windows.

BASIC KNOTS

SQUARE KNOT: The basic tie for joining two ropes, also called a reef knot. Make by forming first a right and then a left overhand knot. Much easier to untie and far superior in holding strength than the granny knot, which it closely resembles.

GRANNY KNOT

BOWLINE: This knot will not slip and is ideal for tying two ropes together, for fastening a rope to a pole, and for rescue operations. Form closed loop in rope, bring end of line up through loop, around standing end of rope, and back down through loop. Pull tight.

SHEETBEND: The best knot for joining two ropes, especially when they differ in size. Form a blight (loop) in the larger line. Bring the smaller through the blight, around the doubled heavier cord, and back under belt.

CLOVE HITCH: Easy to tie and untie. Holds well. This is one of the most useful of all hitches for fastening tent ropes and guys to stakes or poles.

BOATING KNOTS

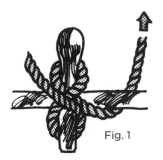

Fig. 1

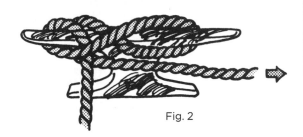

Fig. 2

BELAYING TO A PIN OR CLEAT: It's always best to make a first turn to take the strain before making one or two figure eight turns to temporarily hold the load (Fig. 1). For more permanent fastening, finish with a half hitch (Fig. 2).

FIGURE EIGHT: Useful as a convenient handhold and for preventing ropes from running through a hole or pulley. Form by throwing a loop near the end of a line, bringing the short end completely around the standing part of the rope and back through the loop. Pull tight.

CARRICK BEND: A strong joining knot. Cross a blight on one rope and work the end of the second line around it in a regular under-and-over manner. Note that at no time does the line pass through a loop.

OUTDOOR KNOTS

SHEEPSHANK: Downright handy for shortening a line without untying it. Follow the diagrams and you can't go wrong. The hitch may be fastened permanently by passing the ends of the rope through the loops.

CAT'S PAW: A good way to secure a rope to a hook. Throw a double loop in the line, twist both ends twice, and slip them over the hook.

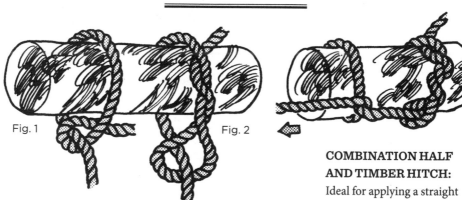

Fig. 1 Fig. 2

COMBINATION HALF AND TIMBER HITCH: Ideal for applying a straight end pull to a pole or pipe. Tie the half hitch first, timber hitch second.

HALF HITCH: For temporarily fastening a line to a pole (Fig. 1).

TIMBER HITCH: A half hitch modified to hold more securely (Fig. 2).

SPLICING & WHIPPING

EYE SPLICE: Useful for putting a permanent loop in the end of a rope and for splicing one line, at right angles, into another. First unlay the rope about five turns and bend it back upon itself to form the desired loop. The two outer strands should straddle and the central strand lie on top of the line. Second, raise a strand in the main line and pass the middle loose strand under it, over the second main line strand, under the third, etc. Weave the two outside loose strands in over the first main line strand, under the second, etc. The finished splice will look like the final drawing above.

THE ESSENTIALS OF A GOOD SPLICE: A good splice must be strong and durable, it must carry the same load as any other part of the rope and—when made out in the middle of a line—it must not increase the rope's diameter enough to bind up in a pulley. Basically, splicing consists of three steps: (1) unlaying the strands of the ends to be joined, (2) fitting the ends together and interlocking their strands, and (3) relaying and weaving the strands into a smooth piece of rope. The splice shown above illustrates all three steps and is an exceptionally handy one to know for making lariats, cinch lines for heavy loads, etc.

WHIPPING: To prevent a rope from unraveling, form a blight in a piece of twine and hold it ¼ inch from the rope's end. Wrap the other end of the twine around the rope until the length of whipping equals the larger line's diameter. Place end of twine through the exposed loop, pull the loop under the whipping, and trim loose end.

FREE STEAM POWER

MODERN MAN—THAT'S YOU AND ME—is power hungry. In particular, we just can't seem to get enough electricity to heat our houses, cook our food, run our appliances, and manufacture all the gadgets we think we ought to have.

On the other hand, we now know that generating all the electrical power we use—especially when we bum fossil fuels such as coal to do it—is one of today's prime sources of air pollution. That puts us between a rock and a hard spot. How are we going to have the power . . . without making the air unbreathable?

Well, there are ways . . . and some of them have been around longer than humankind. I guess we've just been too contrary to use them.

Have you ever heard of geothermal energy, for example? Geothermal power—sometimes called magma power—is heat energy taken from the earth itself.

We know that the core of the earth is molten rock, or magma, and that only the thin outer crust of our planet is cool. On average, for every mile we bore into the surface of the earth, the temperature climbs about 113°F. In some areas this temperature rise can be as much as 720°F for every mile we drill down and, in the Imperial Valley of California, a jump in temperature of 3,632°F per mile has been recorded by test wells.

Now, heat *is* energy but—to make that energy readily available for the generation of electricity—we need one more ingredient: water. Heat plus water, as you know, equals steam.

If it happens, then, that directly above a hot spot on the earth's crust the ground is porous and filled with water, there will be created a natural boiler. And if this steam is captured, we have—ready-made—a tremendous reserve of usable power that we can tap. That doesn't happen often but it

HORSETAILS HAVE THEIR USES

THE COMMON HORSETAIL—THAT STRANGE, angular, rush-like plant with the jointed stems and scalelike leaves—is a miniature descendant of the thirty-footers that grew in prehistoric swamps. One peculiarity of this refugee from 300 million years ago is that its walls have a very high silica content—so high that some gardeners soak horsetails in water and use the liquid as a spray to strengthen the cells of their garden crops.

The early settlers in this country didn't use the horsetail as a garden aid, as far as we know. They did, however, take advantage of the plant's stiffness by tying the stalks into bundles and using the trimmed ends as a scraper when they scoured pots. If you have a good supply of "scouring rush" growing near you, you'll find that this old method still works very well. It makes the scouring more fun too.

COMMON HORSETAILS

happens often enough . . . and this is exactly the situation that exists in California's Imperial Valley.

Tests there have shown that geothermal wells sunk into the huge natural boiler under the valley will tap enough live steam to drive generators capable of supplying a significant portion of California's electrical needs for years and years to come.

Maybe geothermal power is not the final answer to our current and projected energy shortages . . . but this clean steam power from the earth itself looks mighty attractive until something better comes along.

TOMATO JUICE DE-SKUNKS DOG

ANYBODY OR ANYTHING NEW to country life is bound to make some mistakes, so—if you're a recent back-to-the-lander—don't be surprised if your city-bred dog tangles with a skunk some evening. After all, even farm pups commit the same error (usually just once except in the case of a really stupid mutt that will, probably, continue to pounce on every skunk it sees for as long as it lives).

Well, whether for the first or the fourteenth run-in with a striped "woods kitty," the traditional deodorizer is tomato juice. Break out several cans of the liquid and douse your fragrant transgressor good in the fluid. Something—most likely the acid in the juice—will neutralize the smell down to a tolerable level.

CLOVES AND SPICES SCENT LINENS

HERE'S AN OLD RECIPE for a pleasant-smelling mixture to be stored with linens: Dry rose leaves in the shade and mix a pound of them with one ounce each of cloves, caraway seeds, and allspice. Pound the leaves and spices together in a mortar or grind them in a mill. Add a quarter pound of salt, mix well, and put the scent, or potpourri, in muslin bags.

To ADD GLOSS TO dull hair, one old recipe calls for simmering a pound of honey and one ounce of beeswax together for a few minutes. The liquid portion of the warm infusion is next strained off, reinforced by one-eighth ounce each of lavender, thyme, and oil of almond, and stirred until cold. The preparation is then ready to go. On the other hand, beer will do the same thing and comes all set to use.

An egg shampoo is no joke—it'll make your hair just as beautiful as that stuff you see in ads. Mix the yolk of one egg into a pint of warm water and throw in a pinch of borax. Rinse with hot, then cold, water.

Good rinsing, by the way, is the real secret of hair-washing success. Use rainwater if at all possible. Even without any special shampoos, rainwater makes your hair shine.

Environmentally conscious makeup artists should be aware that beet juice lightly brushed on the cheeks imparts a rosier glow than most high-priced cosmetics.

Fine oatmeal mixed into a paste with cold water is said to be good for the complexion too. But my grandpa used to claim there was nothing better for a facial than stump water (the water that collects in the hollows of stumps, logs, and tree trunks). I'm not sure how he'd know, though, since he never had much complexion when he was seventy and his face was just as leathery when he was ninety-four.

INSULATE YOUR HOME-CANNED FOOD

THE SHELF LIFE OF home-canned food can be increased by packing the jars in sawdust or hay to insulate them from extreme heat or cold.

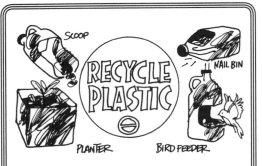

REPURPOSING PLASTIC CAN BE quite a challenge, but one exception—at least—is the bottle with a built-in handle (the kind water, milk, juice, and other liquids come in). This model—with its top on—can be cut down into a handy scoop to keep in a big bag of dried beans, grain, flour, or other stored food.

The same kind of bottle—with the spout and handleless shoulder cut out—is a fine piece of play and storage equipment for kids (good for mixing mud pies, holding puzzle pieces after the box gets stepped on, or collecting shells, pine cones, speckled pebbles . . . you name it).

TOY SNAKES KEEP BIRDS FROM FRUIT TREES

BIRDS CERTAINLY ARE WONDERFUL to have around the farm, backyard, or homestead . . . until the fruit trees start to bear and the feathery little rascals turn into robbers of the first order. If only they'd steal *part* of the crop and eat it *all*, instead of taking one or two bites from every piece of fruit on each tree! What we need is some method of making the greedy little characters keep the heck off the groaning branches and down on the ground snatching bugs, where they belong.

Well, a good number of folks claim that one or two toy snakes coiled around the top branches of each cherry, apple, peach, plum, or other fruit tree will do exactly that. Commercial fruit growers also seem to have good luck setting a carbide cannon or two (timed to fire every three or four minutes) out in their orchards during the fruiting season. The only trouble with the cannon, of course, is that it keeps the birds away entirely as long as it's operating— but that's still better than killing the flying fruitnappers outright.

OLD PAINT BRUSHES CAN BE RECYCLED TOO

BEFORE YOU THROW AWAY that next old paint brush, consider the idea of trimming off its frayed bristles and recycling the tool into a duster for your workshop. It'll get back into those blind corners on the drill press, lathe, and other machinery, and it'll pick up grime and shavings without once allowing you to snag your fingers on a metal splinter.

PAINT OVER PAPER PLATES

YOU'LL KEEP THE FLOOR neater during that next painting job if you simply glue a paper plate to the bottom of your paint can . . . instead of trying to move newspapers under the container every time you set it down.

HOW TO LOCATE A MISFIRING SPARK PLUG

EVEN A NONMECHANIC CAN find a missing spark plug on an engine in minutes if he knows this simple trick: Start the power plant and let it run until warm, then shut the engine off and feel the base of the plugs. The good ones will be warm, the bad ones cold.

PLANT FLAVOR AND NUTRITION IN YOUR GARDEN

IT'S UNFORTUNATE THAT—BRAIN-WASHED AS many folks have become by the "biggest is best" philosophy—our growers grow, consumers consume, and developers develop big and bright fruits and vegetables almost entirely at the expense of flavorful and nutritious produce. It has become a vicious circle.

One organic gardener in Ohio has studied the situation, however, and has found a few noteworthy exceptions. "The picture is dark," he says, "but not entirely black. There *are* a few new fruits and vegetables that have been bred expressly for taste and food value. Every gardener should know about them."

And it's true that with the explosion of farmers markets and home gardens, more and more people are coming to realize that smaller fruits and vegetables can be ten or more times as flavorful as their grocery-store counterparts.

For example, the Double Rich tomato, developed by the University of New Hampshire, has twice the vitamin C content of ordinary varieties. Another tomato—Purdue University's Caro-Red—contains an almost unbelievable ten times more vitamin A than most strains of its kind.

Illini-Chief sweet corn is a hybrid that is not any more vitamin-packed than other varieties, but

PROTECT THOSE FISHHOOKS

LAY YOUR EXTRA FISHHOOKS down on half a long strip of masking tape, fold the other end of the strip over, stick it to the first, and you'll (1) no longer lose the hooks from your tackle box one by one, (2) protect the points of the hooks and keep them sharp, and (3) do away with the constant annoyance of snagging a finger every time you reach into the box.

PEPPER NEUTRALIZES CABBAGE ODOR

THERE ARE TWO KINDS of people in the world: those who relish cooked cabbage and those who can't stand the smell of the dish. Both can be kept happy at the same time if half a green pepper—with the seeds removed—is boiled with the cabbage. The pepper will both add to the flavor of the dish and leave the kitchen odorless.

it IS twice as sweet . . . a feature sure to be appreciated by any dyed-in-the-wool sweet corn eater.

And what about strawberries? "For lip-smacking flavor," says our Ohio gardener, "one berry—Fairfax—stands head and shoulders above all the others." And a researcher at Ohio's Agricultural Research and Development Center agrees: "The Fairfax is neither as big nor as bright as many other varieties of strawberry, but it is vastly superior in flavor. There's just no comparison between the Fairfax and any other strain."

When it comes to peaches, neophyte orchardmen should concentrate on Champion and Belle of Georgia trees. "They lead the flavor parade," says our organic gardener. "Both are white and the Belle of Georgia is generally classified as semifreestone while the Champion is a freestone peach. And be sure to wear a bathing suit when you eat a Champion fresh from the tree because the honey-sweet juice will squirt and run in all directions!"

Folks who enjoy beets and squash owe another debt of thanks to the University of New Hampshire. That school, you see, is responsible for the extremely tasty Sweetheart beet. In case you're wondering, the Eat-All squash was so named because the whole vegetable—seeds and all—are edible. That makes the plant a little unusual . . . but not nearly as unusual as its cousin, the spaghetti squash.

Spaghetti squash—famous for its spaghetti-like strands that result when it's cooked—is loaded with vitamins and minerals. "Regular" spaghetti—the kind you get from those long boxes—is a poor (nutritionally speaking) comparison.

In addition to the above, all kinds of flavorful and nutritious fruits and vegetables are available for growing at home. Check with your local nursery or spend time with your favorite seed catalog and give 'em a try.

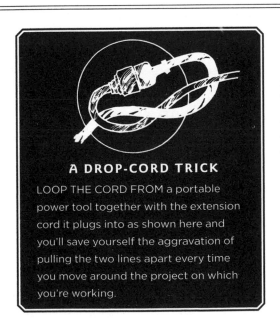

A DROP-CORD TRICK

LOOP THE CORD FROM a portable power tool together with the extension cord it plugs into as shown here and you'll save yourself the aggravation of pulling the two lines apart every time you move around the project on which you're working.

WEATHER PREDICTIONS

SOME TRADITIONAL WEATHER PREDICTORS can be relied on and some can't. For example, a fair February is supposed to denote unseasonable conditions all year, but that doesn't actually tell you much. Likewise, a rainy April portends a good crop—maybe. On the other hand, it's quite right to join tradition when it says "Rainy April and cool May, means lots and lots of grass and hay." There's also a smidgen of savvy in the old saw that states, "If you see grass in January, lock your grain in the granary." That's because an open January—one with no snow on the ground—is hard on wheat and other fall-sown cereal crops.

THE CHEAPEST WAY TO RAISE HOGS

THE EASIEST, CLEANEST, AND cheapest way to raise hogs—if you have good fencing—is out on pasture rather than confined in a barn.

House your sows and pigs—one sow and her litter to a structure—in the traditional, small, movable A-frame hut that hog raisers long ago found most efficient for the purpose. (The A-frame design is simple to build and gives a maximum floor space for a minimum investment in materials and time.)

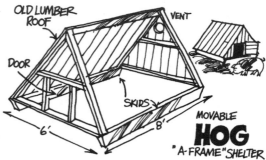

Each hut should measure about 6 feet across the ends and 8 feet down both sides. Nail together the two sides (make them about 4½ feet high) and lean them against each other to form the *A*. Then board up the ends, leaving one entrance large enough for a sow to get in and out. There should, of course, be a skid of something like a 4x4-inch beam down both sides of the house, but the structure doesn't need a floor.

In colder weather, throw some straw or other bedding inside for the little pigs and—during the winter—position the A-frame so that its entrance faces east or southeast (away from the prevailing winds).

When the hogs have trampled, wallowed, and dirtied the area where their A-frames stand, you simply move the sheds to a clean location, *instead of having to haul manure away*, as you would for pigs confined in a barn.

You'll rarely have disease problems raising hogs on pasture in this manner; whereas the animals reared in those supposedly efficient "hog factories" you've heard about would be sick all the time if they weren't constantly pumped full of antibiotics and other feed supplements.

WOVEN WIRE PROTECTS FLOWERS FROM CHICKENS

CHICKENS ARE GREAT TO have around the farm or back lot—until, that is, they start scratching in the flower bed. You can nip that problem in the bud next year, however, by rolling some old, woven, wire fencing out across the flower patch early in the spring. It won't show once the plants come up, but it will prevent the birds from digging around the flowers.

MULCH BONANZA

LOVERS OF MULCH GARDENING, rejoice! The perennial problem of finding all the organic material you really want could be solved by your own backyard. Summer grass clippings and fall leaves can enrich your lawn and protect and fertilize your plants.

When you mow your lawn, set the deck on the higher side (clippings should be an inch or less in length), and let the cut grass rest on top of the mowed lawn. The decomposing grass will fertilize your lawn, giving it 25 percent of the nutrients it needs. (A bonus: The taller lawn retains moisture and so won't need to be watered as often.) Lawn clippings can also be mixed with soil for added nitrogen, and they can be put into your compost pile.

You can get the most grass clippings during June . . . just when you should start mulching your garden. The leaves are available in late fall when you need bedding for livestock and poultry (they work fine for this purpose if they're dry).

Shredded leaves are also good for mulching around any permanent planting: fruit trees, blueberry bushes, raspberries, blackberries, and the like. Cover strawberries with them over winter —it's just another way to save money by not buying expensive straw. Pile leaves on rows of carrots, turnips, parsnips, and potatoes in cold weather to keep such root crops from freezing (the produce will stay usable directly from the garden all winter). Shred extra leaves and pile them for compost.

FENCEPOST WISDOM

IF YOU USE WOODEN posts the next time you build a fence, you should know that those posts will last a whole lot longer (under most conditions) if they're set in well-drained holes. Dig the holes down an extra 9 or 10 inches deeper than you have to and fill in the surplus depth with gravel. That way, excess water can trickle down into the ground more readily than it can stand around the posts and rot them.

OLD PLOW PULLS STUMPS

CLEARING THE LAND OF woods and brush is the hardest work there is, bar none. If you can't afford a bulldozer to push the stumps out right away, sow the ground to grass after you get the trees down and the undergrowth cleared up. Then, use the acreage as pasture for a couple of years until the stumps have rotted a little. A good pasture can be just about as profitable to you as cultivated land anyway.

Once the remaining butts of trees have rotted a few seasons, you can jerk 'em out of the ground with a tractor and a stump puller made from an old plow.

You may be able to get an old plow at an auction. If you can get yourself one cheap, take it apart until there's nothing left except the plow *beam*. This beam—or backbone of the tool— is shaped like a huge fishhook and has just the right cant to make an excellent stump puller. Simply sock the "point" end of the beam under or at the base of the tree butt and pull away with the tractor. Your log chain may break, but the stump puller won't.

SALT KEEPS SCORCHED MILK FROM SMELLING

SCORCHED MILK HAS A terrible odor that seems to linger long after the burning is done. A little salt sprinkled on any milk that boils onto the stove, however, will both stop the burning and—to a large degree—neutralize the unpleasant smell.

DOUBLE THE CAPACITY OF A HANGING SCALE

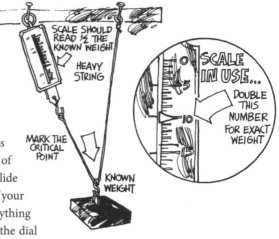

IF YOU'VE EVER TRIED to weigh something on a hanging scale, found the blamed thing too small to handle the object in question, and given up in disgust, you're going to be doubly disgusted in just a minute when you learn how easily you could have solved the problem.

Hang up the scale, tie a string to its hook, and fasten the other end of the twine about as high as the top of the scale. Then take something of known weight, suspend it from the string, and slide it back and forth until the scale reads exactly half your test weight. Mark the twine at that point—anything hung there will actually weigh just twice what the dial indicates. You've just doubled the capacity of your scale!

THE NEXT TIME YOUR family's collective appetite becomes jaded, try perking it up with—are you ready for this?—onion butter. That's right, onion butter. With just a little kitchen alchemy, you can transform the common, lowly bulbs of the lily family into an exotic spread.

You'll need five pounds—yes, *five* pounds of onions (they contain a lot of liquid and cook down amazingly), some water, and salt. That's all.

Peel the onions, quarter them, and throw the skins into your compost pile. Then put the cut-up chunks in a big, heavy pot and scantly cover them with water. Bring the contents of the kettle to a boil, top with a lid, and simmer gently for twenty-four long hours—one whole day and one whole night. You could also set this up in your slow cooker overnight as further insurance against burning the developing ambrosia inside.

When the butter has concentrated into about two and a half pints of dark brown, slightly lumpy "honey," break it up into a paste of uniform consistency, salt to taste, and simmer uncovered until the final excess liquid evaporates.

This spread is absolutely delicious on hardy homemade bread, biscuits, and even pancakes! Try it with Asian dishes, and melt a plug of the butter over a plate of almost any country vegetables you can mention. One couple we know even likes this form of onions on cereal! It's *that* good.

MANURE IS A VALUABLE COMMODITY

IN SOME RURAL AREAS of Switzerland, animal manure is treated as a valuable possession (which it is) and status accrues to the farmer with the biggest stack of the stuff. That's how much people appreciate manure's fertilizing benefit over there. We should too, over here.

But having manure for fertilizer available from your own farm animals is only half the advantage. You must handle the resource correctly. Besides its tremendous worth as organic matter, a ton of manure holds about ten pounds of nitrogen, two pounds of phosphorus, and six pounds of potassium. Most of the phosphorus is in the solid excreta, but nearly half the nitrogen and potassium is in the urine. You must save as much of the latter as possible by supplying your stock with ample bedding to soak it up.

If you pile manure out in the weather, you'll lose about half the nutrients as rainwater percolates through the piles. It's much better to stack the stuff under a roof and pack it tight so that loss of nitrogen (in the form of ammonia) is minimal.

Your best bet is to let the manure build up on the barn or chicken coop floor until you're ready to put it on your soil. Meantime, keep adding fresh bedding on top so that the livestock stay dry. Enough heat will build up in your manure pack to warm animals a little on cold winter nights.

When you do spread the manure on your fields, time your schedule so that you can plow it under as soon as possible.

FLANNEL BLANKETS MAKE SLEEPING-BAG LINERS

WHEN YOU'RE SCROUNGING AROUND in the thrift store, keep an eye open for a used, light flannel blanket or two. They can easily be sewn into very good, warm, washable sleeping-bag liners.

SOAP MAKES CANVAS SEW EASIER

SEWING HEAVY MATERIAL LIKE canvas can be as hard on the needle as it is on your hands. If, however, you rub the fabric well with soap before you stitch, the job will be a lot more comfortable and the needle will slip through the cloth without nearly so much danger of breaking.

SET A LIVESTOCK FEED or water bucket in the center of an old automobile tire and the animal or animals won't be able to overturn the container.

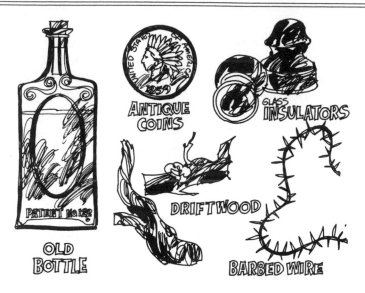

HOW TO BE A DRY-LAND BEACHCOMBER

IF YOU HANKER TO be both beachcomber and homesteader but can't make up your mind which occupation to try, combine 'em! A farm—especially the old abandoned kind of place that so many back-to-the-landers are moving to—offers plenty of opportunity for "dry land" beachcombing. Here are *some* of the possibilities:

OLD GLASSWARE AND POTTERY. Every bygone farm had its junk pile someplace out of sight behind the barn or in the woods. Sometimes a little digging there will uncover glass bottles or crocks that are very desirable to collectors. It's like hunting for buried treasure . . . in fact, that's exactly what it is.

Look for old whiskey and bitters bottles along New England stonewalls or on top of beams in midwestern barns. Grandpa often hid his liquor from grandma out where he could take a snort undetected.

LARD OR WATER MAKES NAILS DRIVE EASIER

TO DRIVE NAILS INTO hard wood without bending them, try dipping the points into lard or other grease. Or—as every carpenter knows—you can accomplish the same end by moistening the points of the nails in your mouth or a can of water. In other words, as long as the fasteners are lubricated, they'll drive easier.

CORK PREVENTS PRICKED FINGERS

STICK YOUR COLLECTION OF loose tacks, small nails, screws, pins, and needles in a large cork and keep it in the kitchen "odds and ends" drawer. The small, sharp items will always be handy that way—and you'll save many a pricked finger as you rummage through your stacks of "make do" materials.

FARM TOOLS. Old barns are also possible treasure troves of yesterday's farm tools, now sancti-fied by the label, "American primitive antiques." In my wanderings (and with full permission of the owners), I've taken from abandoned barns: a wooden buggy jack, a butter churn, an old musket, bottles, a nifty milk stool with an iron ring attachment for holding the milk bucket, a hand-operated grain mill (half-buried under a chicken roost), brass-knobbed horse hames, two corn knives, and—as the auction notices put it—many more items "too numerous to mention."

INSULATORS. Wherever telephone lines are strung, or were strung in the past, you stand a chance of finding aged and valuable insulators. Linemen in the old days often chucked a bushel basket's worth of the things into a hole at the base of a pole and buried them there. Find one of those caches and, if the fixtures are of a rare design, you've got yourself a hunk of spending change.

OLD COINS. The latest craze in rural beachcombing is hunting for coins around abandoned, run-down, overgrown—and even currently farmed and well-maintained—old farmsteads. That might seem like an unlikely place to find money, but farmers used to be smart enough to distrust banks. Instead of depositing their cash in checking accounts, they squirreled it away in tin cans and glass jars buried at the base of a certain fencepost, or at any other secret spot they could remember. The trouble was, of course, that they often *didn't* remember, or they sometimes died without telling anyone else where the loot was hidden.

Searching for these "fencepost banks" is done with a metal detector and an understanding that you will split any treasure found with the present owner of the farm . . . if there is one.

DRIFTWOOD. Any forest or riverbank can yield beautiful specimens of driftwood or gnarled roots that look like driftwood.

BARBED WIRE. Collectors of this commodity—they call themselves "barbarians"—know the difference between "moonshine" wire and "patented" wire.

Keep your eyes open. Back in your woods somewhere may well be a strand of barbed wire 300 feet long that you can cut into 18-inch lengths (the standard size for display in a collection). Remem-ber to check with that farmer or rancher before going onto private property. Also check with them before you make a cut!

THE AUTOMATIC OUTDOOR DISHWASHER

SOONER OR LATER, FOLKS who cook outdoors a lot usually discover a super-simple and super-easy way to clean their pots and pans. What they do is they fill the containers with water, add a handful of wood ashes, and set the kettles and fry pans over the fire to simmer. And what happens is that the grease in the containers combines with the lye in the wood ashes to make a natural soap that—in combination with that simmering water—can slick up a dirty pot or pan "automatically" while the chief cook and bottle washer enjoys his meal with the rest of the gang.

And for the few *really* tough spots that always seem to cling to the bottom and sides of every kettle? Well, a good handful of hay or coarse grass does make a wondrous scouring pad.

HOW TO MAKE HUSH PUPPIES

A REAL, OLD-TIME, traditional southern fish fry or barbecue never seemed to be complete without a whole gaggle of bluetick hounds hanging around the edges of the action. Naturally, the canines always set up a horrendous din when the folks began to eat . . . which—just as naturally—always inspired the people at the gathering to throw together something cheap and filling to shut the dogs the hell up.

For this purpose, dogs and humans kind of compromised on thumb-size cakes of cornbread—deep-fat fried in whatever grease was handiest. The improvised canine chow was good enough to quiet the hounds (hence the name "hush puppies"). It also, as many Southerners soon learned, went mighty well with whatever the people were eating. The word spread, and hush puppies are now regarded as a genuine Southern delicacy. The following recipe is as traditional as any we've found:

2 cups fine cornmeal
2 tablespoons baking powder
1 teaspoon salt
1 cup finely chopped onion
1¼ cups milk
½ cup water
cooking oil

Mix the cornmeal, baking powder, and salt together, and then stir in the onion. Stir in the milk and water next, adding more cornmeal as necessary to make the dough stiff enough to be handled. Shape the batter into small, round (or elongated) cakes, drop them into deep, hot oil (360°F), and turn them occasionally until they're well browned.

Hush puppies are most flavorful when fried together with fish and served piping hot.

NEWSPAPERS AND TIGHT OVERSHOES

TIGHT OVERSHOES WILL SLIP over rubber-soled shoes much easier if a piece of newspaper is held around each shoe heel during the operation.

A SOAP RECIPE

THIS RECIPE MIGHT NOT make the *best* soap in the world, but it's surely the easiest. Get yourself six pounds of potash, four pounds of lard, and one-quarter pound of pine resin. Break up the resin, mix all the ingredients together, and let the batch set for five days. Then put the whole schmeer into a ten-gallon cask of warm water and stir twice a day for ten days. That's all there is to it (but better not let Procter and Gamble find out).

A SOLDERING-IRON HOLDER

FOR A REALLY QUICK and inexpensive soldering iron holder, drive two spike nails into a scrap block of wood to form an *X* and rest the tool's hot end in the cross.

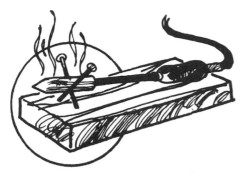

TIPS FOR BERRY PICKERS

AN EXPERIENCED WILD BERRY picker can bring home as many (or more) foraged strawberries, raspberries, and blackberries as a good gardener can raise in a well-tended patch. One of the main secrets of an expert, free-for-the-gathering berry nabber is his ability to "start picking six months before the fruit is ripe." That is, the way he scouts out all the best locations long before the harvest is ready to pluck (so he can zero right in on the choice spots when the big week arrives).

All old hands (probably stained) at this game know well the effects that picking for size can have when it comes to wild berries. Some of those untamed vines out there along the roadsides and in the woods actually bear bounty that is twice the size of their sister plants. And, obviously, an hour spent picking the "big 'uns" will produce just that many more bucketfuls (or pints, if you eat three for every one you save) of berries.

Before you spend a lot of time gathering, then, you should put in a good number of hours just looking. It's more fun that way, anyhow.

SIMPLE GATE LETS COWS— BUT NOT HOGS—THROUGH

IT'S OFTEN NECESSARY, on the small homestead or farm, to allow cattle and hogs to mingle together in—say—a feed lot once or twice a day, and then separate the animals when the cows are turned out to pasture. This can be a time-consuming and miserable job when done by hand but becomes delightfully easy when the rig shown here is used.

Place two planks across a gate with the boards spaced far enough apart to allow a hog to walk between—but not turn around in or step over—them. The cattle will pass in and out at will while the pigs will invariably pass in one end of the passage and out the other . . . never once attempting to jump over.

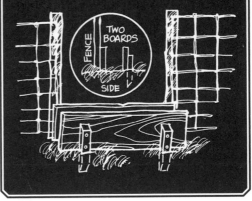

RUBBER BALL "CUP" CATCHES PAINT

THE NEXT TIME YOU find yourself facing the unpleasant prospect of painting a ceiling or under an overhang, cut a hollow rubber ball in two and slip one half—open side up—over the handle of your brush. The cup will catch the drippings and prevent them from running up your arm.

COTTON COLLECTS GLASS SLIVERS

It's easy to sweep up the big pieces of glass when a bottle or tumbler is broken on the kitchen floor—and just as easy to overlook the smaller slivers until they wind up in someone's fingers or bare feet. You can quickly collect those small shards before they do any damage, however, by patting them up with a piece of absorbent cotton that has been moistened in water.

A BAKING HINT

Put a small dish of water into the oven when you bake bread and you'll find that it helps to keep the crust of the loaves from getting too hard.

BRAN CLEANS LARD FROM BUCKET

There's nothing in the world more difficult to clean than a bucket that has contained lard. The job can be made much easier, however, by warming the container and then rubbing it with cornmeal or bran before washing.

METHANE POWER

Municipal solid-waste landfills make up the third-largest source of methane emissions in the United States. But rather than releasing methane into the atmosphere, where it exacerbates climate change, the gas can be captured to produce electricity. According to the U.S. Environmental Protection Agency, about 600 US landfills capture methane to use in a variety of ways, including firing glass-blowing and pottery kilns, heating greenhouses, and even powering an ice rink. Other planned projects will convert landfill gas to methanol for use as an alternative fuel for vehicles.

You can tap into natural gas on a smaller scale by using many household organic "waste" materials to produce your own natural gas for cooking, lighting, and space and water heating. This gas, known as *biogas*, is a mixture of primarily flammable gases—mostly methane—along with carbon dioxide that forms anywhere organic material decomposes anaerobically (without oxygen), such as in water, deep in a landfill, or in the guts of animals, including you.

By constructing a home biogas generator, you can make enough fuel to at least provide your cooking energy. A family with modest daily cooking needs will at a minimum require the output of a warm, well-fed, 200-gallon (27-cubic-foot) generator. This much biogas will allow for about one hour of daily stovetop cooking. Start small to develop an understanding of biogas by making a small generator.

If you can compost it, you can digest it. Ideal biogas ingredients are those materials of which you have a plentiful, convenient, and consistent supply, so you can make steady and useful quantities of biogas. Nearly any combination of vegetables, food scraps, grass clippings, animal manure, meat, slaughterhouse waste, and fats will work as long as your recipe contains the correct ratio of carbon and

PARAFFIN PROTECTS PAINT

IF THE SURFACE OF a partly filled can of oil-based paint is sealed with melted paraffin, the remaining paint will not harden in the container.

LINSEED OIL REMOVES ROAD TAR

ROAD TAR AND ASPHALT that splatters up and sticks to a car is almost impossible to remove —unless, however, you first saturate the spots with linseed oil. Allow the oil to soften the tar for a few minutes and you'll find that the grime rubs right off with a piece of coarse cloth.

A TRICK FOR UNLOADING
HEAVY ITEMS FROM A TRUCK

IF YOU REGULARLY UNLOAD full barrels or other large, heavy items from a truck, keep a few old car tires on hand to lay down in the unloading area. You'll find you can safely drop the barrels the last foot or two onto the rubber casings . . . thereby saving your back from the hardest strain of letting such items down.

---

nitrogen. Avoid using too many woody products, such as wood chips and straw, which contain large amounts of lignin (a part of plant cell walls resistant to microbial breakdown), which tends to clog up the digestion process.

A methane generator usually contains a feeding tube for filling the digester vessel, an effluent outlet to remove digested solids and liquids (called the "digestate"), a gas outlet, and a collection tank for storing the biogas.

In most cases, material you put into a well-maintained methane generator operating in a temperature range of 70 to 105°F will be fairly well-digested in about a month (you'll continually add feedstock as material digests).

The conditions you'll try to mimic within the generator are similar to those inside an animal's gut. Biological activity within the generator will produce some heat, but depending on your climate, you may need to supply additional heat.

Never make biogas indoors or in enclosed spaces. Methane is a flammable gas that will burn when mixed with air and exposed to a flame. A biogas generator could explode if the pressure drops and the flame is allowed to toll back through the piping. The risks are the same as with handling and storing conventional natural gas. Before embarking on making biogas, it is imperative that you understand the process, safety requirements, and risks.

Having a biogas generator is like having another mouth to feed, but with the right setup and a steady supply of feedstock, you'll produce fossil-free natural gas for a variety of energy needs on your homestead.

BIRDS IN THE ORCHARD

THERE'S NO PRETTIER SIGHT than robins or catbirds or orioles warbling away from the flowery boughs of a cherry tree. The only trouble is that the same birds aren't going to be nearly so welcome later in the season when their sharp eyes spot the ripening cherries and their sharp bills peck holes in the fruit you were counting on for your own eating.

All right. The flying bandits outnumber you heavily, they're faster than you are, *and* they have nothing to do by midsummer except hunt food. So if they've zeroed in on your fruit trees, you're going to have some trouble fighting 'em off.

Instead of fighting, though, why not try distracting the feathered raiders? It's not hard to do, once you understand that the luscious, sweet orchard produce that looks so delicious to you is only second choice for the birds. What they really like—if they can get them—are the sharper, stronger-tasting wild fruits and berries. If you're crafty enough to provide these favorites near the fruit you want to eat yourself, the chances are that your bird problem will be greatly reduced.

The "companion planting" principle encourages organic gardeners to grow flowers, fruits, and vegetables next to other growing things to discourage pests. In this case, you can grow wild fruits to protect your cultivated varieties. When you put in cherry trees, for instance, leave room for a mountain ash and a few chokecherries. Dogwood and crab apple will help keep your apples unpecked, or—if it's the grape arbor that you're worried about—elderberry, Virginia creeper, wild grape, or wild black cherry are the preferred bird delicacies you'll want to cultivate. Guard the berry patch with any of the beautiful wild berry bushes and vines: holly, hackberry, elderberry, Russian mulberry, and bittersweet.

With the birds' real preferences catered to, you can enjoy their company, have the pleasure of seeing handsome native plants thrive along with the cultivated trees and bushes, *and* harvest a good store of unpecked fruit at picking time.

MAKE THIS SIMPLE SANDING BLOCK

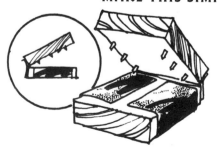

CUT TWO PIECES OF 1x4 to an easy-to-handle size. Then, hinge them together with a piece of leather and drive a few 1-inch-long finishing nails into the top chunk of wood (about ½ inch in from each edge). Then, when you wrap a piece of sandpaper around the bottom block and clamp the top chunk down, you'll have a very inexpensive—and very effective— sanding block.

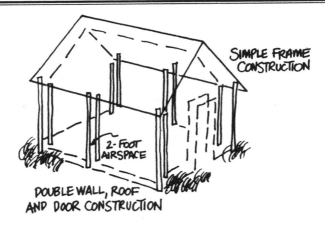

SIMPLE FRAME CONSTRUCTION

2-FOOT AIRSPACE

DOUBLE WALL, ROOF AND DOOR CONSTRUCTION

BUILD AN ABOVEGROUND ROOT CELLAR

YOU CAN BUILD A pretty good root cellar *aboveground* if you construct it with double walls and a double roof. Set the posts for the inner walls, then—2 feet farther out in all directions—the uprights for the outer walls. Board up the enclosure within an enclosure and stuff the space between with dry leaves or straw. If you use sawdust or ground corncobs for insulation, you can cut the width of the space all the way around to only 1 foot.

For the roof of your storage shed, build a double set of rafters designed so that the gap between the inner and outer beams is the same as the space between the walls. Lay boards on the lower rafters, stack on the leaves, straw, sawdust, or whatever, and add the second set of supports and a roof.

It's best to design two doors for the entrance to your aboveground root cellar, with the outer one built double and filled with 6 inches of sawdust.

Construct the vegetable storage shed's floor a foot off the ground of either logs or boards spaced so that there are cracks between them. The narrow gaps will provide some air circulation and heat from the earth below. And, as a bonus, dirt carried in on root vegetables will conveniently sift through the cracks and out of the way.

FINISHED "CELLAR"

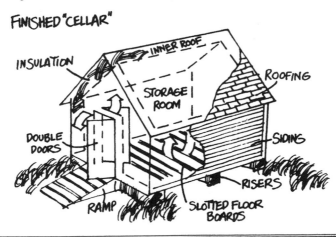

INSULATION

INNER ROOF

STORAGE ROOM

ROOFING

DOUBLE DOORS

SIDING

RAMP

RISERS

SLOTTED FLOOR BOARDS

WHITEWASH

WHITEWASHED OUT-BUILDINGS GIVE THE FARM A NEAT, CLEAN APPEARANCE

PAINT IS PRETTY EXPENSIVE stuff, especially for folks who are just getting started at farming or homesteading. If you're in that group, you may like to try another way of protecting your farm buildings and smartening up the place at the same time. Whitewash does a good job for both purposes and saves some pennies too.

Many of the old "household helps" books contained recipes for whitewash, most of which included lime, salt, Portland cement, and water as the key ingredients. After a lot of boiling and mixing, and sometimes days of waiting for your wash to set up, you would end up with a mixture you could then put on your walls.

If you want to get to your project sooner, however, a quick trip to the local hardware or home-improvement store, and a gallon or so of budget, white latex or primer paint later, you can get started on your project. To make the whitewash, mix one part water and one part paint in a clean bucket. (If you want a thinner wash, use two parts water instead.) As with any painting project, make sure your surfaces are clean and your floor (if working inside) is protected. Use a sponge or a brush to apply the paint, working in small sections and brushing in the direction of the wood grain. Any excess paint should be wiped off—again, in the direction of the wood grain—using a lint-free rag.

Whitewash works best on a slightly damp wall . . . and if you want to do a really good job on a surface that's been whitewashed before, wash off the old coating with hot water and vinegar.

HOW TO REMOVE BOULDERS

SOONER OR LATER—ONCE YOU'VE committed yourself to raising your own food—you're going to run into a huge boulder that disputes your title to the land. Move it the heck out of the way if you can . . . but, if the blamed thing's too heavy to move, just dig a monstrous hole beside the rock and roll it in so that the stone is dropped well below plow level. That won't solve the problem *entirely*, you understand, but it should take the boulder a good twenty years to work its way back up to where it can argue with you again.

Should you decide to persuade the rock to leave your premises by the application of a good dose of dynamite, pause first—please—for a word of advice from One Who Found Out: do NOT dig a hole down under the chunk of grandfather granite, shove in an assortment of high explosives, and necessarily expect the boulder to move.

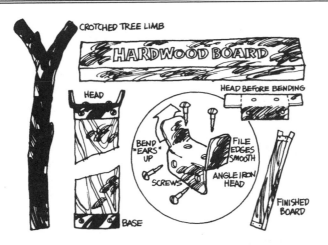

A POWERFUL FENCE PULLER

YOU CAN CLEAR OLD fence posts and stumps from the back forty—or even the front yard—with this ingenious use of simple leverage. The lever, in this case, is nothing more than a heavy piece of hardwood edged on both ends with angle iron.

Notch the "top" of the piece of wood or turn up "ears" on the iron to keep the chain from slipping off (a crotched tree limb, if stout enough, will work just as well). Loop the length of chain around the post at ground level, run it through the "holder" on the lever, hitch it to your team, tractor, or Jeep . . . and—chances are—you'll be able to ease that contrary rascal right out of the ground.

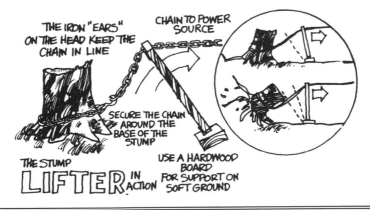

HOW TO MAKE LOOSE SCREWS HOLD IN WOOD

AS FURNITURE AND OTHER wooden structures age and dry out, the screws that hold them together frequently become loose. This situation can often be remedied quite rapidly by removing one of the offending screws, breaking off a wooden match stem in its hole, and replacing the screw.

RULES OF THE THUMB FOR THE CREATIVE COOK!

FOLLOWING RECIPES THAT SOMEONE else has developed is a lot of fun. Conjuring up food formulations of your own, however, can be even more exciting and—sometimes—disastrous.

The next time you're tempted to experiment in the kitchen, keep the excitement of accomplishment as high as possible—and the drag of disaster as low as reasonably can be expected—by bearing in mind the following "general rules of thumb":

- 1 cup of liquid to 1 cup of flour for pour batters
- 1 cup of liquid to 2 cups of flour for drop batters
- 1 cup of liquid to 3 cups of flour for dough
- ⅓ to 2 or more cakes of compressed yeast* softened in ½ cup water to 2 cups of liquid (⅓ yeast cake to 2 cups of liquid is used in bread mixed at night—1 cake or more, according to the time available for rising, when bread is mixed in the morning. By using several yeast cakes to 2 cups of liquid, bread may be baked in three or four hours from time of mixing)
- ½ cup of liquid yeast (either compressed yeast* dissolved in ½ cup liquid, or any other yeast such as potato yeast) to 2 cups of liquid
- 1 teaspoon of baking soda and 3½ level teaspoons of cream of tartar to 4 cups of flour
- 2 teaspoons of baking powder to 1 cup of flour, when eggs are not used
- 1 teaspoon of baking soda to 2 cups of thick sour milk
- 1 teaspoon of soda to 1 cup of molasses
- ¼ teaspoon of salt to 4 cups of milk for custards

- ¼ teaspoon of salt to 1 cup (or 1 teaspoon to 4 cups) of sauce or soup
- 1 teaspoon of flavoring extract to 4 cups of custard or cream
- 1 tablespoon of flavoring extract to 4 cups of mixture to be frozen
- ⅔ cup, or less, of sugar to 4 cups of milk for custards and the like
- 1 cup of sugar to 4 cups of milk or cream for ice cream
- 4 eggs to 4 cups of milk for plain cup custard
- 6 to 8 eggs to 4 cups of milk for molded custards
- ¼ package, or ½ ounce of gelatine to 2 cups (scant) liquid
- 3 cups of water, or milk or stock, to 1 cup of rice
- 1 ounce (2 tablespoons) of vegetable shortening, ½ ounce (2 tablespoons) of flour to 2 cups of liquid for soups
- 1 cup of cooked meat, or fish cut into cubes, to ¾ or 1 whole cup of sauce
- Meat from 3½ pound chicken equals about 2 cups or 1 pound

*Compressed yeast is available in limited markets, usually as 1-ounce cakes.

TIN CAN CANDLE HOLDER

YOU'LL GET A MUCH better light from a candle if you place it in a simple reflecting holder made from a metal can. Choose a container with a shiny inside and cut away about two-thirds of the wall, with about a half-inch rim left at the bottom. If you wish, you can taper the reflector at the top and pierce the point with a nail so you'll be able to hang the candleholder on the wall or a convenient post.

TIN CAN COOK STOVE

YOU CAN TURN a large metal can into a simple camp stove for preparing a quick hot snack. Just cut one hole at the open end (for fuel) and another opposite and near the closed end (to make a cross draft). A few twigs, a couple of candles, or a little canned heat under the can will be fire enough to cook bacon or warm up your beans.

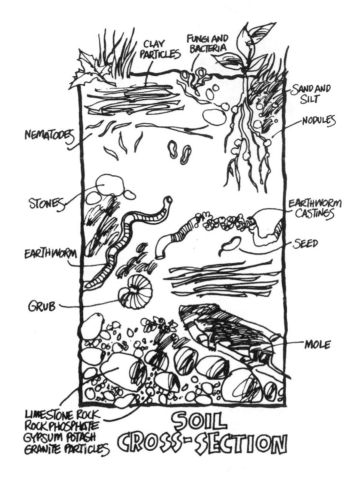

CLAY PARTICLES

FUNGI AND BACTERIA

SAND AND SILT

NODULES

NEMATODES

STONES

EARTHWORM CASTINGS

SEED

EARTHWORM

GRUB

MOLE

LIMESTONE ROCK ROCK PHOSPHATE GYPSUM POTASH GRANITE PARTICLES

SOIL CROSS-SECTION

SIR ALBERT HOWARD AND "ORGANIC" FARMING

IT TOOK MANY DECADES for organic gardening to become a regular part of our vernacular and landscape. Years of hard promoting by a handful of enthusiasts ultimately made organic gardening a *natural* part of putting food on our table.

Back in 1905, Sir Albert Howard of England was appointed Imperial Economic Botanist to the Government of India. Upon arriving in that country, Sir Albert immediately noticed that in the region where he was stationed, the crops were almost entirely free of disease and insect infestations. So free, in fact, that the natives there had never even heard of such things as insecticides or fungicides. Nor did they use any chemical or artificial fertilizers. They *did*, however, return to the soil every possible bit of plant and animal matter.

"Hmmmm," Sir Albert wondered, "could there be a relationship?"

Howard began experimenting on a 75-acre farm and, by 1910, he had taught himself how to grow almost perfect crops using absolutely no chemicals or sprays. In the course of his experiments, Sir Albert developed an interesting idea about insect pests and plant disease. He said, "Insects and fungi are not the real cause of plant diseases because they only attack unsuitable varieties or crops which are imperfectly grown. They point out the plants that are improperly nourished and I look upon these pests as Nature's professors of agriculture."

Sir Albert next applied that reasoning to the animals he raised and he found that oxen fed only healthy, organically grown plants were, in turn, so robust that they could rub noses with other oxen infected with hoof-and-mouth disease and *never* catch that highly contagious sickness.

During the next twenty years, Sir Albert Howard's ideas on farming and plant nutrition were tested on coffee plantations in Kenya, on farms in Tanzania, in Zimbabwe's potato and cornfields, on plantations in Costa Rica, and in many other parts of the world.

By 1938, about one million tons of compost were being made each year on the tea estates of India and Ceylon, and expert growers of the crop claimed that—for the first time since the introduction of chemical fertilizers—tea was again of first-rate quality.

Municipalities in South Africa and Malaysia began converting all refuse into compost during the early 1940s and, by 1945, the organic gardening and farming movement was well established in both New Zealand and Australia. Organic gardening converts can now be found around the globe.

In addition to thanking Sir Albert Howard for getting the ball rolling in this country, Rodale Press (publisher of *Organic Life* and the well-known but now retired *Organic Gardening*) in Emmaus, Pennsylvania, championed natural farming, gardening, and sustainable living. Thank you, Rodale.

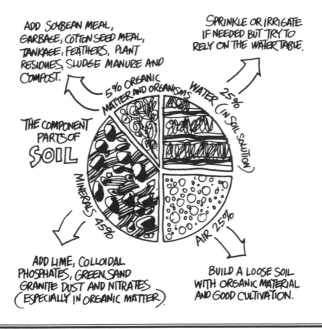

THE COMPONENT PARTS OF SOIL

ADD SOYBEAN MEAL, GARBAGE, COTTON SEED MEAL, TANKAGE, FEATHERS, PLANT RESIDUES, SLUDGE MANURE AND COMPOST.

5% ORGANIC MATTER AND ORGANISMS

WATER 25% (IN SOIL SOLUTION)

SPRINKLE OR IRRIGATE IF NEEDED BUT TRY TO RELY ON THE WATER TABLE.

MINERALS 45%

AIR 25%

ADD LIME, COLLOIDAL PHOSPHATES, GREEN SAND GRANITE DUST AND NITRATES (ESPECIALLY IN ORGANIC MATTER)

BUILD A LOOSE SOIL WITH ORGANIC MATERIAL AND GOOD CULTIVATION.

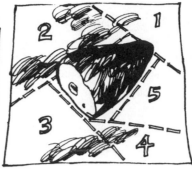

PROTECT HOME-CURED MEAT FROM INSECTS

THE RED-LEGGED HAM BEETLE—a bright greenish-blue beastie with red legs and antennae—may be quite a handsome creature in his way. He won't, however, be a welcome sight if you discover him feeding on the surface of your home-cured ham (especially if you know that, as a larva, he did his eating by tunneling around *inside* the meat). You can, however, ward off the ham beetle—and several other pests that get into cured meats—by taking some precautions.

One way to keep your hams insect-free is to bury them in cottonseed hulls or in oats or other grain. Find a box that will allow 3 or 4 inches of extra space on all sides of the meat, cover the bottom of the carton to that depth with your packing material, center the ham on the layer, and fill the box with the cereal or hulls.

It's a good idea to check your embedded ham about once a month, especially since meat isn't the only food that's attacked by insects. If grain beetles seem to be getting into the packing, throw it out and replace it with fresh material.

Another and more common way to protect hams is by wrapping and hanging them. Look over each chunk of cured meat to be sure that the beetles haven't already moved in, lay it on a sheet of heavy wrapping paper, and remove the string that held the meat when it was smoked. Fold the paper as shown in the drawing.

Now put the wrapped pork in a closely woven cloth bag with no holes in it, tie the top with string or rustproof wire, and hang the sack—where rats can't get at it—in a cool storeroom (between 55 and 60°F). Hams shouldn't touch each other as they hang.

Again, inspect the meat monthly and replace any broken or grease-spotted wrappings.

A CABBAGE RECIPE

CABBAGE DOESN'T RESPOND WELL to boiling and is more fragrant and tasty when stir-fried: Slice the vegetable coarsely and toss it briefly in hot oil along with a chopped clove of garlic. Then add a little boiling water—a couple of tablespoons is enough—and steam the cabbage under a tight cover for a couple of minutes so that it's tender but still crunchy. Be sure to drink the liquid too. It can be thickened, if you like, with a little cornstarch mixed with cold water and soy sauce.

Folk Medicine

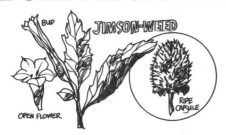

AN OLD NEIGHBOR of mine says that the juice of jimson weed—which is poisonous to eat—makes an excellent poison ivy lotion. I don't get poison ivy, so I've not been able to test that one out, but the same neighbor told me that milkweed juice would take away warts and, by golly, it sure took away mine.

- Boil oak bark in water until you've made a strong tea and you'll have a good treatment for blisters.

- For chapped hands, nothing in the world is as good as Bag Balm, an ointment formulated for the treatment of sore cow teats and available at farm supply, hardware, and (even) some larger national chain stores almost everywhere.

- A poultice of cobwebs will stop the flow of blood from even bad wounds. I've seen it work like a charm on de-horned cows.

- Folks with dry hands should keep sheep. Their wool contains lanolin and simply rubbing your hands across a sheep's back once in awhile will keep them soft as goose down.

HOW TO JOIN POSTS

FENCE, CLOTHESLINE, OR OTHER wooded posts that are too short may be salvaged in the following way: Take two of the shorties and cut halfway through each timber 12 inches from one end. Then split off the cut pieces and nail, or bolt, the two posts together as shown. The result is one post that is long enough to be serviceable.

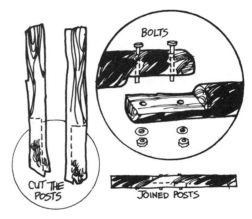

A BUTTER-AND-VEGETABLE-OIL SPREAD

EQUAL PARTS OF BUTTER and unsaturated vegetable oil, mixed in a blender and chilled, make a healthful, good-tasting table fat that's easy to spread and goes a long way.

HOW TO TELL THE AGE OF A WILD RABBIT

TO JUDGE THE AGE of a wild rabbit, look for smooth, sharp claws, soft ears, and a narrow cleft in the lip. These are all signs of a young, tasty animal. (Like other game, bunnies should be handled with gloves and cooked thoroughly.)

SILAGE FOR HOMESTEAD LIVESTOCK

YOUR CRASH COURSE IN sustainable farming is not complete until you can pronounce "silage" (sigh'lij) correctly and know what it is. Silage is grass or grain plants cut and chopped green and stored in a silo. And the crop most successfully made into silage is corn. When the ear reaches the "dent" state, the whole plant is cut, chopped and blown into the silo, where it turns brownish and ferments into a feed cows love.

Air spoils silage quickly and must be kept out of the chopped feed. The least expensive way to store the food is in a trench silo, which is nothing but a basement-size hollow scooped out of the ground. The silage is dumped in, tightly packed by running heavy-tired machinery over it, and then covered with tarp or heavy black plastic. The forage is also packed tightly enough to exclude most air when it's stored in the old wooden upright silos, and the newest vertical silos are coated inside with glass or plastic to make them airtight.

Corn silage is a good cheap feed for subsistence farmers. If you have just a few livestock, though, it won't pay you to get all the equipment necessary to make silage (to say nothing of the silo). You can, however, store a small supply of the forage by piling it on the ground, covering it with tarp or black plastic and burying the edges of the film in the ground. Ancient, stationary silage choppers can be found in dairy country, and most of them will still work if the blades are sharpened. You can cut and tie green corn into bundles and haul them to the chopper.

You can also avail yourself of farmers who have a custom service of chopping silage and filling silos for others.

If I had just one or two cows or goats to feed year-round, I'd chop up all the stalks from the garden sweet corn patch (right after roasting ear season) with my rotary mower, and put the shredded plants into plastic bags. Instant silage!

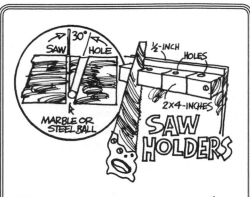

Most amateur carpenters hang their saws flat against the workshop wall simply by hooking the tools' handles over a nail or nails. It works but a lot of fingers get dinged every year on those exposed blade teeth. A much better idea is to park handsaws with their cutting edges turned directly to the wall—and this clever rack does exactly that.

Saw a series of slots 1½ inches deep into a length of 2x4 and drill one hole as shown to intersect each slot. Drop a marble or steel ball into each hole and, when a saw is slipped in and down into a slot, the ball will act as a wedge that grips the blade firmly.

THE PROPER TEMPERATURE FOR SCALDING AND PICKING CHICKENS

A TEMPERATURE BETWEEN 140°F and 160°F is best for scalding chickens before picking. Test the water with an instant-read thermometer and maintain this range while doing the job. You'll find the work much easier and results far more satisfactory than when using water that is either hotter or colder.

FEED YOUR HENS GROUND-UP EGGSHELLS

THE LAYING HEN USES a lot of calcium to package her eggs, and she will appreciate getting the shells back, crushed, in her food. If you don't keep chickens, the houseplants or compost pile will be the better for the minerals in ground-up eggshells.

MOSQUITOES AND THE COLOR BLUE

FOR WHAT IT'S WORTH: The mosquito is attracted more to wet clothing than to dry and is especially fond of the color blue.

SNOW KEEPS MICE FROM GNAWING TREE BARK

To PREVENT MICE FROM gnawing the bark of young apple trees in winter, the early American settlers used to pack snow very firmly around the base of the tree.

BIRDS INDICATE WEATHER

IF SWALLOWS FLY HIGH, expect fair weather, but if they stay near the ground, look out for rain.

AUTUMN

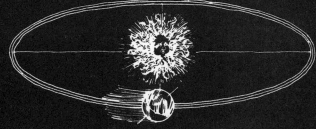

September 23, Autumnal Equinox

THE TIME OF MATURING

Sᴇᴘᴛᴇᴍʙᴇʀ 23 ᴍᴀʀᴋs ᴛʜᴇ second and final time (the first is March 21) each year that day and night are of equal length at all points on the earth's surface. On this date (the autumnal equinox for the Northern Hemisphere and the vernal equinox for the Southern), the sun sweeps across the globe's middle on a three-month journey toward the Tropic of Capricorn. It's the official astronomical beginning of fall above the equator and the start of spring below.

There are longer nights and shorter days ahead for the cornfields of Iowa, while just the opposite increasingly holds true in South Africa. Purple martins will soon be leaving the Mississippi River Valley for their annual flight to the towns and countryside of Brazil. Folks in Canada and the United States are starting to think about raking leaves, carving jack-o'-lanterns, and sitting down to turkey dinners, while their counterparts south of the equator turn the soil, herd animals to spring pasture, and doze in the first warm rays of the brightening sun. It's a good time to be alive wherever you live.

THE ART OF MAKING SAUERKRAUT

MAKING SAUERKRAUT IS NOT difficult if you wait until cool fall weather to tackle the job. All you need is a large earthenware crock and a cabbage slicer (or mandolin). I found both in an antique shop, but they can be purchased elsewhere too.

Slice up your cabbage heads by sliding them over the blade (or blades) of the "krautcutter." Then salt the shredded mass at the rate of three and a half tablespoons of seasoning to five pounds of kraut.

Work up five pounds of cabbage at a time, thoroughly mix in the salt, and place the kraut in a good-size farm crock. Keep mashing the kraut down in the container with a potato masher or similar tool (I use a baseball bat)—you want the cabbage packed in as tightly as possible—and fill the crock to within 5 inches of its top. By then, juice should cover the kraut when you press it down hard with the potato masher, bat, or whatever.

Cover the mass with several thicknesses of clean cheesecloth and top that with a plate that fits the circumference of the crock. Weight the plate down with a rock or other heavy object (a jar of water will do) to keep the kraut down under the juice.

A scum forms on the surface of the kraut juice as the cabbage ferments. Remove the deposit, or—as usually happens— if the cloth soaks it up, change the fabric covering often.

When the weather's hot, the kraut may spoil. (I like a temperature of about 65°F best for kraut making, though some prefer 70°F.)

In about a month, the kraut will stop fermenting. You'll know it because the bubbles will stop coming up in the juice, even when you tap the crock.

You can leave the sauerkraut right in the crock, *if* you can place it where the temperature remains no higher than 55°F and *if* you'll eat it all up before the end of winter. Otherwise, you should can the sauerkraut following the canning instructions in any cookbook or freeze it.

HOW TO HARVEST CORN

SIDE VIEW

SPIKE

LEATHER

CORN HUSKING TOOLS

CORN KNIFE

SPIKE

Farmers pay very big bucks for big combines so they can finish harvesting their corn before Thanksgiving. Then they spend thousands of dollars more to get the grain dried artificially. That leaves them all of January, February, and March to sit in town and complain about how they can't make enough money to meet their bills.

There's no need to play that silly game on the small family farm, however. Not when you can still harvest corn by hand—with no expensive machinery at all—in amounts sizable enough to make the project practical. One man can cut and shock at least 5 acres of corn in a season without overextending himself. (Dad did three times that much and grandpa handled five times the acreage.)

You can harvest 5 acres of corn, that is, if you cut the stalks and shock them. Once the stalks are shocked, you'll have the entire winter to husk out the ears and—all the while—the corn will be drying naturally before it's put safely in the crib.

HOW TO TOAST PUMPKIN SEEDS

Come Halloween—when you're carving out that jack-o'-lantern—or Thanksgiving, with its pumpkin pie—don't throw away the seeds from your festive yellow-orange gourd. Properly toasted, pumpkin seeds make for some mighty tasty and very nutritious munching.

Separate the flat, slippery little rascals from the stringy pumpkin fibers, rinse away the stickiness, and drain the seeds. Then preheat your oven to 425°F, melt one tablespoon of butter in a large, shallow pan, and spread a cup of the pumpkin seeds around until each one is coated with the butter. Toast, stirring occasionally, for fifteen minutes or until each morsel is lightly browned. Season to taste with onion or garlic salt and store the crunchy snack (if you can somehow resist eating it on the spot!) in a tightly covered container.

GHOST TOWNS

There are numerous ghost towns in the United States. "They range from the abandoned silver mining towns of the Rockies to once-famous eastern spas and southern sawmill communities," said one researcher. "A handful have already become tourist attractions but many are still unmarked, unnoticed, and—some people think—unrivaled as locales for leisure living."

Evidently a few farmers still agree with this philosophy because I bought a corn knife and husking peg—the tools you'll use to handle your corn crop this way—in a small town in southern Indiana. The manufacturers certainly wouldn't be producing this equipment if there weren't at least some demand for it.

The proper way to cut corn is to grasp a stalk about head high with your left hand and then cut the stem off approximately 6 inches above the ground with the knife in your right hand.

You'll soon develop a certain rhythm that will allow you to move steadily down a row of corn and easily whack off one stalk after another without slashing your own leg. When you can't hold any more stalks in your left arm, drop them in a neat bundle. Later, you'll come back, tie each bundle, and set every twelve to fifteen up in a shock.

Yep, it's hard work. But if you do a little every day, you'll find that it's a very satisfying job. Start as soon as the corn is dented good—about Labor Day—and continue cutting and shocking until Halloween or later. Then you can husk out a few shocks as you need them until spring. In addition to the ears of corn, you know, the stalks and leaves of the plants can also be fed to sheep and cows.

Husking corn is an art. Basically, you pull the husk down from around an ear of corn and snap the covering off. Old-timers using husking pegs (you don't really need a peg, by the way) got very good at this. However, it's one of those arts you cannot describe in writing. You'll get the hang of it after you've husked a couple of bushels yourself.

Another way to harvest those ears, when you don't want to feed the stalks and fodder, is by stripping them directly from the standing stalks. Then knock the fodder down with a disc or stalk chopper and plow it under.

HOW TO KEEP BOILED RAW MILK FROM CURDLING

RAW MILK IS BECOMING increasingly popular with health food enthusiasts who are sometimes surprised to find that "the real thing" often behaves differently from the pasteurized, homogenized, vitamin-enriched, standardized version sold by supermarkets. In particular, raw milk seems to have a greater tendency to curdle when it's boiled . . . but that can often be overcome by stirring a pinch of baking soda into the liquid before setting it on the stove.

AN EASY WAY TO PEEL TOMATOES

SOME COOKBOOK AUTHORS DO their readers a disservice when they state that tomatoes are easily peeled if first dipped in boiling water. Were those same authors to actually try the idea, they'd find the following method much superior:

In a heatproof bowl, completely cover the tomatoes with boiling water for thirty seconds, then place the fruit in another bowl of chilled water until they're perfectly cold. At that point, the skins can be slipped off quite easily, leaving the tomatoes as firm and as unbroken as before they were scalded.

HOGS ARE MORTGAGE LIFTERS

FARMERS USED TO call hogs "mortgage lifters" because a hog is the most efficient of all farm animals for converting plant material into meat. A hog also dresses out a higher percentage of its live weight than beef. A word to the wise for modern homesteaders:

The old saying "root, hog, or die" came proudly from pioneer lips because they knew no self-respecting hog was about to die, even if left in the woods without grain. Hogs can live on grass and acorns.

But pigs will live much better with corn and alfalfa hay. To fatten a hog to 180 pounds takes about ten bushels of corn or the equivalent in other grains. The more hay, pasture, roots, vegetables, waste fruit, and the like (a hog will eat most anything you will) you get into your porker, the less grain you'll need. But if you feed it no grain, the animal's meat will be soft and of lower quality.

If you range your hogs on pasture, they'll root the sod up in a most unsightly manner. Rings in their noses stop that nasty habit, but if you're as kindhearted as I am, you'll probably keep your hogs penned in a lot where you can let them dig to their hearts' content.

If given enough living space (no less than a 10x10-foot pen per six pigs), the porkers will not dirty the bedding where they sleep. Hogs are very smart and naturally housebroken. Which is more than you can say about most humans.

THE CASE FOR WELDING

ANYONE DECIDING TO FACE life on his or her own terms in the country would do well to learn how to weld. Sound ridiculous? Not at all. I can say unconditionally that a welder is the most useful tool on the farm.

But there's more. You can profit from welding—not only by being able to make your own repairs, and those of your neighbors—but also by building farm machinery from junked parts. Farmers with engineering talents in this direction save themselves thousands of dollars.

And there's still more. Welding can also reward you as a creative art. Metal sculpture never seems to go out of fashion, especially arty pieces made from scraps of steel, brass, and copper.

Start learning this skill on an acetylene torch rig. Then try an electric arc welder. Fear not. Without any training at all, I started keeping company with a red-eyed electric welder and, in two months, could put two pieces of heavy machinery together again so they'd hold. If I can do it, believe me, anybody can. I've got about as much natural mechanical ability as a tree stump has.

THE ADOBE HOUSE

BLOCK MOLD

Looking for an antique home in the country . . . or a Colonial in the suburbs . . . or a fixer-upper in the city? Old houses suit some just fine, but it's not surprising that many folks want to build their own homes. Homesteaders and people who are interested in living sustainably have brought different perspectives to the American dream. All kinds of people are building themselves all kinds of dwellings—everything from homes made from steel shipping containers to tiny homes on wheels (some less than 800 square feet in size) to handcrafted adobe abodes.

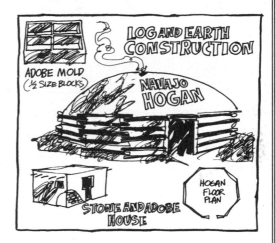

Adobe? Yep. Earth houses are being built again. As one inhabitant of a soil home said, "The best way to build a dwelling dirt cheap is to build it out of dirt itself. Adobe, rammed earth, whatever . . . our earliest ancestors had a pretty good idea after all."

Maybe that fellow's right. Soil, you know, is available everywhere—or, at least, everywhere you're likely to want to live. It's extremely economical, no special skills are needed to work with the material, it's durable enough to last for centuries when properly stabilized, it's fireproof, decay and termite proof, cool in summer and warm in winter, and either an adobe or a rammed earth house can have a warm, rustic look to it.

On the other hand, it takes both time and hard work to build a house of earth . . . but then, you

never get something good entirely for nothing, and the folks who construct earth houses generally seem to be pretty darn happy working for themselves in this way.

I mean, just stop and think about it for a minute. Which would you rather have: A warm, snug, substantial home that should last at least a hundred years and which you built yourself, *or* a plywood and plastic contractor's "development" house that threatens to self-destruct just about the time you finally finish off its thirty-year mortgage?

continued on next page

WEST FACADE OF
LA LUZ
AN ADOBE TOWNHOUSE CLUSTER
IN NEW MEXICO... WINDOWS
OPEN ON THE EASTERN SIDE, PROTECTED
FROM PREVAILING HARSH WINDS AND
STRONG SUNLIGHT

LIVING UNITS

ADOBE WALL

ADOBE WALL

Quite a few modern pioneers are choosing the first and that's why the age-old earth house is an option. Some books on the subject include: *Adobe Houses for Today* by Laura and Alex Sanchez (Sunstone Press), which details twelve plans for adobe homes; and *Adobe Homes for All Climates* by Lisa Schroder and Vince Ogletree (Chelsea Green Publishing), which shows how to build these homes. Look for these and other books at your local library or ask any bookseller about them.

WEATHER WISDOM

FOLKLORE HAS WAYS UNENDING of helping you to predict the weather. "Rain before seven will stop by eleven." Often true. "If the sun shines while it's raining, it will rain again tomorrow." Very often true. "Whirlwinds bring rain tomorrow." Also very often true. "Heavy morning fog portends a nice day." Usually true. "When smoke hangs low, expect rain." Always true. "Rain from the east will last twenty-four hours at least." In my experience, always true. And a snowstorm that moves in from the east, ditto . . . at least in the section of Pennsylvania where I live.

It's when folklore tries to predict weather by the calendar that it gets as daffy as the fellow who plants by the zodiac. "Whatever weather you have on St. Swithun's Day (July 15), you'll have for forty more days." "Ice in early November means the rest of the winter will be mild." And so on. Mere drollery.

I'm not so sure, however, that the legend about St. Martin's Day—November 11—isn't true. This date (the English call it St. Martin's Little Summer) is always supposed to be warm and doggone if it usually isn't. I've kept close records for a number of years now and almost every November 11th (or sometimes the 10th or 12th) will be a beautiful, summer day . . . again, at least in my part of Pennsylvania.

A NEW-FANGLED VERSION OF AN OLD IDEA

NOTHING BEATS WHAT THE old-timers used to call a "stone boat" when it comes to moving rocks, firewood, pumpkins, and other heavy, bulky items around the farm. You can make an easily fabricated, modern version of this age-old sled-type implement quite easily by equipping a discarded automobile hood with a length of chain. Pull the makeshift carrier behind your tractor, Jeep, or horse, and—when the bottom begins to wear through—take the hood to a junkyard and trade it in on another. To make a larger stone boat, weld two of the auto engine compartment covers together in a canoe shape.

Wild Foods

IT'S A REAL PUZZLEMENT that so many modern parents refuse to allow their children to eat mulberries. Sure, the fruit is messy when dead ripe (mulberry eaters always have dark-purple lips and tongues) and more than one kid has fallen out of a tree while gorging himself on these "aerial raspberries." That's still a small price to pay for the sheer delight of cramming handful after handful of the natural sweets into a stained mouth.

There's no real lack of the trees in this country. The red mulberry is native to the whole eastern half of the United States and has been planted as far west as the Oregon coast. The white mulberry, imported from Asia more than a hundred years ago when various promoters were trying to establish a silk industry on this continent, has since found its way into most parts of the United States too.

The quality of both red and white mulberries (and what seems to be a cross between the two) can vary tremendously and ranges from "good enough to eat" to "darn hard to resist." In general, most folks prefer the red variety (which is really purple when ripe) because the white (which can also be somewhat purple in its eating stage) is—believe it or not—just too dang sweet for many palates.

The easiest way to harvest the fruit is by spreading a blanket, sheet, or newspapers on the ground under a tree and then giving the tree a good shake. The best way to eat the berries is as rapidly as you can stuff them into your mouth.

Folks with a little more composure sometimes like to mash the fruit and use the juice for a summer drink. One quick recipe is to fill a glass one-third full of the fluid, squeeze in the juice of half a lemon, add two teaspoons of sugar and some ice, and then fill the container with plain soda water. Mulberries also make fine jelly (if pectin is added) and pie.

HOW TO STORE CABBAGE

CABBAGE WILL KEEP CRISP and fresh all winter if you leave the outer leaves on a number of good heads and put them into a large wooden box. Then bury the box in the garden under protective boards, a layer of straw, and—finally—dirt.

HARVESTING HICKORY NUTS

BEFORE YOU SPEND a lot of time picking up hickory nuts under any particular tree, crack a few of the fallen delicacies first. If three out of four are rotten, there's obviously not much sense in gathering at that spot. Move on to another tree.

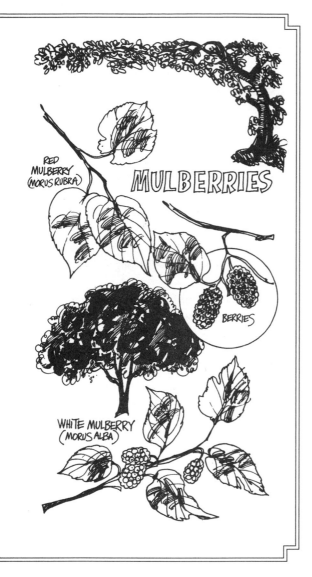

RED MULBERRY (MORUS RUBRA)

MULBERRIES

BERRIES

WHITE MULBERRY (MORUS ALBA)

HOW TO COOK AN OVERSIZE TURKEY

IT'S EASY ENOUGH TO buy a Thanksgiving or Christmas turkey that's too big to fit into your roaster, and not so easy to know what to do about it. One quick solution is the mixing together of four cups of white flour with enough water to make a stiff dough. Place the turkey in the pan and cover it with a blanket of the mixture instead of the usual lid. The bird will cook through and through with no basting although the dough—which is sure to burn on top—will have to be discarded.

USE A WATCH AS A COMPASS

IT'S WORTH NOTING, AS the Lone Woodsman never tires of demonstrating, that an ordinary watch can be used as a compass. Just point the hour hand of the (correctly set) timepiece toward the sun and—anywhere in the Northern Hemisphere—south will always be halfway between that very same hour hand and "12" on the watch's face. When asked if the idea—suitably modified—holds true south of the equator, the Lone Woodsman reckoned that it would but "since I ain't never been there and don't intend to go, I'll leave it to someone else to apply this principle to the underneath half of the planet."

MILK CLEANS SILVERWARE

FEW FOLKS SEEM TO have real, genuine *silver*ware these days, but those who do might be interested in this traditional method of removing stains from a whole set of such utensils at once: Place the knives, forks, and spoons in a pan and cover with sour milk. Let stand overnight, pour off the milk in the morning, rinse the silver in cold water, rinse again in hot water, and wipe dry.

TELL A STORY WITH STRING

MODERN SOCIETIES GENERALLY REGARD playing cat's cradle—the weaving of patterns into a loop of string passed around the hands—as a simple game, worthy only of children. The practice is actually far more than that.

Native tribes the world over traditionally illustrated the telling of their legends with intricately formed string figures, named for the animals, objects, or actions they performed. Lightning, little boat, turtle, yams, sun, two stars, fish spear, dressing a skin, one chief, carrying wood . . . the list of patterns woven into a loop of string by the peoples of the world runs into the thousands.

It's definitely worth your time to recreate at least one of these traditional designs (it'll give you a healthy respect for those native cultures, if nothing else), and the Apache Door is as satisfying a figure to experiment with as any.

Start the pattern by holding your loop of string as shown in fig. 1. Then bring the hands together, put the right index finger up under the string crossing the left palm and, by separating the hands, pull the loop out on the back of the finger (fig. 2).

Bring the hands together again, slip the left index finger up under the strand crossing the right palm *between the strings on the right index finger* and, by separating the hands, draw that loop out on the back of that finger (fig. 3). You should now have a loop over each thumb, index, and little finger as shown in fig. 4.

Now with the right thumb and index, pick up the near string on the left index finger close to that finger, lift the loop completely over the left hand, and let it drop down on the left wrist. Using the left thumb and index, pick up the near string on the right index finger close to that digit, lift the loop completely over the right hand, and let it drop down on the right wrist. Separate your hands and pull the strands tight. You now have loops over each thumb, each little finger and each wrist (fig. 5).

At this point, use the right thumb and index finger to pick up the left little finger near string (not the whole loop this time) close to that finger. Draw the strand toward you and release it between the left index finger and thumb. Then, still using the right thumb and index, pick up the left thumb far string close to the left thumb. Drawing it away from you, pass the strand between the left ring and little fingers, and release it.

Next use the left thumb and index finger to pick up the right little finger near string (again, not the whole loop) close to that finger. Draw the strand toward you and release it between the right index finger and thumb. Then use the left thumb and index to pick up the right thumb far string close to that thumb. Draw the strand away from you, pass it between the left ring and little fingers, and release it.

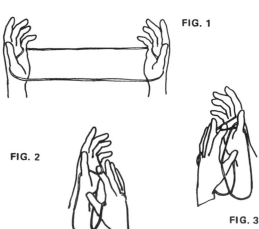

FIG. 1

FIG. 2

FIG. 3

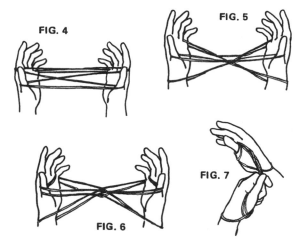

FIG. 4

FIG. 5

FIG. 7

FIG. 6

You now have a loop around each wrist and double loops around the thumbs and little fingers (fig. 6).

Now, *while holding all loops in position on both hands*, use your left hand to pick up all the strings where they cross in the center. Pass the collection of strands over the right thumb so that they lie on the back of the right hand between the thumb and index finger (fig. 7).

Next use the left thumb and index finger to take hold of the two loops already on the right thumb. Without pulling the loops out, slip them up over the tip of the right thumb as shown in fig. 8. Then, *still holding the two loops*, let the collection of strands lying on the back of the right hand slip around to the front of the right hand. This leaves the right thumb entirely free.

Without untwisting the two original right thumb loops (which you still hold between the left thumb and index finger), replace the two loops on the right thumb as they were before you removed them (fig. 9). Separate the hands to draw the strings tight.

Now repeat exactly the transfer of the collection of strings from the front to the back and again to the front of the left hand while manipulating the two loops on the left thumb just as you handled the two loops on the right thumb. Separate the hands and draw the strings tight.

You now have two twisted loops on each thumb, two twisted loops on each little finger, and a loop around each wrist as shown in fig. 10. You're almost finished.

Pick up the loop around the left wrist with the right thumb and index finger and drop the string across the bundle of strands in front of the left hand. In the same fashion, use the left thumb and index finger to pick up the loop around the right wrist and let it fall across the collection of strands in front of the right hand.

Finally, retaining two loops on both thumbs and both little fingers, separate the hands and draw the figure tight. The finished pattern will look like fig. 11.

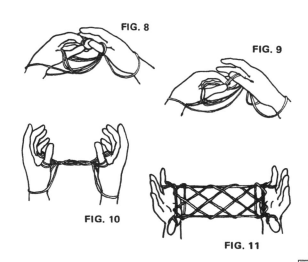

FIG. 8

FIG. 9

FIG. 10

FIG. 11

HOW TO JUDGE FRUIT TREES

RELIABILITY IS THE MEASURE by which you should judge the fruit trees on a subsistence farm—that and economy of production. It's a good bet, then—when you plan your orchard—to accentuate the positive: apples. Year in and year out, apple trees generally bear *some* fruit . . . even if you mistreat them.

From the standpoint of economy, pears are even a better bet than apples, since you can get by without spraying them as much. Sour cherries are reliable too.

Peaches, plums, apricots, nectarines, and sweet cherries, however, are more difficult to grow in most areas. If you want a bushel of any of these fruits, it may be less expensive and less hassle to buy that bushel rather than try to raise it.

A QUICK WRENCH

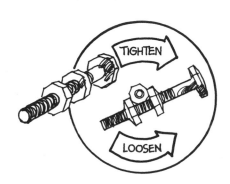

NEXT TIME YOU NEED a wrench in a hurry and you don't have one handy, try this: Screw two nuts—flat sides together—onto a good-size bolt. Space the nuts apart so that the head of the one you want to remove fits snugly between the "jaws" of your makeshift arrangement. The device can then be used just like an adjustable wrench.

SHELLAC KEEPS GREASE FROM SOAKING THROUGH WALLPAPER

ONE OF THE EASIEST and fastest ways to brighten a renovated house is by applying new wallpaper right over old. This can do the trick when the old paper is merely dingy and dirty, but if it's grease-splotched, forget it—the oil will bleed right through the new layer too. It will, that is, unless you coat the spots with shellac.

The same idea also works on machinery that's being painted. Put a layer of shellac over the equipment before you apply the final coat, and any grease that was on the items in question will be unable to bleed to the surface of the finished job.

AIR PRESSURE POPS DENTS OUT OF LARGE TANKS

SOMETIMES A GOOD OLE plumber's helper is all you need to remove a dent from a gas can or tank . . . and sometimes it isn't. To pop out the more stubborn dings, try plugging all the container's openings and filling it almost full of water. Then pump in fifteen or twenty pounds of air pressure and tap around the outer edges of the indentation until it is no longer visible.

UNUSUAL DOWN-HOME TABLE DECORATIONS

TABLE DECORATIONS DON'T HAVE to be flowers or even fruit. How about a shiny purple eggplant in a wooden bowl with lemons, or a fresh cauliflower set off by scarlet tomatoes? Or green peppers with a couple of crookneck yellow summer squash?

HOW TO GROW GOURDS

YOU'LL PROBABLY NEVER GET rich doing it, but you can pick up a little welcome spending money every year raising gourds. The plants—even those that bear the fancy, decorative fruit—take up little space, are so hardy that they require practically no attention, and generally yield a heavy harvest. Best of all, the bright colors and interesting shapes of that harvest are dang nigh irresistible to a lot of people—thus, making gourds what marketing experts call an *impulse item*. Roughly translated, this means that many folks who walk up to a roadside stand with no intention of ever buying a gourd, stagger away with fewer dollars in their pockets and their arms full of the blamed things.

Gourds grow well anywhere that pumpkins or squash do and should be planted as soon as all danger of frost is past. Drop four or five seeds into individual hills spaced 1 foot on center in rows 1 foot apart. Thin each hill to the three best plants, and weed the seedlings until they're big enough to take care of themselves. Then forget 'em. Come fall, you'll have gourds.

The folks who tend to make gourd cultivation somewhat more of a science than the above would indicate seem to split into two schools: (1) those who like to stake the plants and (2) those who prefer to mulch their patch well and just let the vines ramble as they see fit. Both methods appear to work and you're welcome to take your pick. Just remember, when you're laying out that gourd plot in the first place, to try to locate it where it'll get plenty of sun with—if possible—just a touch of shade during the hottest afternoon hours.

The only disease that ever seems to bother this member of the squash family is wilt, and you can avoid that by raising your ornamentals in a different spot every year. Assuming that you do, your next order of business in the gourd patch will be cutting off the mature fruit when it feels very hard to the touch (or at the first sign of frost).

Leave a couple inches of stem on each of the ornamentals and wash them carefully in warm, soapy water. Then rinse the fruit in clear water to which a little household bleach has been added (to remove any soil-borne bacteria that might cause mold). Most growers, by the way, don't use this bleach treatment, which means that—after a while—you'll become known as "the fellow whose gourds don't have all those icky spots on them."

OK. You're now ready to (1) offer your harvest for immediate sale or (2) dry the crop and peddle it all winter. If you choose the latter, lay the melon-like fruit out in the sun or—if there's a chance of rain—in a warm attic or barn loft. Turn the gourds daily and throw out any that are spotted or shriveled.

continued on next page

After about seven days of the above treatment, wipe the ornamentals again with the bleach solution and spread them out (out of the direct sun so they won't fade) to dry for another three or four weeks. Then wax or shellac the gourds to give them a protective finish and to bring out their colors.

Gourds make great centerpieces just as they are. They may also be cut and carved into bowls, spoons, ladles, dippers, birdhouses, flower holders, pencil holders, masks, stocking darners, doll cradles, and many other useful items. Use your ingenuity to whittle out a few of these things and display the finished pieces with the fruit—it'll give your customers ideas and noticeably increase sales. You may even create a demand for your handiwork!

And don't forget to round the ends of their stems and leave a few of the gourds "natural" or unprotected by wax, shellac, or lacquer. When completely dried, this special stock will rattle delightfully and can safely be chewed, making them ideal "pioneer-type" toys for small children.

BAKE THOSE STRING BEANS

THERE'S HARDLY ANYONE WHO doesn't like baked beans. But did you know that the delicious dish can be made with the dried string beans that you didn't eat when they were fresh? Pole beans are especially good this way.

Let them mature on the stalk and when they're dry in the fall, pick the pods. Then dump the pods in a sack and whale the living daylights out of the bag to shatter them (stomp on the sack if beating doesn't do the trick). Finally, winnow away the chaff in a strong breeze or in front of a big window fan. Kidney, marrow, and white northern beans can be shucked out the same way.

When they're good and dry, store the beans in closed containers (such as glass jars). There's a little bug (see the insect chart in the back of this book) that gets into beans and eats them full of holes. By heating the beans in a pan in a 140°F oven for five to ten minutes before sealing them away, however, you should solve that problem before it begins. Or you can store the beans in the refrigerator.

A NEW IDEA FOR BATHTUBS

ALTHOUGH IT GOES AGAINST the hoariest of traditions, consider the idea of installing the faucets *opposite* the drain end of the tub if you're remodeling or building a bathroom. Fresh water let into one end of the tub will then wash dirt and grime right out the other . . . instead of forcing it back into the receptacle as is the case in a standard installation. Makes cleaning the bathtub a lot easier.

TIPS ON RAISING CATS

IF YOU'RE THINKING OF getting yourself a kitten to raise as a house cat, you might do well to get two. Felines—especially the young ones—are more sociable than they usually get credit for.

There's a good reason why a kitten needs company. He has a fantastic amount of energy to spend on exercising his muscles and practicing the skills of a hunting animal—climbing, pouncing, and darting after anything that moves. If there's nothing better to take out his friskiness on, he'll swarm up the curtains and attack your bare feet . . . but he'd really prefer another young cat to play with. Two aren't twice as much trouble to keep—half is more like it. And they'll enjoy each other's company—in a quiet way—even when they're grown.

Any cats you decide to live with should have all their shots as soon as possible. Feline infectious enteritis—almost always fatal to young kittens—is a nasty way to die. Once you've got them protected from this widely spread contagious disease, though, you'll find that these delicate-looking beasties are remarkably tough and suffer from illness very little when they're well nourished.

EVER THINK ABOUT OWNING A CAT (OR TWO)?

A final note on cats: While exterminators have plenty of poisons to eliminate unwanted rodents, a cat can be a very green way to take care of this too. The cat has been domesticated since before the time of the ancient Egyptians, and a good mouser using age-old tactics (pounce and bite) will keep your home Mickey free.

SAFETY PINS MAKE GOOD COTTER KEYS

TRY USING A BIG safety pin (instead of a cotter key) the next time you need to secure a shaft, nut, or whatever on a piece of machinery. The safety pin is handier and should outlast several cotter keys (since they have to be bent every time they're put on or taken off).

SALT IS GOOD FOR A CLOTHESLINE

IF YOU DRY YOUR clothes on an old-fashioned cotton line, try boiling the next replacement rope in salted water for a half hour before you put it up. This will take out all the tangles and prevent wet articles of wash from freezing to the line in cold weather.

THE JOYS OF HOME CANNING

BACK IN 1809, a French experimenter named Nicholas Appert discovered that food—sealed into airtight containers and heated until all harmful bacteria were killed—could be preserved for a year or more. As we all know, this relatively simple breakthrough—canning—revolutionized the off-season eating habits of millions of people. Over time, the process was refined and it developed into a multibillion-dollar business.

There's no reason, though, for you to let the large packers corner the market on canning, especially when one of the most satisfying feelings in the world is that of walking into the pantry and looking at row after row of glistening jars packed full of fruits, vegetables, and meat that you've "put up" yourself. No wonder that self-sufficient homestead living and canning-on-the-kitchen-stove go together so well.

And if you don't live on the land and raise your own garden or livestock? No problem. You can still buy quantities of produce in season—when they're inexpensive—and can them right in your home or apartment for use all year. Sure, it's work—if you want to think of it that way. But it's also a great family project, a lot of fun, extremely satisfying, and it'll give you an almost sinful feeling of self-reliance and independence.

Grandma and great-grandma knew all the tricks of home canning but, chances are, you never acquired that knowledge from them. If that's the case, you'll probably be pleased to learn that there are many excellent books containing all you'll probably ever need to know about canning at home.

One guide that I like is the *Ball Blue Book* (Alltrista Consumer Products). This book just overflows with information on proper canning procedures and contains hundreds of recipes for canning, preserving, and freezing nearly everything your family will ever want to eat. Check with your library or local bookseller for a copy.

SUNSHINE PRESERVES

You CAN PUT UP strawberry or red cherry preserves very easily by cooking them in sunshine. Mix equal weights of washed fruit and sugar and place the mixture in pans so that the fruit is no more than ¾ inch deep. Cover the containers with plain window glass and stand them in full sun. Stir morning and evening, and bring the preserves inside when the sun goes down. When the mixture is thick enough—after several days—heat it almost to boiling on the stove, pack it in hot sterilized jars, and seal the containers.

CANNING YIELD

Legal weight of a bushel of fruits or vegetables varies in different states.
These are average weights:

FOOD	FRESH	CANNED
APPLES	1 bushel (48 pounds)	16–20 quarts
APRICOTS	1 bushel (50 pounds)	20–24 quarts
BERRIES (except strawberries)	24-quart crate	12–18 quarts
CHERRIES, as picked	1 bushel (56 pounds)	22–32 quarts
PEACHES	1 bushel (48 pounds)	18–24 quarts
PEARS	1 bushel (50 pounds)	20–25 quarts
PLUMS	1 bushel (56 pounds)	24–30 quarts
STRAWBERRIES	24-quart crate	12–16 quarts
TOMATOES	1 bushel (53 pounds)	15–20 quarts
ASPARAGUS	1 bushel (45 pounds)	11 quarts
BEANS, lima (in pods)	1 bushel (32 pounds)	6–8 quarts
BEANS, snap	1 bushel (30 pounds)	15–20 quarts
BEETS, without tops	1 bushel (52 pounds)	17–20 quarts
CARROTS, without tops	1 bushel (50 pounds)	16–20 quarts
CORN, sweet, in husks	1 bushel (35 pounds)	8–9 quarts
OKRA	1 bushel (26 pounds)	17 quarts
PEAS, green (in pods)	1 bushel (30 pounds)	12–15 quarts
PUMPKIN	50 pounds	15 quarts
SPINACH	1 bushel (18 pounds)	6–9 quarts
SQUASH, summer	1 bushel (40 pounds)	16–20 quarts
SWEET POTATOES	1 bushel (55 pounds)	18–22 quarts

Above table reprinted from U.S. Department of Agriculture Bulletin, AIS-64

"CHAW" THAT SPEARMINT

A PATCH OF WILD spearmint (transplanted from down along the creek) proliferates at the corner of our garage. My wife uses the leaves to make mint juleps (once a year at Kentucky Derby time), but I have an even better and more constant use for the plants' foliage.

Whenever I'm going somewhere, am in a hurry, suspect that my breath is offensive, and haven't had time to brush—all normal conditions for me—I pull a leaf or two from the plot of mint and "chaw" on the bits of greenery as I drive away. Works better than chewing gum.

THE SOLAR-POWERED HOUSE

THE LATE 1940s AND early 1950s were an exciting time for technology in the United States. An amazing variety of clever new machines and scientific breakthroughs came on the heels of World War II, and these things inspired business leaders, government officials, and popular press to predict that we were all going to ride into the future in nuclear-powered cars, and live in prefabbed solar-heated houses when we got there.

One "reliable" source even forecast a total of 13 million solar-heated homes in the United States by the mid-1970s. There were about twenty such homes then, and now . . . well, there aren't quite one million such homes, but it's close, at approximately 700,000 and counting . . . even the White House has solar panels.

Now, individually and collectively, this foot-dragging development of the solar home has cost us all a great deal. It's hurt our pocketbooks because—obviously—if your home and my home were each capable of getting free power from the sun, then you and I wouldn't have to spend more money than we like to think about every year for electric, oil, or gas heat.

And that, in turn, would be a very good thing for the planet. With global warming a reality these days, it would eliminate the need for much of the strip-mining and the damming of rivers that is done to produce electricity. And there'd no longer be a need for many of the pipelines, tankers, and railcars that carry heating fuels to our cities because we wouldn't need the fuels themselves. (And let's not talk about what happens if something goes wrong when the fuel is being moved from point A to point B.) And, if the power companies were no longer burning all that coal and gas and oil, the air we breathe would be much less polluted.

If your home were solar-heated, in other words, you would still be warm and comfortable all winter, but at a price, to both you and the earth, of only dollars . . . instead of the many hundreds of dollars and foul air and climate change that the heat now costs.

SALT CLEANS VARNISHED FURNITURE

VARNISHED FURNITURE TOPS WILL develop white rings when glasses or plates are set on them, and folks still wonder what to do about it—although grandma long ago discovered that salt and shortening would remove the blemishes.

Sprinkle salt on the marks and then rub them gently with a clean cloth dipped in shortening. Wash and rewax the area as soon as the stain is gone. In extremely stubborn cases, of course (when the discoloration has gone completely through the varnish), the surface will have to be sanded and refinished.

Decades have passed since the original predictions about solar homes, and now it is relatively easy to install clean, environmentally friendly solar power at home. If you have a south-facing roof, you'll be able to install solar photovoltaic (PV) panels and start collecting those rays. Also, you'll have options for not only heating your home, but also your water . . . and you can get electricity to power all your lights, refrigerator, and whatnots. Now, jumping on the solar bandwagon isn't without some costs. Initial installation fees might make you swoon. HOWEVER, there are so many federal and local government incentives and tax rebates that you'll find the cost of the project decrease before you make the first payment. AND some electric companies will buy any excess electricity you generate. Not a bad deal, eh?

As Cheryl Long in a MOTHER EARTH NEWS report said, "A straight cost/benefit analysis is not the only factor to consider. If you choose to go solar, you will be supporting an industry that is poised to make a major contribution to the looming energy crisis and our global warming predicament. Buying a solar-electric system is one of the best things you can do to help protect our environment and to give your family some protection from skyrocketing energy prices and the uncertainties caused by climate change. Every homeowner who opts for clean, renewable solar power is taking us one more step toward a wiser, more sustainable human presence on Earth."

HOW TO MAKE HARDTACK

IF YOU'RE GOING TO be camping, or otherwise cut off from a supply of fresh bread for some time, you might consider mixing up a batch of hardtack. Made with rye or other whole-grain flour, it's nourishing and will keep well as long as it's baked very thoroughly.

To make hardtack, take a teaspoon of salt and a teaspoon of sugar for every five cups of flour and mix well. Add just enough water to make a stiff dough. Roll the paste ¼ inch thick, cut it into pieces, and bake on a greased pan in a slow oven until it is very dry.

DAMP NEWSPAPER CLEANS GLASS

DAMP NEWSPAPER CLEANS AND polishes glass much better than cloth does, without getting lint all over it.

NATURAL FLEA AND TICK CONTROL FOR YOUR DOG

PEOPLE WHO KEEP CATS and dogs almost invariably (knowingly or unknowingly) keep fleas too. An infestation of the ornery critters *can* get heavy enough to severely bother an animal and even weaken a pup or kitten through loss of blood.

Believe it or not, there are some completely natural down-home controls for these pests. The little bugs, for instance, do *not* like the odor of some aromatic plants that are quite pleasant to most humans: pennyroyal, mint, sassafras, and the like. Try boiling a good quantity of such herbs in water and washing your animal, or animals, in the liquid. If the fleas don't leave, at least you'll have a fragrant pet!

You can also soak pieces of cord or clothesline rope in oil of pennyroyal to make flea collars (which should be renewed every two weeks). Hang a couple of bunches of the herb in the dog-house, too, if Lady is the well-disciplined kind of pooch that sleeps outside. If she's the indoor type, put a pillow stuffed with camomile flowers in her bed. (And if Lady gets on *your* bed at night? Maybe *you'd* better use the pillow.)

Folks who've tried letting their dog or cat sleep on a blanket that's been used to wipe off a sweating horse claim that fleas hate the equine smell even more than they dislike the herbs mentioned above. If you can live with a pet that's been scented with *eau de Ole Gray Dobbin*, then, you've sure enough found your bug repellent.

On the other hand, if you want to attempt an internal cure for your dog or cat's external parasites, you should know that fleas don't care for vitamin B1 in the blood they suck. Regularly sprinkle a little brewer's yeast in your pet's dinner if he or she will take it (most animals will) and you should cut the flea problem drastically.

A DANDY FIRE EXTINGUISHER FOR MINOR FIRES

WE ALL KNOW THAT we should have a fire extinguisher or two in the kitchen, another in the car, and yet others within handy reach in the shop, barn, and so on. Few of us do because . . . well, *because* . . . the dang things are too big and bulky, and they have to be recharged, and they *cost* too much.

OK. Right now, today. You're going to go out and buy a whole half dozen compact, low-cost, ever-ready fire extinguishers. They'll weigh less than two pounds each (so they're not too large), they'll never have to be recharged (so there's no objection there), and they'll be inexpensive.

Talking 'bout—are you ready?—baking soda. Good old baking soda in one-pound cardboard boxes. Each carton contains enough powder to douse almost any minor fire you're ever likely to encounter in the kitchen, basement, home workshop, or car. How? By generating flame-snuffing carbon dioxide when sprinkled on a blaze.

Now, to prevent moisture from caking the soda over the years (and to keep the weak-willed at your house from using the contents of the fire extinguishers for other purposes), protect each box of

WARM MILK HELPS SLEEP . . . SORTA

THE OLD CUSTOM OF drinking warm milk as a cure for sleeplessness is an old wives' tale with a little bit of truth. Scientifically, the jury is still out as to whether or not milk has any chemical properties that will help you sleep. Psychologically, the warm milk may remind you of nighttime routines with your parents when you were little, causing you to relax with thoughts of stuffed animals, footy pajamas, and being tucked in for the night.

RAW APPLES CLEAN TEETH

NO MATTER WHAT THE dentist says, no children—and precious few adults—brush their teeth after every meal. You can get somewhat the same effect, though, if you pass around chunks of raw apple when everyone's finished eating.

A TIP FOR FEEDING HOGS

MORE THAN ONE FIRST-TIME farmer has learned the hard way that getting into a pen of hungry hogs (and they're always hungry) with a couple buckets of feed can be rougher than playing goalie on a professional hockey team. It's a much better idea to position the porkers' trough under a steeply slanted spout that runs right through the pigpen fence. Then you can mix all the hogs' dry feed with water or milk and pour the food into the trough with no muss, no fuss, and—at least to you—no jostling.

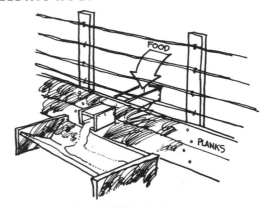

the powder in a tightly sealed, double wrap of aluminum foil. Then glue a band of red paper around every package or clearly label the foil on the individual boxes (with something like a marker) "FOR FIRE ONLY."

Put one of the soda containers in the kitchen, another in the bedroom, a third in the basement, a fourth in your workshop, a fifth in the car glove compartment, and carry the sixth on your tractor (or put it in the baby's room, near the heat lamps in the barn during spring farrowing, in the chicken house next to the brooder stove, and every other place you can think of).

At the first sign of fire, grab the nearest box of soda, tear off the protective foil, and sprinkle the powder over the blaze. It won't take much, so spread the soda thin. As the powder hits the flames, it'll produce a dense cloud of carbon dioxide that will quickly extinguish grease, electrical, and most other kinds of minor fires. Just be sure to keep a regular fire extinguisher on hand for anything more than a minor flare-up.

Remember now . . . do it TODAY!

THE MANY USES OF **LYE**

WATER

HARDWOOD ASHES

ASHES

STRAW

GRAVEL

HOLES

NON-ALUMINUM CONTAINER

MAKING LYE

The average farmer these days goes about his business with the help of many chemicals. So many that the total would probably amaze him if he stopped to add up all the veterinary preparations, disinfectants, cleansers, orchard sprays, rust removers, painting aids, and the rest of the cans and bottles he keeps in his barn and sheds.

That farmer's grandfather, though, didn't have specialized substances for all those purposes . . . and chances are that he made one single chemical—lye—do most of the jobs listed above.

Now, lye—whether leached from wood ashes or bought at the hardware store in the form of sodium or potassium hydroxide—is a powerful agent that has to be treated with respect . . . and some old-timers still have scars to show for their careless handling of this caustic substance. There's no doubt that a person who intends to use *any* strong chemical should know its properties (lye, for instance, must never be put in an aluminum container because it eats right through that metal) and should have antidotes on hand in case of accident. Nevertheless—used with caution—lye was a good friend to the old-time farmer.

And what did that prudent man of the soil do with lye? Well, to begin with, he made soap at slaughtering time . . . and if you're butchering your own hogs, you might consider following his example. (Most lye manufacturers will provide instructions for making soap.)

In fact, grandpa passed lye around among his stock and barns pretty freely, with good results. His cows—for instance—stayed healthier because he scrubbed their stalls and stanchions with a 1:150 solution of this powerful disinfectant (one 13-ounce can in 15 gallons of water). Dairy utensils like

HOW TO STORE BROTH

Don't hesitate to boil up your chicken/turkey/ham/beef bones for stock just because you won't have a use for the broth in the next few days. It's true that meat soup is tricky stuff to keep (labs, in fact, use it for a bacteria culture medium), but you can cook the liquid down to a concentrate and freeze it in ice trays. Transfer the stock cubes to plastic bags and store them in the freezer for future use. Diluted to normal strength, your frozen soup gives you a useful base for pilaf, gravy, or just a good hot pick-me-up when you need it most.

churns, bottles and crocks—not to mention the hard-to-clean parts of the cream separator—were sweetened by a wash with a weak lye mixture made by adding a level teaspoonful to a gallon of water.

The chicken house, also, was a cleaner and healthier place after grandpa disinfected it with the 1:150 lye mix to kill lice, mites, roundworm eggs, and disease germs.

The orchard, too, got the benefit of lye solution (as a spray to remove mosses and lichens). Then, if an old-time farmer wanted to spray other remedies on his trees, he mixed up a batch of fish-oil soap to blend with the chemicals so they'd stick to the foliage. And you *know* what he used to make the soap!

That's not all, either. If the plowshare got rusty and hard to pull, grandpa took a strong lye solution and an old broom and scrubbed the metal bright again. He made his own paint and varnish remover too, and here's the recipe: Put on rubber gloves. In a wooden pail or stone crock, mix four tablespoonfuls of cornstarch with two quarts of water. In another container—*not* aluminum, remember—dissolve one can of lye in one quart of water. Pour the lye solution into the cornstarch mixture, while stirring well. Still wearing gloves, cover a small area of the painted surface with this paste, leave the mixture on until it begins to dry and scrape off the loosened paint with a putty knife, wire brush, or steel wool.

Grandma also found lye very handy to have around the house. In diluted solution it was good for all kinds of cleaning jobs, and—when used to scrub the cellar walls and floor—kept the basement from getting musty. The same chemical took the skin off fruit at canning time and the hulls off corn to make hominy. In concentrated form, the caustic stuff kept drains open, of course . . . and the occasional canful emptied into the outhouse pit made the privy a more pleasant and sanitary place.

That's a lot of mileage from one cheap, simple chemical, isn't it? Again, lye can be dangerous stuff to have around, and many of us will probably stick to more sophisticated products to clean canning jars (though it's possible that the modern chemicals may be just as hazardous—or more so—in their own subtle ways). Nevertheless, it's good to know that—if we were cut off from our suppliers of veterinary preparations, disinfectant, and plain old soap—we'd have something to fall back on. And even if we couldn't get our hands on a can of potassium or sodium hydroxide from the hardware store, we'd still be in business . . . because, when you get right down to it, all we *really* need to make our own lye is water and wood ashes.

MAKE A TOOL HOLSTER
FROM AN OLD GLOVE

IF YOU'LL CUT THE worn fingers off an old work glove and then add two slots to the back of what's left, you'll have a quick, recycled tool holster that you can slip right onto your belt and put into immediate use.

PROTECT TODDLERS FROM POWER TOOLS

TODDLERS HAVE BEEN KNOWN to injure themselves by plugging in power tools and appliances that grownups have carelessly left within the babies' reach. Cure this problem once and for all around your house by locking tools in a toolbox or buying a number of the small, inexpensive, jewelry chest padlocks and snapping one onto a prong of each electrical tool that you want to keep safely out of your young'uns' reach.

BLACK WALNUT FORAGING TIPS

MY OLE DADDY-IN-LAW KNOWS more ways to survive than a cat does —and I've learned to argue with him at my own risk. One of his more curious rules of thumb (which I've never yet been able to explain nor find a way around) has to do with gathering wild walnuts (black walnuts) in the fall.

Every autumn this wily old woodsman cracks the first few mature walnuts he finds and sizes up—are you ready for this?—the *color* of the skin on the meats inside. If the coverings are dark, my wife's father wouldn't forage walnuts that fall if you threatened him with a loaded shotgun. "No use," he says. "When the nutmeat skins are dark, the meat will shrivel up to nothing in storage."

If, on the other hand, the skins of the meats are light-colored, daddy-in-law picks up at least a bushel of the hulled nuts (enough to last him and mamma-in-law two full years). "Light-skinned nutmeats will store that long without drying up," the ole trapper and trader explains.

All I can say is that I've collected walnuts every fall for the last ten years and, as my son puts it, "Grand-dad ain't been wrong yet."

BUILD A LOW-COST CORN CRIB

TOP VIEW

CORN SHOCK ROOF

←—12-FEET—→

RAILROAD TIE RISERS AND OLD LUMBER FLOORING

AIR VENT

OUTER FENCE

TWO SNOW FENCE RINGS

YOU CAN BUILD A low-cost, convenient crib for ear corn in less than an hour with snow fence. It won't be permanent, but such a storage facility has done a good job of temporarily (for a year or two) holding and protecting a bumper crop of corn on many a small family farm.

First make a platform on the ground large enough to accommodate a round bin 12 feet in diameter. The easiest way to do that is to lay down a few logs or old telephone poles on a level spot and nail boards across them. That's your floor.

Then set up a long enough piece (almost 38 feet in length) of snow fence to form a circle 12 feet in diameter on the floor. Securely fasten the ends of the snow fence together with wire.

HOW TO DIVIDE A BOARD IN HALF

SOME FOLKS NEVER DO seem to learn the easiest way in the world to divide a board, piece of paper, or other sheet of material into halves. Just lay a 12-inch ruler diagonally across the width of the piece so that each end of the measure is flush with one edge of the sheet. The 6-inch mark will always be right on center, no matter how wide the piece being scribed. The same idea can be used to locate thirds, quarters, etc., and—for sheets of plywood or other wider-than-1-foot spans—substitute a yardstick or tape measure for the ruler.

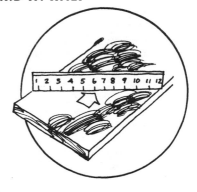

VINEGAR PROTECTS HANDS FROM COLD

THE NEXT TIME YOU'RE obliged to do some fine work outdoors on an extremely cold day, rinse your hands in vinegar and dry them before going out. For some reason, the vinegar wash makes the frigid temperatures easier to take and seems to keep the fingers a little more limber a little longer.

HOW TO UNSTICK TWO GLASSES

YOU HAVEN'T EXPERIENCED ALL the frustrations of life until you get two glasses stuck together that neither gentle pressure, violent cussing, nor—like marriage—any man can put asunder.

Relax. There is a way. Place the bottom glass in *hot* water and fill the top (inside) one with *cold* water. They'll come apart quicker than a June bride can say "I do."

Next, cut a 6¼-foot-long piece of snow fence and set it up to form a 2-feet-in-diameter circle in the center of the first ring of fencing. When the larger circle of snow fence is filled with corn, this middle "flue" will be left empty so that air can circulate through the middle of the pile. (You may have to put some cross bracing inside this central "chimney" to keep the pressure of the corn from collapsing it.)

Once you've filled the first section of temporary crib with corn, you can add another tier of fencing right on top. Make it smaller, though (8 to 10 feet in diameter), and don't forget the center air vent. I've seen third sections put on top of these quickie corn bins, but they can become a little "iffy." It's better to start a second snow fence crib, if you have that much extra corn to store.

When your bin is filled, top it off with cornstalks that are tied in bundles and sloped away from the center of the crib to direct rain and snow off—rather than into—the stored grain. Old metal roofing or sheets of plastic can also be used as roofing for the bin. Don't worry about the rain that may be driven through the fencing that forms the sides of the crib. What little gets into the outside layer of ear corn won't hurt it.

Take the corn out of your snow fence bin by cutting a hole—big enough to allow easy access with a scoop shovel—into the bottom of the lower circle of fencing. If the corn won't feed down, ram a crowbar into the ears that are packed above this scoop hole and work the bar around vigorously.

GOING NOMAD

You know, an awful lot of children dream about running away from home and traveling with the circus, but very few ever try. That's the way it is with many of us grownups too: Down in our secret heart of hearts we often feel like walking away from the job, selling the house, buying a big ole bus, and taking to the road. But not many of us ever try.

Or, at least, not many of us *used* to try. It's a different story today, because a number of folks are now actually making that dream come true for themselves.

Folks like a couple from North Dakota, who decided to live and travel in a twelve-ton bus that was converted to a rolling studio. The family of nine—count 'em—nine roam far and wide during the summer on the former sixty-six passenger bus. (While their seven kids are in school, they park semipermanently.)

The dad is a landscape painter and he makes a living by selling his work. Since he can whip out a made-to-order landscape in less than thirty minutes, and since his prices are extremely reasonable, he sells a lot of paintings.

You've got to give the family credit for organizing their own brand of Good Life . . . a Good Life that allows the dad to feed, clothe, and educate

A RUBBER BALL IS A HANDY TOOL

There are times—when busting out a chunk of concrete or modifying a piece of heavy farmstead equipment—that a home handyman has to put in a long stint with hammer and cold chisel or star drill. This can be dang fatiguing on the hand and arm that holds the chisel or drill. Kill that impact shock and resulting strain by cutting a hole (to fit the shank of the tool being held) through a sponge rubber ball and slipping the new "handle" over the implement. You'll be able to grip the shank tightly, but in much greater comfort.

RUBBER BALL ABSORBS THE SHOCK

his children while still working only when and where he chooses. Not many of us can say that.

Which brings to mind another fellow who's made the itinerate life and a box of paints work for him. Al doesn't do landscapes, though. He paints signs, and he's not above slapping a coat of preservative on a whole building, for that matter, or working as a day laborer once in a while. One way or another, he always makes enough money to get by.

Al and his son live in a converted step van and they ramble the West from Idaho City to Mexico. The two pretty much come and go as they please and they particularly enjoy camping for weeks at a time in some of Idaho's old ghost towns.

Some modern wanderers make better-than-average money with more down-to-earth jobs. Marvin, for instance, does very well indeed as a traveling farrier. He works only the racetracks and fairgrounds of his choice and—as he says—really has it made.

For others, the nomadic life is a way to reduce their carbon footprint and live sustainably. One couple discovered that an Airstream trailer was their ticket for this kind of living. Cece and Brenda travel the United States and Canada in a solar-powered Airstream that is fueled by vegetable oil. They got rid of their excess things, and moved into a 25-foot-long Airstream. Their rolling home includes green features too: a composting toilet, solar panels, cork flooring, and more. Their goal is to share a message of conservation, exploration, and inspiration with the people they meet in their travels.

Yes, it is possible to be a substantial, law-abiding, tax-paying citizen while living on the road. In fact, there seems to be a whole slew of ways to find both the Good Life and a Good Living as a modern-day nomad.

PUT RUBBER HOSE ON YOUR PLIER HANDLES

SLIP A 13 TO 15 inch length of rubber hose over the handles of a pair of electrician's pliers and (1) the handles will be a lot more comfortable to hold; (2) the pliers will automatically open whenever you release your grip; and (3) they'll be insulated for work on "hot" wires.

THE FINE OLD ART OF BARTER

WITH FEDERAL TAXES, STATE taxes, city and county taxes, and sales taxes whittling each dollar down to quarter size before we even get a chance to spend it, it's not surprising that an increasing number of folks are turning once again to the age-old practice of barter.

The trend away from money and back to swapping is gaining in popularity again. If you don't have a lot of cash on hand but you do have something worth swapping for, then bartering is a good way to get what you want—without the tax implications to boot.

Barter offers ironclad protection against inflation too. When goods and services are traded directly, their value is apparent and the folks making the transaction couldn't care less about whether the dollar is going up or down. In other words, it doesn't matter what the eggs sell for in the market— an egg is still an egg and, if I think one egg is worth five strawberries, that's exactly what I'll give you and no more.

But isn't barter a lot of trouble? Not at all. Every time you buy a new car or furniture or an appliance and trade in an old item, you're using a little bit of barter. You're also making use of barter when you swap magazines or books or garden produce with a neighbor, or place an ad offering to trade something you no longer want for something you need.

Barter also plays a far more important part in really big business deals than you might have imagined. Very few of those multimillion-dollar corporation mergers or real estate transactions are made with cash. Instead, a percentage of ownership in the form of stocks is simply swapped, or one piece of property is traded for another (usually for the primary purpose of beating taxes).

A few folks are even turning barter—this oldest-of-old business idea—into some of the newest and most satisfying self-employment enterprises around.

One fellow noted that most newlyweds receive a great number of duplicate wedding gifts, many of which they don't want, need, or care for. He decided to help remedy that situation by setting up an evening and weekend wedding gift exchange in the basement of his home. Brides and grooms would be allowed to swap duplicate presents at the exchange by paying him a 10 percent cash fee of the known, or reasonably estimated, value of the articles in question. Any overage on a particular swap would be

THERE'S MONEY IN JUNK

THERE HAS ALWAYS BEEN money in junk, but never on such a ridiculously broadscale as now. Every farm trash pile and city dump, it seems, contains potential buried treasure in the form of bottles, jars, crocks, and thousands of other items.

But we all know that. So, if you have the beachcomber's itch, you might do better to go junk hunting with a *map*. Yeah. A map from the county courthouse or local historical society will show the location of *yesterday's* dumps and used-car lots. Because what you're looking for are old car parts.

Replacement items for Hupmobiles, Model Ts, and the odd antique Essex are dang nigh worth their weight in gold (or more), and you might as well cash in on the bonanza as the next fellow. Searching out

recorded as a credit balance on a future trade.

His idea caught on immediately and—within a year—his part-time business was holding a reasonable stock balance and netting him a profit every week.

Or how about organizing a small-scale food co-op? The operation of such a services-exchange is simplicity itself. The organizer first lines up as diverse a collection of tradesmen, laborers, and professional people as possible into a "club." Each member qualifies merely by agreeing to provide his services IN HIS SPARE TIME to any other club member on an exchange basis. All such work is billed at each participant's regular rates, but no money changes hands. Instead, the doctor, lawyer, music teacher, mechanic, house painter, dry cleaner, or whatever has his or her account credited with "work units" that the individual can collect from any other club member in the form of services and labor. The organizer of the operation, of course, draws his or her credits for keeping the club's books and overseeing the work exchanges.

The services-exchange idea is feasible because all the work for the club is done after regular hours (hence no one loses out on regular income), members spend no out-of-pocket labor money for car repairs, dental work, construction, and so forth, done by exchange members, and the whole setup neatly sidesteps all sales and other taxes.

Individuals with any kind of skill, of course, can work the same idea on their own. As an example, one artist has swapped portraits and sketches for dogs, furniture, fancy fish, a life-size model of a quarter horse, rugs, veterinarian care, art paper, driving-school lessons, and—occasionally—money. "Whatever I trade for," she says, "I always come out with the best."

old and forgotten radiator caps and rumble seats is good clean (if somewhat dusty) fun, and the chances of stumbling across a treasure trove of fenders and engine blocks in a long-closed garage are still good enough to add a generous dollop of spice to the hunt.

After you've collected an assortment of parts (throw nothing away—the door handle from a '38 Nash may be just what some collector needs to finish his restoration), ooze into a few local antique car shows, and have a go at selling your loot to the highest bidder.

THE REAL MAGIC BEAN

AMERICANS, AS A WHOLE, have high-protein diets, and we eat—on the average—more meat, milk, and eggs than almost any other people in the world. But did you know that there's something else, which isn't on a lot of our tables, that contains twice the protein of meat and over ten times the protein in milk? We're talking about soybeans. They are both delicious and exceptionally nutritious, and you should know more about them.

For centuries, soybeans—sometimes called "the meat that grows on vines"—have been known as the meat, milk, cheese, bread, and oil of Asia. Selected varieties of the beans are reputed to contain one-and-one-half times as much protein as cheese, peas, or navy beans; double the protein found in meat and fish; three times as much as eggs or whole-wheat flour; and a fantastic eleven times more protein than fresh milk.

Chemical analysis has further shown that the amino acids (protein) in soybeans are present in nearly the maximum amounts essential for the diet of both man and animal. This means that properly prepared soybeans (forget trying to eat them raw, they're basically undigestible that way) alone are a sufficiently complete food (they contain fat and carbohydrates too).

In short, soybeans are an excellent vegetable source of protein and have become an

TREAT CUTTING BOARDS WITH BEESWAX

SALAD BOWLS, CUTTING BOARDS, and breadboards will be more pleasant to use, remain much more attractive looking, and stay in tiptop shape if they're occasionally treated with beeswax. Apply the fluid with a soft cloth, let the wooden articles set overnight, and wipe away the excess liquid in the morning. A little buffing with a dry cloth will then bring out a warm shine. Repeat the procedure periodically.

A HALLOWEEN RHYME

HALLOWEEN IS APPLE TIME and here's an old rhyme that's supposed to help a girl tell her fortune as she counts the seeds in the fruit she's eaten:

One I love,
Two I love,
Three I love, I say . . .
Four I love with all my heart
And five I cast away.
Six he loves,
Seven she loves,
Eight they both love.
Nine he comes
Ten he tarries
Eleven he courts
And twelve he marries.

important ingredient in many of the dishes enjoyed by vegetarians . . . and they can be eaten in a wide variety of recipes. Folks who are really into the beans use them in everything from cereal to pancakes, and they use soy milk to drink as well as make everything from puddings to cake.

For an easy and tasty introduction to eating soybeans, put one cup of the dry seeds in a bowl, cover with four cups of water, and soak them overnight in the refrigerator. The next day, dry the beans between two towels and spread them in a thin layer on a cookie pan. Roast 'em in a 200°F oven for two hours.

Peek in occasionally to make sure the beans don't burn and—after the two hours—turn the oven to broil and stir the soybeans almost constantly for five or six minutes, till they're brown and crunchy.

Eat the beans hot out of the oven "as is" or shake 'em up in a jar with just a couple drops of olive oil and a little salt. They taste like roasted nuts when they're cold and you can enjoy them lots of ways (such as ground up and sprinkled on ice cream). Or just munch 'em as a snack.

Note: Make sure you buy *organic* soybeans and their offshoots (e.g., edamame, tempeh, miso)—and avoid genetically modified versions.

Once you've proven to yourself that soybeans *are* good to eat, you'll probably want to get a copy of Dorothea Van Gundy Jones's collection of recipes called *The Soybean Cookbook* from your local library or book purveyor.

RECYCLE YOUR THREAD HOLDERS

Years ago, some unknown backwoods farmer inserted a nail through an empty spool and then drove the spike into his outhouse door to make an improvised handle. Ever since, folks have been recycling these wooden castaways from the sewing basket into useful articles.

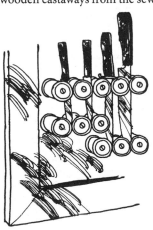

If you can find old wooden spools, fasten a row of the discarded thread holders—jammed shoulder to shoulder—inside a kitchen cabinet door and—presto!—you've got yourself an instant knife holder. The handles of the cutting tools will rest on the spools while the implements' blades fit through the gaps between each set of the wooden rollers. It's a perfect marriage and, once you try it, you're going to be dang proud of yourself for thinking of the idea in the first place.

Attach the spools to the cabinet door with both screws (through each roller's center) and glue (on the base of the discarded thread holders) for safety. You may also want to run a second full or partial row of spools under the first as added security for your butcher and other extra-long knives. A coat of varnish, shellac, or paint that matches the inside of the cabinet finishes the project.

HOW TO START AN HERB BUSINESS

IT'S ONE THING TO speculate idly about building a new life for yourself . . . and quite another to roll up your sleeves and put that new existence on a self-sustaining basis. That's why the folks here at MOTHER EARTH NEWS spend so much time digging out good, ole-timey home businesses that are (1) environmentally sound, (2) something almost anyone can do, (3) easy to finance, (4) downright fun, and (5) healthy enough to put a family on a secure financial basis.

One of the best of the back-to-the-land businesses we've found so far is the occupation of growing specialty crops such as herbs. It's an enterprise the whole family can enjoy. It's also an undertaking that you can start inexpensively (for just the cost of a pack or two of seeds), and build into just as big and profitable an operation as you want.

We, in fact, know one couple who actually and honestly began an herb business with an investment of one seed pack. They grew their business into 2½ acres planted in herbs, a beautiful retail store of their own, and a number of other outlets that handle their produce.

Now that's a darn enviable position to be in, especially when you realize that our herb growing friends are not only living quite well, they're having the time of their lives doing it! That herb farm of theirs—which they love—is what they dropped out to from stifling city lives, which they hated. For them, then, growing herbs is both a good life and a good living. And, if you've been looking for a paid

BALING WIRE AND OTHER FARM TOOLS

SOONER OR LATER (AND usually sooner) on the farm, you'll be handling hay and straw bales—either your own or some you buy. Just remember, when you remove the wire or twine that holds each bale together, to hang it up. Baling wire and binder twine are the two handiest "tools" on the farm, as you'll eventually learn, for holding things together. Besides, if you drop twine into bedding, it'll cause you to invent new curse words later on when you try to fork the manure out. The string catches in each fork you lift and, once in the manure spreader, snags in the tines.

ticket back to the land, there's no reason why you can't make the growing of specialty crops give you the same winning combination.

There are numerous garden suppliers across the country that can get you started. The people at Nichols Garden Nursery in Albany, Oregon, for example, have worked with folks starting their own businesses. This nation's appetite for both culinary and aromatic herbs isn't slowing down, and many more producers are needed to keep up with the demand.

Even if the idea of raising and selling herbs sounds attractive, you may find you prefer to keep such an undertaking on a "puttering around" scale, and that's OK too. Herbs are hardy, most grow well in relatively poor soil, and few insect pests bother the pungent plants. It doesn't take a very large bunch of herbs to be worth several dollars, either, so the smallest backyard patch has the potential of producing a cash crop.

As a final frosting on the cake (for all you folks who've decided that business doesn't have to be conducted for profit alone), the raising and marketing of herbs can offer a number of creative challenges to you and your imagination. Will you sell your produce as seeds or sets? Fresh or dried? Bulk or packaged? Made into tangy ketchups and flavorings or sewed into sachets and catnip mice? Will you cater to the gardening or the consumer market? Retail, wholesale, or mail order? The sky's the limit in the herb business.

If you don't use hay and straw bales, keep baling wire and binder twine on hand anyway. You can't farm without 'em. Other useful tools necessary to a practicing farm, but which you might not think of, are: (1) buckets; (2) vise-grip pliers; (3) Liquid Wrench (an oil that helps loosen rusty bolts and burrs); (4) an engineer's squirt oilcan and a grease gun; (5) a jack; (6) a post-hole digger; (7) a wrecking bar; (8) pocketknife; and (9) shovel, axe, and pitchfork.

You'll find many uses for these tools of the trade, some of which uses you haven't even dreamed of. Yet.

Money *does* grow on trees—in the form of fruit and nuts—and every homestead (even if only city-lot size) should have at least a mini-orchard. Plant yours in the spring and never try to make the trees fit in little bitty, squinched-up holes. Lean on that shovel and dig out an excavation big enough so that those seedlings' roots can spread out in comfort. Then hold off on fertilizing the newly set orchard until it's growing well.

Shade trees, of course, have a dollars-and-cents worth all their own, and can make any home more valuable. Their leaves make good compost, so burning each autumn's offering makes about as much sense as lighting a cigar with a bill of large denomination.

All leaves will rot down into rich soil faster when they are shredded, and it's a good idea to sprinkle lime (which sweetens the final product) on any that you intend to use around the vegetable patch. Evergreen trees, holly, azalea bushes, and blueberries—all acid-loving plants—can take their leaves straight, however, and a good 10-inch mulch of the unshredded variety is all the fertilizer azalea and holly need.

A SIMPLE MITER JIG

About the only thing more difficult than arm wrestling an octopus is trying to glue a mitered corner together so that the dang thing is square. Oh sure, there's some complicated and rather expensive jigs and fixtures made especially for the job, but what amateur ever uses such equipment often enough to justify the investment?

No problem. The simple little rig shown here (two C-clamps and a cigar box) shouldn't set you back more than a couple of dollars, and it will hold all the mitered corners (one at a time, of course) you care to stick together.

THE SELF-HEATING, SELF-COOLING HOUSE

How WOULD YOU LIKE to live in a house that cools itself in the summer and warms itself during the winter *automatically*, without a furnace or an air conditioner? That would be fabulous, wouldn't it? Because (1) it would save you an initial investment of thousands of dollars for the furnace and air conditioner; (2) it would save you additional money each year for fuel; and (3) having cut all that consumption of hardware and fuel, it would be a very good thing for the environment.

Such a home is not a dream. A fellow named Wendell Thomas first built one years ago in North Carolina's Celo Community. And, although Celo is located in the mountains where weather extremes can be most severe, the temperature inside that house never dropped below 60°F nor climbed to over 75°F. Incredibly, the only supplemental heating the dwelling ever required was a small blaze in the fireplace on only the coldest mornings in winter.

Now that's almost unbelievable when you compare the Thomas home to other houses in the area, because the others required the consumption of oil or coal or cords of wood for winter comfort.

How did Wendell do it? Well basically, he designed his house to be a "lithospheric" building. This means that he used the earth itself as the major regulator of his home's temperature, and that's easier than it may sound.

What Wendell did was (a) he dug a generous basement under the house; (b) he cut a series of vents in the main floor of the building just inside the exterior walls; and (c) he installed a large grill—again, in the main floor—and a stove right in the center of the dwelling.

Now the basement was nothing unusual but those vents around the outside edge and the grill in the center of the main floor WERE. They were also the main secret of the Wendell Thomas self-heating, self-cooling home because they allowed an unusual circulation of air in that house.

What happened was, in the winter, cold air flowed down the inside of the building's exterior walls, through the vents in the main floor, and into the basement. There, since the surrounding ground was warmer than the outside atmosphere, the air was somewhat heated and rose back to the main level through the grill in the center of the house.

The normal winter air circulation in the Thomas home, then, took the shape of a giant two-story donut that rolls up in the middle and down around the outside edge.

In the summer, this donut was still there, but it flowed the other way. The air on the main
continued on next page

floor, just inside the building's exterior walls, was warmed by the heat coming in through those walls, and that air rose. As it rose, it flowed toward the center of the house where it was forced down through the grill in the main floor. As the air sunk into the basement and passed across the basement floor, it became cooler and cooler and would have been quite happy to stay down there. But, as the air above it warmed and rose, this cooler air in the basement was pulled up through the vents around the edges of the main floor to start the cycle over again.

Thus the two-story donut of air in the Thomas home sunk in its center and rose around its outside edge during the summer. And the main floor was thereby cooled with "air conditioning" from the basement.

Thanks to this largely vertical circulation, the upstairs walls of homes built this way never dry out and crack in the winter, nor does the basement become damp and moldy in the summer. These homes, in short, work the way houses SHOULD work . . . and by adding just a touch of solar heating in the winter, Wendell Thomas developed a home that automatically maintains an almost-ideal living temperature.

TWO SIMPLE NAIL HOLDERS

INSTEAD OF SMASHING YOUR fingers the next time you drive a batch of small nails or brads, slit the end of a pencil eraser and use the improvised tool as a holder while you start the little rascals. A bobby pin also makes a good brad holder.

HOW TO KNIT WITH A SPOOL

WHEN MA GETS HER knitting out, the kids often want to try too—even the children who are too young to handle a set of needles. For these tykes, a good introduction to yarn craft is spool knitting.

If you can acquire old wooden spools, take a good-size, empty spool and drive four finishing nails into one end to form a square. Leave about ½ inch of each nail sticking out. Now find some yarn—lightweight is best—and poke the free end of the ball down through the hole in the spool so that it hangs out the bottom.

Hold the loose end of the yarn at the bottom of the spool and pass the strand at the top end once around the outside of all four nails. Now start a second round higher up than the initial wrap. As you come to the first nail, hook the lower strand on the head of a large pin, lift it past the second round of yarn and pop it over the top of the nail to make a loop on the inside. Continue around the nails in order and keep the tension loose enough to allow the loops to slide easily over the tops of the "posts."

As you work, gently pull the free end of the yarn now and then to draw the knitting down through the hole and—after a while—a soft wool tube will appear and grow at the bottom of the spool. Make it as long as you like, with new colors tied on whenever you want. To bind the creation off, slip the knitting off the nails, cut the upper end of the wool, pass it through all the loops, and tie it firmly.

The finished knitting can be rolled in a spiral and sewed loosely to make rugs for doll-houses or mats for Christmas presents. Other uses will occur to children, especially when they find that the wool tube—while stretchy—is almost unbreakable.

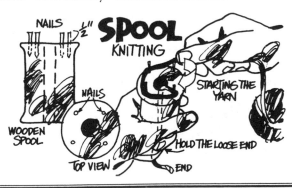

HOW TO MAKE COFFEE FROM THE BEAN UP

GRABBING A CUP OF coffee at home is easier, cheaper, and probably a lot tastier than heading out to the nearest coffee shop. There's also nothing more satisfying than pouring a cup of the brew directly from freshly ground beans. Since there are a good variety of coffee pots, old-time coffee mills, and whole and ground beans, perhaps some general instructions in the fine art of making coffee are in order. The following directions originally appeared in *The Ohio Farmer* dated March 7, 1942—long before national coffee chains could be found coast to coast.

OLD-FASHIONED COFFEE POT. USE one heaping tablespoon of coffee for each three-quarter measuring cup of water. Measure coffee into the coffee pot. Bring freshly drawn water to a boil; pour over the coffee, stir well, cover tightly and over low heat or in a warm place eight to ten minutes. Strain coffee immediately into a hot serving pot. Serve at once. A second method for making this kind of coffee is to measure the coffee into the pot and then add cold water. Place over heat, stir mixture well, and just bring to a boil. Stir again, remove from heat, add one-quarter cup cold water to settle the grounds. Cover tightly and let stand as above for five minutes. Strain immediately into hot serving pot. Serve at once.

PERCOLATOR METHOD. Use one heaping tablespoon of coffee for each three-quarter measuring cup of water. A percolator may be started with either cold or hot water. Measure water into the percolator. Place basket in pot and measure coffee into it. Cover and place on the heat. When water begins to percolate reduce heat and allow to percolate slowly over the coffee for seven to ten minutes. Remove the basket containing grounds as soon as coffee has percolated a sufficient length of time. Serve at once.

GROW YOUR OWN RABBIT FEED

COMMERCIAL RABBIT FEED IS a "scientifically balanced complete diet." It's also unnecessary and expensive. I feed my bunnies *dried* clover and *dried* grass clippings (fresh grass can give rabbits diarrhea if they aren't used to it), lettuce, cabbage, anything green from the garden, carrots, turnips, rutabagas, and grain that I raise myself.

When my soybeans are ripe, I cut and store them—stalks and all—in the barn. A fistful of the dried plants a day gives the bunnies needed protein. The rabbits even eat the beans right out of the pods (often consuming the pods themselves in the process), which saves you the trouble of threshing. Same with wheat.

I cut my wheat patch by hand, tie the stalks in small bundles and give about a third of a bundle to each rabbit every day. The critters eat the grain out of the heads and gnaw the wheat's stems into pieces. The straw that then falls from the bunnies' cages into the manure pit below, and soaks up the urine down there. I work almost the same deal with my chickens.

It sure is nice to raise livestock that can thresh its own grain and bed itself down.

DRIP METHOD. Use one heaping table-spoon of coffee for each three-quarter measuring cup of water. Scald the pot with boiling water. Measure coffee into coffee compartment. Pour fresh, briskly boiling water slowly into the water container. Cover and place over low heat or in a warm place where coffee will keep hot but not boil. When dripping is completed, remove upper compartment containing grounds. Stir the brew before serving as the last of the coffee to drip through is weaker than the first. Cover and serve at once.

VACUUM METHOD. Use one heaping tablespoon of coffee for each three-quarter measuring cup of water. Measure cold or freshly boiled water into lower bowl. Place on heat. Do not place upper bowl in position until water boils. Adjust filter and measure coffee. Place the upper bowl on the lower bowl, giving it a slight twist to make an airtight seal between the two bowls. Water will almost immediately be forced through center tube into the upper level. When all but the small amount of water below the bottom of the tube has risen, stir the mixture well in the upper bowl. Remove from heat. When the brew has returned to lower bowl, remove the upper bowl. Serve at once.

EXTEND THE LIFE OF YOUR GARBAGE CAN

PAINT BOTH THE INSIDE and outside of your new metal garbage can's bottom with asphalt roofing sealer and the container should last ten years or more, instead of the usual one or two.

WHY LADDERS ARE NOT PAINTED

HAVE YOU EVER NOTICED that wooden ladders are very seldom painted? There's a particular reason for that: Paint can hide cracks and splits until they've developed far enough to become dangerous. It's far better to put a coat of linseed oil on your ladder if you feel duty-bound to protect and preserve it.

PLAIN OLE SALT

WHAT'S THE HOUSEKEEPER'S BEST friend—the single most useful item you can have around your home? In a popularity contest, there'd be plenty of votes cast for a really good set of kitchen knives, and another big block for a pile of old, often-washed cloth diapers (which make the best dishtowels and polishing cloths you could find anywhere). But the overall winner—on the basis of general, all-round handiness—might well be an extra box or two of common salt.

You probably already know that a cracked egg will stay neatly inside its shell when you boil it if you add a teaspoonful of salt to the cooking water, and that a tiny pinch makes egg whites or chilled cream beat up easier. But did you know that a smidgen of the same seasoning will keep raw milk from souring quickly? Or that fish are easy to clean if you douse them in hot saltwater until the scales curl?

Salt will also help you extract nutmeats unbroken, it's said, if you soak the nuts in brine overnight. Then, tap the end of each shell with a hammer and it'll break easily, leaving the kernels whole.

What's more, if your winter store of apples starts looking a little wrinkled, you can try washing and soaking them in brine made by adding one handful of salt to every three gallons of water. Change the solution every six hours until the fruit perks up. (The old recipe says to use a stone crock for this process.)

Pancake breakfasts are more fun for the cook, too, if you make a little salt bag to rub the griddle with instead of greasing it. The flapjacks won't stick, and the hot metal won't smoke.

And speaking of smoke, if the pie boils over in the oven, just throw a big handful of salt over the spilled juice. The mess will stop smelling up the kitchen and the salt will cook into a light, dry, porous crust that you can sweep off the oven bottom when the stove cools.

LET YOUR LIVESTOCK HARVEST YOUR CORN

FOLKS WHO ARE TRYING to make a small farm pay out for the first time should know that one of the easiest and cheapest ways of all for harvesting corn is simply to let the livestock do it.

Now, this isn't at all ridiculous. Yesterday's farmer used the method frequently. When your corn is tall but still green—in August when the pastures are drying up—turn fattening lambs in on it. The lambs will eat off the lower leaves without harming the rest of each plant.

Then, as the corn matures and the lambs go to market, let the hogs into the field. This practice, called "hogging off" is somewhat wasteful, but the cut in machinery and labor-costs more than makes up for that.

Finally, after the fattened hogs have been shipped to market, you can turn your beef cattle in on what's left of the corn. They'll clean up the ears that remain and winter graze the stalks and fodder.

Another surprising talent of good old sodium chloride is that it seems to make some things wear better. Brooms and toothbrushes, for instance, last longer if you soak them in hot saltwater before you use 'em for the first time. You can also toughen glassware and lamp chimneys by setting them in a pan of cold brine, gradually bringing the solution to a boil and then letting it cool.

While we're on the subject of lamp chimneys, folks who are homesteading off-grid may want to try polishing these glass covers with salt after washing them. Brightens 'em up and allows them to transmit a better light.

In fact, salt—used like scouring powder—cleans all sorts of things: discolored coffee pots and cups, wood tabletops, or oilcloth. In a hot water solution, the same chemical cleans bamboo furniture . . . and drains . . . and the insides of bottles. Made into a paste with flour and vinegar, it does wonders for tarnished brass or copper. (Leave your homemade polish on for an hour or so, rub it off with a soft cloth, and wash the metal.)

One of the few things you *don't* want to use salt for is melting ice on paths and roads—you know what the residue does to car exteriors *and* to the plants that you hope will come up in the spring—but if you have to hang out your wash on a cold day, you can take advantage of sodium chloride solution's low freezing point in a different way. Used in your final rinse water, salt will keep the clothes from freezing on the line.

There's no need to go overboard about salt, of course—like the folks who try to detect poisonous mushrooms by sprinkling a little of the seasoning on the gills of the fungi they've gathered. The idea is that if the gills turn black, you can eat the mushroom, but if they turn yellow, the fungi are not edible. Forget it. This old rule of thumb has no real basis in fact and—if used—stands a good chance of killing you.

In general, though, you really can't go wrong with salt. It's a cheap, harmless, handy replacement for a whole shelf full of expensive chemicals that may be none too good for you or for the water they'll eventually wind up in. And knowing the uses of this household wonder makes the job of chief cook and bottle washer a lot simpler and more fun.

TEA CLEANS VARNISHED WOODWORK

DON'T KNOW IF IT'S the tannin or what, but if you steep old tea leaves in water for half an hour and strain the liquid, the tea is excellent for cleaning varnished woodwork. Put a little on a damp flannel and rub the wood lightly to get rid of finger marks and that dull, gummy look. The same infusion also brightens mirrors and windowpanes.

REMOVE TAR WITH LEMON PEEL

YOU CAN GET TAR off your hands by rubbing the spots with a piece of orange or lemon peel and wiping immediately.

"NATURAL" FOOD STORES

A FEW DECADES AGO, the average "health food store"—and there weren't many of them—was tucked away on a low-rent side street in a run-down section of town, and business wasn't very brisk.

Since then, however, that's all changed. Hundreds, if not thousands, of "health" and "organic" and "natural" food stores have sprung up in every corner of the North American continent. Folks of all ages, incomes, and hair lengths—it seems—are demanding foods free of chemicals and additives . . . and business is booming.

But wait a minute. Just what the heck do terms like "natural" and "organic" mean on food labels anyway? And why is the stuff these stores sell so much better than supermarket produce . . . or is it?

Well, to start with, the term "natural," as used by food manufacturers, doesn't mean a thing. In fact, the word is completely *mis*used in that context to greenwash products and interest buyers who are looking to buy *actually* healthful foods.

A much more defined label is "Certified Organic." The "Certified Organic" label is, at its core, a consumer protection law. It's the US Department of Agriculture's (USDA) assurance that you're buying food that has been produced and processed according to its National Organic Program

(NOP) standards: **Vegetables and fruits** have not been produced using irradiation, sewage sludge, synthetic fertilizers, prohibited pesticides, or genetically modified organisms (GMOs); **livestock** has been fed 100 percent organic feed without antibiotics or growth hormones and were raised with at least some access to the outdoors; and **multi-ingredient processed foods** must contain at least 95 percent Certified Organic ingredients.

The Certified Organic label is backed by regulations developed by the USDA and the National Organic Standards Board, an advisory committee of consumers, environmentalists, farmers, and scientists. Part of the board's job is to advise the USDA regarding the "National List of Allowed and Prohibited Substances." But it aims to be more than an organic referee that rules a farming substance or practice either "fair" or "foul play." The board also makes recommendations about sustainable agricultural practices, and if its recommendations are approved by the USDA, the law requires farmers who seek organic certification to demonstrate that they follow such methods.

To obtain organic certification, applicants must have their operations reviewed by a third-party certifying agent. The review process includes annual inspections, and inspectors can request samples of soil, water, and plant and animal tissue to test for chemical residues. Producers must also pay certification fees that range from a few hundred to several thousand dollars. For some growers, the financial cost and the rigorous path to gain a Certified Organic label are daunting. The law thus makes allowances for small operations. Producers who market less than $5,000 of organic products annually may call their products organic (but not Certified Organic) without going through the certification process, provided they comply with other regulations. (For more information on certification requirements, go to the USDA's National Organic Program FAQ). Labeling a product Certified Organic without receiving USDA authorization is illegal and can result in prosecution and a fine.

Although some of the USDA's decisions have been criticized by organic watchdog groups (such as The Cornucopia Institute), we've come a long way in organic food labeling. Before the national organic standards went into effect in April 2001, consumers had no way of knowing whether food labeled as organic was in fact produced using sustainable, environmentally sound practices. Today, we can know that farmers have produced food without using toxic pesticides, harsh fertilizers, and unsustainable—and sometimes inhumane—systems. Year-over-year increases in sales show that more and more consumers prefer to eat Certified Organic products.

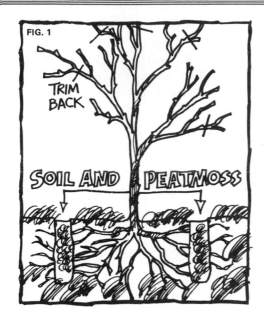
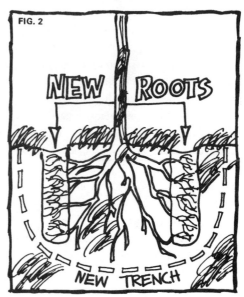

HOW TO TRANSPLANT A TREE (WITHOUT KILLING IT)

TRANSPLANTING YOUNG TREES IS a task that most of us approach on a rather spur-of-the-moment basis and carry out in a more or less haphazard manner. Which probably explains why a somewhat alarming number of our transferred trees shrivel up and die.

Professional nurserymen, on the other hand, plan the movement of their growing stock months in advance, execute the transfer in a systematic and orderly manner, and then have the satisfaction of watching almost all the transposed trees thrive and flourish in their new locations. Here's how they do it:

In the spring, prepare the roots of each sapling you want to move by digging a circular trench around the tree (fig. 1). Use a sharp trenching spade and make the excavation as wide and deep as the digging tool itself. Remember to keep the inner cut of the circle at least 8 inches away from the trunk of any tree up to 6 or 8 feet tall (allow more distance for larger saplings). This will cut the plant's roots back to a manageable size for the later move and—since the healthiest trees always have about as large a volume of roots below the surface as branches above—you should trim the upper portion of each sapling accordingly at this time. The trench should also be filled with a mixture of topsoil and peat moss so

BLACKBOARD ERASER CLEANS CAR WINDOWS

WHEN YOUR WINDSHIELD STEAMS up on you, a clean blackboard eraser kept in the glove compartment of your car or truck can be quite handy for wiping off the moisture. The eraser is less bulky than a cloth and doesn't shed lint on the glass.

FIG. 3

BURLAP SQUARE

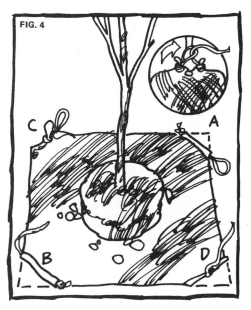

FIG. 4

that the tree's new growth of more compact roots (fig. 2) can proceed as easily and rapidly as possible.

By autumn or the following spring (most nurserymen prefer to transplant during spring when the cool, damp nights and warm days make for near-perfect growing conditions), your sapling will be ready to move. Cut a new circle (fig. 2) just outside the first one to completely free the soil ball containing the tree's roots.

A 4x4-foot square of burlap (an old feed sack opened out will do) should be a nearly ideal "container" in which to wrap the lump of dirt for its move. Roll up half the piece of fabric, tip the tree and its chunk of earth over far enough to allow you to tuck the bunched burlap under the ball of soil, rock the root cluster back in the opposite direction, and unfurl the rolled fabric right up the other side of the lump of earth (fig. 3).

Secure two looped (A and C in fig. 4) and two straight (B and D in fig. 4) pieces of cord on opposite corners of the square of cloth and gather the burlap around the clump of earth by drawing B through A and D through C. Pull the corners together at the trunk of the tree as shown in the detail in fig. 4 and tie them off. Extra lashing may be added for more support and strength.

continued on next page

HOT WATER TAKES DENT FROM TABLE TENNIS BALL

IF A TABLE TENNIS ball is dented—but not cracked—you can put it back into tiptop shape by dropping it into a pan of boiling water to which you've added a pinch of salt. Turn the ball over and over with a spoon for a few minutes, and the collapsed area should pop right out.

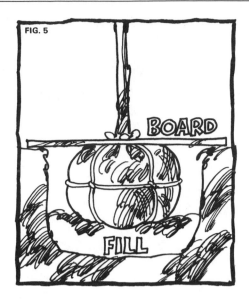

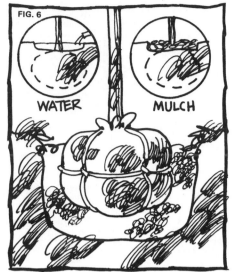

Dig your sapling's new "home" twice as wide and one and a half times as deep as the wrapped root cluster (fig. 5). Loosen the earth at the bottom of the hollow and add a healthy layer of peat moss. Then shovel in just enough nesting soil (two parts earth to one part peat moss) to bring the top of the root ball level with the edge of the hole. Check your calculations by placing a piece of lumber directly across the opening and ball of earth as shown in figure 5.

Hold the tree up straight, fill the space around its base with wet soil, and carefully tamp the fill dirt each time a new shovelful is added. Leave a 2 inch deep "saucer" around the sapling, water the tree generously, and fill the depression with bark-chip mulch. Thereafter, keep the sapling well watered (but not drenched) until it's substantially rooted. It's also a good idea to trim the tree's branches back (almost severely) at the time of transplanting to "take the load" off those roots until they're firmly established in the new location.

HOW TO CUT PLYWOOD SHEETS SO THEY'LL FIT TOGETHER

TRYING TO PLANE THE edges of a couple of pieces of plywood so that they'll fit neatly together is noooo pleasure at all. Matter of fact, it's nearly impossible. Forget even trying. Instead, just butt the two sections as tightly together as possible, tack 'em down, and run a power saw right up the seam. Even if the saw wavers a little (as—say—a sabre saw will), the edges will vary from true exactly the same amount and exactly in "step." Shove the two sheets together (after making the pass with the blade) and they should fit absolutely perfectly.

KITCHEN TIPS

3 teaspoons of liquid equal . . . 1 tablespoonful

4 tablespoons of liquid equal . . . ½ gill or ¼ cupful

½ cup equals . . . 1 gill

2 gills equal . . . 1 cupful

2 cups equal. . . 1 pint

2 pints (4 cups) equal. . . 1 quart

4 cups liquid equal . . . 1 quart

4 cups flour equal . . . 1 pound or 1 quart

2 cups vegetable shortening
(solid) equal . . . 1 pound

½ cup vegetable shortening
(solid) equals . . . ¼ pound or 4 ounces

2 cups granulated sugar equal . . . 1 pound

2½ cups powdered sugar equal . . . 1 pound

1 pint milk or water equals . . . 1 pound

1 pint chopped meat (solid) equals . . . 1 pound

10 eggs (without shells) equal . . . 1 pound

8 eggs (with shells) equal . . . 1 pound

2 tablespoons vegetable
shortening equal . . . 1 ounce

4 tablespoons vegetable
shortening equal . . . 2 ounces, or ¼ cup

2 tablespoons granulated sugar equal . . . 1 ounce

4 tablespoons flour equal . . . 1 ounce

4 tablespoons ground coffee equal . . . 1 ounce

1 tablespoon liquid equals . . . ½ ounce

AT ONE TIME ALMOST everyone cooked with lard, but now most folks use nothing but Crisco or one of the other vegetable shortenings. If you're in the latter group, the following hints are handy to know:

When using vegetable shortening in place of butter, add one level teaspoon of salt to each cup of the shortening.

When there is smoke in the kitchen, the shortening has burned or heated too high for frying. Or, some may have been on the *outside* of the pan or kettle.

When using vegetable shortening in your regular recipes remember that—since it contains no moisture—it is much richer than butter and, therefore, one-fifth less should be used.

In making sauces, thoroughly blend the flour and vegetable shortening before adding the milk. When using melted vegetable shortening in boiled dressing, croquettes, rolls, fritters, and other like recipes, be sure that the shortening is cooled sufficiently so that the hot fat will not injure the texture of the foods. Shortening, like butter, is susceptible to heat and cold. When it's too hard simply put it in a warm place.

WINTER

December 22, Winter Solstice

THE TIME OF REST

O**N DECEMBER 22**, the sun appears to circle the earth directly over the Tropic of Capricorn, 23½ degrees south of the equator. This is the winter solstice for the northern half of the planet (and the summer solstice for the southern). It is also the longest night and shortest day for the top half of the globe (and vice versa for the bottom).

"Winter" is Anglo-Saxon for *to make wet* and is generally the season when the most precipitation falls in the temperate areas of the world.

During the approximately ninety days following the December 22 solstice, folks in upper Pennsylvania will become reacquainted with their snow shovels; a small boy in North Dakota will be taken on his first ice-fishing trip; a young lady from Greenville, South Carolina, will be kissed under the mistletoe; at least 6,000,010 snowball fights will be fought on the North American continent; the cat and dog will spend a lot of time sleeping under the kitchen stove; and grandma will read the seed catalogues and dream of the coming spring.

WOOD ASHES DE-SKID DRIVEWAY

HERE IT IS ALREADY, the first ice storm of the winter, and you never did get around to filling yourself a box of sand with which to de-skid your paths and driveway. Naturally, you don't want anyone breaking his neck on the back steps. But you know that the same rock salt that does such a fine job on the slippery places *now* will still be lying in wait on the ground *next spring* when you want to plant morning glories by the porch.

Well, who needs rock salt, anyway? There are other materials that won't melt the ice for you but *will* provide excellent traction underfoot and be kind to your soil too. Wood ashes, for instance. Or plain old garden earth, if it isn't already frozen too hard to dig up. Or—if you're reduced to using a store-bought product—try cat litter. It has the advantage of not tracking into the house as much as some of the other nonskid substances, and you'll find that most of it will still be lying around on the walk after the ice is gone (where you can sweep it up and save it for the next storm).

While you're sprinkling your footpaths, you'll want to fill a container of whatever material you use and put it in the back of your car or truck along with the extra snow shovel. Then, when your wheels spin on ice, you can provide enough purchase to get going. And, since you're not using salt, you won't have corroded car bodies or yellowed roadside flowers on your conscience.

If you invest in too much cat litter, by the way, it won't be wasted the following summer (even if your cat thinks indoor plumbing is for sissies). The absorbent clay takes up almost any kind of spill—like oil puddles on concrete, or hot bacon grease on the kitchen floor, or the sort of accident that happens when you're house-training a pup (or a child). Just pour the litter over the mess, let the moisture absorb it, and sweep up the whole business (but don't put it in the toilet— cat litter gums up plumbing).

CHIHUAHUA DOGS SEEM TO "CURE" ASTHMA

AN OLD WIVES' TALE notes keeping a Chihuahua dog as a personal pet will relieve the symptoms of asthma for many people. Many years ago, an editor of *Mechanix Illustrated* magazine, reported this amazing "fact," and received a steady stream of letters from folks who swore the method worked. The truth, however, is that the Chihuahua is not a very furry critter and, thus, the asthma sufferer will not be debilitated by the dog's shedding fur. If you're afflicted with the disease, and like animals anyway, then this method of "self-medication" would seem to be worth at least a try. At best, it may help you to "take up your bed and walk." At worst, well, you'll still be ahead one small, big-eared, bug-eyed friend.

A CREATIVE WILD FOOD GARDEN

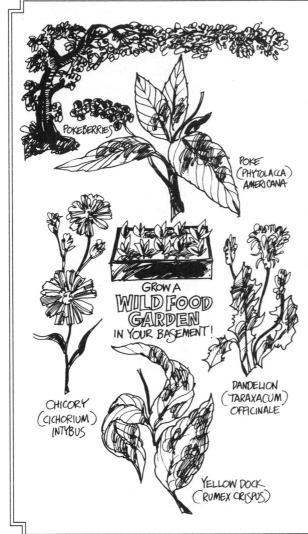

KNOWLEDGEABLE WILD-FOOD FORAGERS EXTEND the harvest of some volunteer vegetables by "forcing" tender shoots of the plants in the basement during the winter.

Dandelions and their cousin—chicory—are two of the easiest wild greens to handle this way. Dig up their roots during the fall, replant them in a box of dirt, and leave the container outside until after the first frost (to fool the plants into thinking that winter has passed). Then bring the container inside, keep it watered, and try to maintain the box's temperature at around 55°F in a semidark spot (a cellar provides near-ideal light and temperature conditions). In about twenty to thirty days you should be able to start gathering crisp, pale, blanched leaves that go well in any salad.

Continue watering the dandelion and chicory roots, and they'll produce several cuttings of greenery. When the first box starts to taper off, you can bring in another,

HOW TO SOUR CREAM

MANY GOOD COOKS PREFER sour cream to sweet for certain recipes, even though sweet cream left to sour by itself often develops an undesirable flavor and odor. You can sour your own cream with consistently good results, however, by shaking up five teaspoons of buttermilk in a fresh pint of the liquid. Let the mixture stand twenty-four hours at a temperature between 70 and 85°F before use.

A HINT FOR ROASTING BIRDS

TO KEEP THE BREAST of roast fowl from drying out while the legs cook, cover the white meat—after the first hour in the oven—with cheesecloth dipped in unsalted fat or oil.

and then another (if you've been clever enough to have them waiting outside), and extend your harvest right on through the winter.

Yellow dock can be forced in the same way, although its shoots (which are multi-colored) add more eye appeal than worth-while flavor to a salad.

Another plant that can be grown in this manner is poke. Dig out twelve or fifteen of the massive roots, trim them to fit a box, and bury them just as you did the dandelions. Let the box remain outside until after the first freeze and then bring it in. If you keep the poke watered, you'll be able to gather delectable shoots (cook 'em like asparagus) every week for most of the winter from that one container. One caution, though: DO NOT try to eat the poke roots. They can poison you . . . but don't let that fact discourage you from enjoying the poke sprouts. They're entirely safe to eat and delicious!

A SEWING TIP

Sewing thread will never kink if you always make your knot in the end of the strand that leaves the spool first.

MAKE *POT-AU-FEU*

If you tend to have a lot of leftovers, you might do what the French (and Americans and Germans . . . maybe everybody) have done for centuries; make a *pot-au-feu*, a kettle of soup that simmers on the back of the stove. (It's vitally important, by the way—to prevent the growth of harmful bacteria—that the rich brew *is* kept simmering, instead of merely warm.)

Start your pot off by mixing up a bigger batch of vegetable soup than your family can possibly eat. Then simply dump in each day's leftovers (plus, maybe, a little shot of vinegar from time to time for flavoring) and keep the kettle bubbling gently. The steady stream of fresh ingredients will constantly change, enrich, and extend the broth's dimensions and character . . . and the soup will always be ready to eat, to boot (a pox on frozen dinners)!

BAY LEAF PROTECTS FLOUR

Try putting a bay leaf in your barrel or sack of flour. Its pungent aroma should help keep out the creepie-crawlies.

POLISH YOUR SHOES WITH A LEMON

You're going out, you want to dress up a little, and you just found out that the shoe polish is down to a few dried up bits rattling around in the bottom of the tin. If you have black or tan leather shoes, fake it! Take a piece of cut lemon and rub the leather all over. Finish off with a soft cloth, just as if you used polish. Nobody will ever know the difference.

NEWSPAPER SHINES GLASS AND FURNITURE

Crumpled newspaper is great for shining up glass and furniture. The ink in the sheets seems to act as a polish.

FIX A HEARTY, NORTH WOODS BREAKFAST INEXPENSIVELY

THERE'S NO REASON TO agonize about overpriced and nutrient-deprived packaged breakfast foods—not when it's so easy to roll the clock back to grandma's robust morning meals at trifling costs. Matter of fact, you can feed a steaming hot, old-time, stick-to-the-ribs breakfast to every member of your tribe tomorrow morning for just a few dollars.

Now this is no light breakfast either. Nope. It's a hearty, satisfying-right-down-to-the-toenails meal that is so good it's a mainstay with modern homesteaders up in the north woods of Canada's British Columbia.

The secret is wheat—*whole wheat*. If you buy the grain that way—before some processor mills it and bleaches it and takes out the germ and throws away the hull and adds I-don't-know-how-many-chemicals—you'll find that it's a surprisingly complete food. Natural wheat berries contain calcium, iron, B complex and E vitamins, and many other nutrients. Whole wheat is GOOD for you.

It's also inexpensive, especially if you buy it from a grower. Sixteen ounces of the grain—there's about sixty pounds of wheat in a bushel—costs a lot less per pound when compared to buying it in little one-pound cartons from a supermarket or fancy health food store. Give it a try: pick up your grain direct from a farmer on your next weekend trip out of the city. Just make sure you get fresh, organic whole grain that has NOT been treated in any way with chemicals or pesticides.

Now, assuming you make a fantastic buy direct from a grower or feed store, you'll probably find yourself holding uncleaned grain. That is, your wheat will have some weed seeds, husks, and a little dirt in it. Nothing to be alarmed about though—it all comes from the field that way. Ask any farm boy. That's the way Mother Nature grows it.

❖ ❖❖ ❖

A TEMPORARY LIVESTOCK SHELTER

IF YOU'RE NEW TO homesteading and don't have your outbuildings up yet, you needn't hold off on getting a cow or a couple of goats. You can provide a cheap and comfortable shelter for the animals in a couple of days by building a framework of poles and stacking a thick layer of loose straw over the support. Overlap the straw bunches on the roof—using the thatching principle—so your improvised stable will shed rain. That's the way countless farmers have done it over the ages.

What you do is you go outside on a breezy day and you pour the grain back and forth between two pans a few times or you dump the wheat—a gallon at a time—into a bucket of water, swirl it around and then spread it out to dry on a tablecloth.

If that sounds like work, it isn't. The breeze-cleaning process (called winnowing) is especially fun and gives you an unbelievably funky, old-time feeling. Besides that, you must bear in mind that you're swapping a few dollars and a little elbow grease for the major ingredient of *600* meals. It's worth it.

Store your cleaned grain in repurposed glass jars (the bigger the better) with screw-on tops, and grind it as you need it.

That grinding can be done with an old coffee mill or a kitchen-size, hand-cranked grain mill. New, the grain grinder won't set you back too much, and the darn thing is made of cast iron and can be used to process several hundred dollars worth of cracked grain and flour every year from now on. It's a good investment.

For that robust breakfast we've mentioned, set your mill to a coarse crack and wind off one and a half cups of cracked wheat. Mix it with five cups of warm water and one and a half teaspoons of salt in a large, heavy pan, and let the mixture set overnight to soften. Stir well in the morning, place the pan on the stove, and continually stir the cereal while you bring it to a boil. Stir the mixture often while you let it simmer for about thirty minutes. The cereal will be quite thick when it's done. Add a little milk and a topping of sugar or honey, and you'll have some mighty tasty eating that'll propel you right through a frosty winter morning. Or just forget the milk and top your cracked wheat with a bit of brown sugar and a spoonful of butter. That's how they do it in Canada's north woods.

HIMMEL UND ERDE

THERE'S A GERMAN DISH called *Himmel und Erde*—Heaven and Earth—that's perfect for folks who like solid, homey cooking. The proportions are up to the cook. All it is, is cubed potatoes, cubed turnips, and sliced apples cooked separately until just tender and then mashed very lightly together. Leave the mixture a bit lumpy, and then add diced, cooked bacon, chopped onion that's been softened in bacon fat, salt, and pepper. Sounds terrible, tastes delicious.

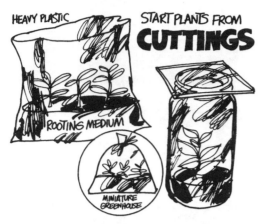

HEAVY PLASTIC

ROOTING MEDIUM

MINIATURE GREENHOUSE

START PLANTS FROM CUTTINGS

Although it does take a little longer, starting trees, vines, and ornamentals from cuttings is the poor man's route to owning fine and expensive yard and garden specimens.

Most plants can be multiplied from cuttings if—in the spring—you clip the starts from last year's wood and—in the fall—you take the sprigs from the current season's growth.

Some folks swear by dipping a cutting into a rooting hormone, others swear at the idea— you'll just have to experiment and find out which approach (dipping or not dipping) works best for you. Either way, put each new start in a glass jar of moist sand or vermiculite, and cover the container with a piece of plastic film or a lid.

Cuttings form roots much faster when kept in a humid (not wet) environment. If it gets too damp inside the jar and mold begins to form, uncover the container for brief periods to allow some drier air to enter.

After a new start has rooted well and is putting forth third and fourth leaves or branches, set it outside in a protected, half-shaded spot. Once the plant is well established, you can transplant it wherever you want.

Willow trees, grass, and most vining plants root so easily that you can simply stick their cuttings directly into the ground at the spot you want them. Then keep them well watered until the new growth has established itself.

A SHOP TIP

Folks who've tried it claim that a small, makeshift cardboard fan slipped over the shank of a wood bit is worth its weight in gold. The fan—which obviously turns as fast as the drill's chuck rotates—blows away sawdust and shavings as fast as the bit brings them to the surface, thereby allowing the tool's operator a clear view of the work in progress.

USE NEWSPAPERS TO BACK CARPET

A thick layer of newspaper under a rug keeps the room warmer in winter and makes the carpet last longer.

HOW TO PEEL AN ORANGE

To PEEL AN ORANGE easily, cut a flat slice of skin off at the stem end and use the tip of a sharp knife to score the rind in vertical quarters that can then be worked off with a finger or thumb. And don't be too particular about removing all the white stuff under the skin, either, unless it really turns you off. That inner membrane isn't bitter and is considerately packaged by nature inside the orange as an aid to the absorption of vitamin C.

HOW TO PICK A DUCK

It's NOT OVERLY DIFFICULT to pick the main feathers from ducks, but the down—which sticks tightly to the skin—is a different story entirely. Farm wives long ago learned to melt paraffin over a low heat and then either dip a partly picked duck into the liquid wax or sprinkle the melted paraffin over the down. As soon as the wax hardens, feathers and all may be stripped away from the duck quite easily.

COOKING OIL IS A NATURAL HAND MOISTURIZER

When you're COOKING WITH any good-smelling fat or oil, rub a little of it into your hands instead of washing it off. This method conditions the skin as well as any lotion can.

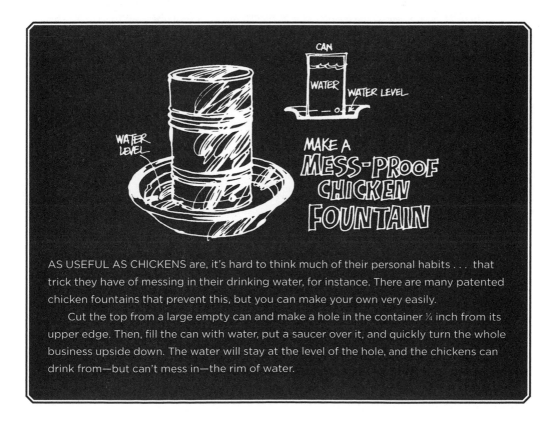

AS USEFUL AS CHICKENS are, it's hard to think much of their personal habits . . . that trick they have of messing in their drinking water, for instance. There are many patented chicken fountains that prevent this, but you can make your own very easily.

Cut the top from a large empty can and make a hole in the container ¼ inch from its upper edge. Then, fill the can with water, put a saucer over it, and quickly turn the whole business upside down. The water will stay at the level of the hole, and the chickens can drink from—but can't mess in—the rim of water.

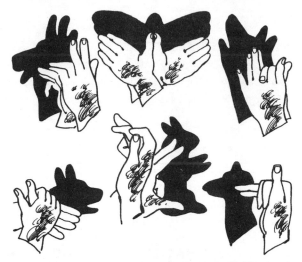

THE ART OF SHADOW PICTURES

Long before different means of entertainment came along, adults often amused children (and themselves) on long winter evenings by casting hand shadows on the wall. This simple pastime, which probably began in the caves of our remotest ancestors, is still entertaining.

All you'll need to start populating a white or lightly colored wall with imaginary figures is a good bright light that can be easily moved. Position the lamp to cast the resulting shadows with maximum effectiveness, while the performing "artist" works in a comfortable position, and begin. It's that simple.

Some suggested illusions are shown here, and many others are described in such books as the classic *Hand Shadows to Be Thrown Upon the Wall*, by Henry Bursill.

Once you've mastered the trick of creating several basic forms, the real fun of animating the characters begins. By wiggling your thumbs and fingers, you'll soon be able to make your figures move, talk, eat, and react in a surprisingly lifelike manner. Complete the illusion with sound effects and you'll be the absolute center of attention of any waist-high audience you're likely to encounter.

MAKE THAT POPCORN POP

Few people realize that popcorn pops because each kernel contains a minute amount of water. When the grains are heated, this moisture turns to steam and the resulting mini-explosions split the kernels open.

It follows, then, that popcorn—if not stored in a sealed container—can become too dry to do its thing. The next time you find yourself up against this situation, soak the grain in cold water for fifteen minutes, drain it, and then try to pop the corn again. You should be pleased with the results.

RESCUING FROZEN FOOD

FOLKS WHO GROW A good part of their own food often store much of those victuals in a home freezer. And that freezer, in turn, relies on electricity that is—unfortunately—subject to interruptions.

If the power does go at your place, the first step in saving your stored food is to try to find out how long the juice will be off. According to the US Department of Agriculture (USDA), a fully loaded freezer will hold its contents frozen for two days (if you keep the door shut).

However, if the unit is just half full, you may have only one day before the edibles within the chest begin to melt.

If you think your food won't stay frozen until the electric company gets the lines back in order, find yourself a supplier of dry ice and buy about twenty-five pounds. This amount should be enough to salvage a 10-cubic-foot cabinet's full load for three or four days (two or three days if the freezer is only half filled). Spread a piece of cardboard or some thin boards over the food packages, place the emergency cooling agent on top, and *keep the freezer closed* until the power comes back on (unless you have to add more dry ice).

Even if the contents of the freezer do become partly or wholly thawed, however—as may happen when, say, you don't realize that the appliance isn't working properly—you haven't necessarily lost your food store.

The USDA says, "To determine the safety of foods when the power goes on, check their condition and temperature. If food is partly frozen, still has ice crystals, or is as cold as if it were

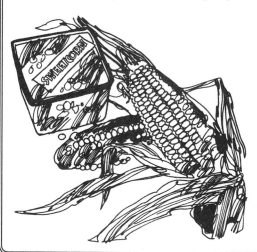

in a refrigerator (40°F), it is safe to refreeze or use. It's not necessary to cook raw foods before refreezing. **Discard foods that have been warmer than 40°F for more than two hours. Discard any foods that have been contaminated by raw meat juices.** Dispose of soft or melted ice cream for quality's sake."

Even when refrozen food is perfectly harmless to eat, however, thawing probably hasn't done its flavor any good. For better taste, it's wisest to use any rescued provisions as soon as possible.

HOW TO REMOVE AND PREVENT MATCH SCRATCHES

If you keep the big, old-fashioned wooden kitchen matches in your home, it's a sure bet that—sooner or later—someone will develop the habit of striking them on the woodwork, leaving unsightly marks behind.

Those match scratches may be removed from the paint by rubbing the area with a wedge of lemon—just apply a little elbow grease to lift the mark. Then, by coating the spot with a light film of Vaseline, the area can be made worthless for any further striking of matches.

MAGNET "MARKS" METAL RULER

Whenever you're using a metal ruler and need to mark a measurement on it for transfer, you'll find that a small magnet "clamped" to the ruler will hold your place easier and neater than any other kind of marker.

RECYCLE THAT GINGERBREAD

Stale gingerbread will still make a good dessert if you steam it and serve it with lemon sauce.

THE TRICK OF REMOVING A BROKEN WINDOWPANE

Replacing a broken windowpane isn't difficult at all, especially, once you've removed the tough, caked putty that holds the old piece of glass in place. That job is a downright cussful undertaking, too, unless you know the trick of brushing a little lacquer thinner or muriatic acid on the congealed putty and letting it set a few minutes to soften. From there on, the task is a breeze.

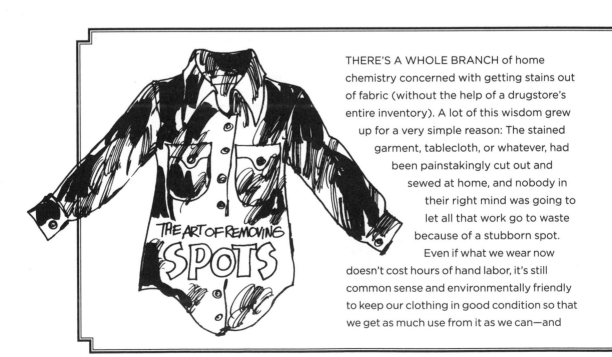

THE ART OF REMOVING SPOTS

THERE'S A WHOLE BRANCH of home chemistry concerned with getting stains out of fabric (without the help of a drugstore's entire inventory). A lot of this wisdom grew up for a very simple reason: The stained garment, tablecloth, or whatever, had been painstakingly cut out and sewed at home, and nobody in their right mind was going to let all that work go to waste because of a stubborn spot.

Even if what we wear now doesn't cost hours of hand labor, it's still common sense and environmentally friendly to keep our clothing in good condition so that we get as much use from it as we can—and

HOW TO OPEN A STUCK DRAWER

DIDJA EVER HAVE THE knobs of a stuck drawer come off in your hands, leaving you no way to open the contrary son of a gun? Try socking a plumber's helper (you know, that suction cup on the end of a stick that you usually keep hidden under the bathroom sink) on the front of the drawer and then pulling straight out. The soft cup on the tool won't harm the surface of the wood (if it leaves any marks at all, they can be wiped off with a damp cloth) and you'll find it "sticks" tight enough—especially if you wet its rim before attaching it—to allow you to give a pretty good tug.

WILD VIOLET FLOWERS CAN CURE THE GRUMPS

IF SOMEONE AT YOUR house has days when he or she is hard to get along with, you could try the traditional Appalachian remedy for grumpy people—a tea of wild violet flowers. Might give 'em a hint, anyhow.

MAGNETS MAKE SOLDERING EASIER

SMALL METAL PARTS ARE harder than the dickens to solder because—as you heat them up to make the joint "take"—they become too blamed hot to hold in position by hand. Burned fingers and sloppy soldering are the usual result . . . unless you're clever enough to keep a few small magnets on hand to temporarily but securely anchor the small items in question exactly where you want them during the job.

---

that means taking out stains whenever possible. The trouble is that a lot of tips that worked fine in centuries past won't work now.

And why don't the old spot-removal hints necessarily work these days? Because back when Aunt Nell found out that she could remove ink stains from colored cottons with a paste of dried mustard and water, the ink she banished was—chemically speaking—nothing like the stuff your pen just leaked into your shirt pocket. Ink just isn't made the same way when Aunt Nell was doing laundry. And, to complicate matters even more, your shirt may not be cotton at all but some fiber that wasn't in use when Aunt Nell was around . . . so don't be surprised if the mustard does no good.

Luckily, some substances don't change—human sweat, for example—and you can still remove a perspiration mark by dampening the spot, sprinkling it thickly with borax, and rolling the cloth up lightly for fifteen minutes. Rinse the area with cold water and, unless a Martian's been wearing that shirt, the stain should be gone.

Iron rust hasn't altered over the years, either, so the old lemon-and-salt trick should still work for you—or, if you want to try something off the beaten track, soak the spot in boiling rhubarb juice. After all, nobody's found a way to "improve" rhubarb . . . so far.

HOW TO FEED HOMESTEAD LIVESTOCK . . . CHEAPLY

IF YOU HAVE TO *buy* very much feed, raising your own meat and eggs barely pays. You'll be wise, then, to follow strict economies when providing for your livestock and poultry. A few hints:

1. There's no need to let a large amount of apples go to waste simply because they're wormy or you have all you want for your family. Horses love the fruit and apples are good for cows, hogs, and sheep too.

2. Table scraps (after the choice tidbits have been given to the farmstead dog and cat) should be fed to the chickens or hogs.

3. Pull all root vegetables that your family can't eat and give them to your rabbits, cows, and other livestock. The cows will also relish any excess pumpkins your garden or corn patch produces,

HOG FEEDERS

if you break the gourd into pieces that the cattle can manage.

Cole vegetables—cabbage, kohlrabi, Brussels sprouts, kale, and more—are good fare for chickens, rabbits, goats, and cows. Yesterday's poultrymen sometimes even grew cabbages specifically as winter green feed for hens. The plant will last almost until Christmas in the field and—pulled and stored upside down—cabbage will keep through January and February.

4. Hay is expensive to buy, and you need equipment and a large barn if you expect to put enough of the crop by to last your livestock through the winter. Except for the far northern sections of the country, you may be better advised to grow Kentucky fescue. This forage crop will provide pasture well into cold weather and—if properly managed—will furnish field roughage for cattle all winter long. The fescue won't grow in hot summer weather, though, and you'll need a brome pasture for that period.

Don't let the prepared-feed boys tell you that it's impossible to raise healthy cattle on a mostly grass diet, either. There definitely are cattlemen who currently make a living raising beef on brome and fescue. One in Kansas said the only other feed he provides his herd is protein supplement and molasses. The cows stay on pasture all year 'round . . . even when it snows.

This cattleman owns no expensive buildings or equipment, and says his kind of farming can be done by every back-to-the-lander south of Nebraska.

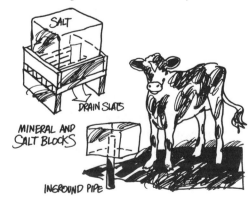

SALT

DRAIN SLATS

MINERAL AND SALT BLOCKS

INGROUND PIPE

START A CO-OP

The co-op idea is no stranger to this country. Inhabitants of many early North American settlements combined orders for tea, herbs, spices, and manufactured goods and then contracted for delivery of whole boatloads of the desired items at attractive discounts.

The simplified, main idea behind a co-op is that no one person is the owner—everyone has a stake in the business—and everyone shares in the profit.

There are more than 29,000 co-ops in the United States, and the number just keeps growing. Modern co-ops are not only about food, but there are also co-ops for things such as housing, banking, electricity, insurance, telephone service, day care, and more. Did you know nationally known outdoor retailer REI is a co-op? And would you believe Land o' Lakes is one too?

Co-ops generate billions of dollars annually and employ millions of people. For the more traditional buying co-ops we're talking about here, the savings to members can be 10 percent or more—that can be a healthy chunk of change left jingling in the pockets of co-op consumers.

There's no deep, dark secret to setting up and operating a cash-saving co-op. The basic idea—at least in the beginning—is simply to pool buying power and then purchase basic necessities direct from wholesalers, manufacturers, farmers, or any other producer your group desires.

Start the ball rolling by talking up the co-op idea with friends and other associates. You'll need about fifteen to thirty people or families—preferably folks who know each other, live close together, and get along well.

When you have your group in hand, call an informal meeting and explain that everyone there can realize an immediate 10 to 20 percent (sometimes more) savings if a few ground rules are followed. This is a possible model for establishing a food co-op:

1. Each person (or family) must put up a small initial deposit. This "seed" money will be used as the co-op's operating capital; the deposits are to be credited to the individual's families' accounts and—should a household withdraw from the buying group—its deposit will be refunded.

2. A couple of people should be assigned to contact wholesale grocers and establish the rock-bottom, cash-and-carry prices you'll have to pay for quantity purchases of fresh fruits, vegetables, and other staples.

continued on next page

3. Your group must agree on, and obtain permission to use, a centrally located parking lot, driveway, garage, spare room, or church basement from which the bulk purchases may be distributed. It is extremely important that the buying club obtain the use of this distribution point free of charge, at least in the beginning. Later, when the operation is a going concern, you can think about renting a "home" for your co-op.

4. Everyone present should understand that each member will be responsible for picking up all purchases from the central supply point. Home deliveries are another expense that your co-op doesn't need.

5. All members will be required to pay cash for their orders at the time they pick up the supplies. Credit plans and deferred payments have no place in your cost-cutting operation.

6. Last, and probably most important, your co-op's members should agree that the buying club will never pay a penny for labor. Instead, each member will keep its food costs at an absolute minimum by voluntarily helping—on a rotating basis—to buy and distribute the co-op's purchases. Make doubly sure this point is well understood because more good co-ops have been scuttled by a lazy "let someone else do it" attitude than by any other cause. Of course, if only a few members always seem to wind up doing all the work for an otherwise healthy buying club, it's only fair that the organization budget a few dollars weekly for these workers. This will mean slightly higher prices for everyone . . . but the compromise should still cut each member's grocery bill noticeably while keeping the operation alive.

Once your group understands and agrees to abide by the rules of your new co-op, the members will have to decide on the organization's basic "shopping list"—the staples that almost everyone uses and that you'll be able to purchase in greatest quantities (thereby realizing the largest discounts). Obviously you'll want to concentrate—whenever possible—on the soaps, paper products, cosmetics, toiletries, and other items that receive the heaviest markups in most conventional stores. Don't be afraid to start small—twenty-five or thirty items are a nice beginning.

Copy your first list of discounted items on Monday; pass the sheets out to members on Tuesday; and hold a hard-and-fast rule that every member must fill in the quantities of each item he or she wants

FIREPLACES ARE FOR COOKING

THE BEST BAKED POTATO I ever ate was wrapped in a ball of clay and buried for about an hour in the hot coals of a fireplace. The best bean soup I ever had was cooked all day in a pot hung from a crane over a fire in that very hearth. Some mighty fine biscuits have also come out of an oven built into the side of the same, identical fireplace.

Moral: Put a fireplace (complete with crane and oven) into your house and you'll be able to cook and keep warm right through the average emergency or power failure. And if you can't afford a fireplace? Glom onto an old wood-burning kitchen stove and enough stovepipe to set it up in the garage, basement, or some other out-of-the-way place.

and deliver the order forms back to headquarters no later than, say, 5:00 p.m. on Wednesday. This will allow your ordering committee to compile a master order that will be given to your wholesaler or wholesalers early each Thursday morning. On Friday, two or three co-op members (a different two or three each week!) will pick up the master order and take it to your club's distribution center where the individual households can collect and pay for their particular array of supplies.

Although you'll always strive to keep your club's bookkeeping at an absolute minimum, it's a good idea to appoint a semi-permanent finance committee to mark up all items slightly above the wholesale prices the co-op is forced to pay. There will always be some spoilage, errors, and breakage for you to cover with that margin and—if your members really get excited about their savings—they'll soon want to build a kitty of excess funds with which to expand your club's services.

If you reach that point, you'll probably want to invest in a used freezer so you can handle frozen meat and other perishable foods. Then your club may decide to expand its dollar-stretching group buying habits to include household appliances, furniture, and other big-ticket items. The sky is truly the limit, as millions of Americans have already proven.

One word of caution, though: GO SLOW. Co-op savings are worth going after, but your group must be solidly organized right from the start. Slapdash buying clubs seldom deliver meaningful dividends or last more than two or three months. A little time invested in the study of proper co-op management before you begin, however, can literally save you thousands of dollars in the future.

KNEE PADS

WHAT'S THAT, BUNKY? YOU say you varnished the back room floor yesterday morning, troweled cement on your knees in the afternoon, and spent half the night—again on your prayer bones—teaching the kids how to play "knuckle down marbles"? And now your patellar joints are all sore and painful?

Well, lift your thoughts from those creeking kneecaps to the next time you have to spend a lot of time kneeling, and resolve to pin a big sponge (with a couple of large safety pins) on the front of each pant leg. It's the only way to fly.

HAVE GARDEN VEGETABLES ALL WINTER LONG

MAKING SURE YOU EAT your own vegetables all winter long is not as formidable a task as you might think. The average family of four needs only about forty quarts of string beans, forty pints of corn, ten pints of peas, fifteen of lima beans, and twenty pints of broccoli stashed away in the freezer. That should be enough "main" vegetables to last from January until the rhubarb, asparagus, and dandelions are ready to eat in the spring. And, since the harvest times for the seven summer vegetables are staggered, freezing the amounts listed above is never an overwhelming task.

Tomatoes are a different proposition and should be canned. To my way of thinking, in fact, tomatoes are about the *only* garden vegetable that is practical to can. Figure on thirty quarts and another thirty quarts of juice.

Sweet potatoes can stay in the ground until frost, and Irish potatoes can remain there until just before a really hard freeze. Once dug, the sweet potatoes will keep best in a dry place held at a temperature of 55 to 60°F. The Irish variety can be stored fairly well until early spring if stashed in a dark bin that has good air circulation and is maintained at 40°F.

Winter squash, picked before frost and kept in a dry place where the temperature does not go below freezing, will last until Christmas—especially if you remember to leave about an inch of stem on each fruit when you pick it.

HOW TO ESTIMATE A HOUSE PAINTING JOB

TO ESTIMATE THE NUMBER of gallons of paint needed to cover the outside of a house, first multiply the distance around the building by the average height (if the building has gables, add 2 feet to the average height before multiplying). Then check the label on a can of the paint you intend to use and find out how many square feet each gallon of the coating will cover. Finally, divide the calculated square footage by the second number and you should be close to an answer.

Close, but not right on, until you allow for the porosity of the surface being covered. A corrugated-metal wall will need one-third more paint to cover it than a flat metal one and you'll find that paint goes 10 percent farther on wide-lap siding than it does on narrow. Any surface that is noticeably dry, rough, and/ or porous will drink up at least 20 percent more coating than a similar surface that isn't . . . and you should always figure on using an extra 50 percent of your paint when applying the first coat to concrete blocks.

Unless the season is very wet, carrots can stay right in the ground in the garden. Cover them with enough leaves to prevent the earth from freezing over them and harvest the carrots as desired throughout the winter. You can store them in dry sand kept in boxes in the root cellar too.

Cabbage will keep for a month after the first freeze when the heads are buried upside down in sand.

If you enjoy fresh salads well into November, endive deserves a place in your garden. Cover it with clear plastic panels (bent into a "half-moon" arch over the row) and the vegetable will hang on until Christmas.

Kale remains harvestable until the middle of December, unless temperatures drop below 15°F for an appreciable length of time.

It takes very cold freezes to do in broccoli, kohlrabi, and Brussels sprouts, and all three usually remain edible until December.

Parsnips should be left in the garden and harvested in February and March, when they taste their best (which is still not very good in my book although, by March, almost *any* fresh vegetable tastes good).

Turnips and rutabagas—especially when planted about July 10—remain good to eat until early winter. When you get tired of the blamed things, feed 'em to your rabbits and/or cows.

Parsley, the herb, can be used directly from the garden into January.

And finally—if you're lucky enough to have wild watercress growing in clean, ever-flowing springs (we do)—you'll find the delicious salad maker, which can be enjoyed all winter, is at its absolute best in February . . . when your hunger for something green is at its peak.

PIPE INCREASES LEVERAGE OF CLAW HAMMER

HAVE YOU EVER BROKEN the handle out of a good-driving claw hammer in your efforts to pull a super-imbedded nail? Sure you have—haven't we all? If you slip a 12 to 18 inch length of pipe over the tool's head the next time you want to do some heavy prying, however, you'll save a whole lot of strain on the hammer handle and—at the same time—dramatically increase your pulling power. Proving, once again, that science and technology can triumph over ignorance and superstition . . . or something.

HOME WINEMAKING

MAYBE YOU DIDN'T KNOW IT, but making wine at home is completely legal, and Uncle Sam says you can produce up to 200 gallons of your own brew—tax free—every year for your family's consumption. That's about 1,000 bottles and, unless you have a very large family or a VERY big thirst, it should be sufficient.

There are thousands and thousands of wine recipes, and you'll find you can make your own from grapes, pears, peaches, plums, blackberries, cherries, strawberries . . . almost any fruit that grows. You can even make wine out of honey. It's called *mead* and is supposed to have been the drink of the Roman and Greek gods.

One of MOTHER EARTH NEWS's friends gave us simple directions for making mead. He said to get a gallon jug—preferably glass, but food-safe plastic will do. Clean it out good, wash the container with soap (NOT detergent), rinse it with baking soda in water, and—finally—rinse again with clear water.

Then put a pint and a half to two pints of honey in the jug (the more honey, the stronger the wine), fill the container with warm water, and shake. Add a packet of yeast—champagne yeast works well, but you can also ferment with the same stuff you use for bread—and leave the jug uncapped and sitting overnight. Expect the brew to foam up and get pretty sticky.

After the workings quiet down a bit, you're ready to put a top on 'em . . . but NOT a solid top. What you want is something that will allow gas to escape from the jug (so it won't explode) without letting air (which can turn the wine to vinegar) get in.

One way to do the job is to run plastic or rubber tubing from the otherwise sealed mouth of the jug, thread the free end of the hose through a hole in a cork, and let the tubing hang in a glass or bowl of water. Or you can make a loop in the hose, pour in a little water, and trap it in the loop to act as a seal.

A POPCORN BALL SURPRISE

FOR A GOOD OLD-FASHIONED Christmas surprise, wrap some tiny gifts in wax paper and conceal them inside popcorn balls. Hang the balls from the branches of your Yuletide tree.

Now put the container of brew away for about two weeks until it has finished doing its thing. The wine is ready to bottle when bubbles stop coming to its top. Old wine bottles sealed with corks are best, and the mead will be ready to drink in about a month.

You can use this same rather crude beginner's recipe with almost any fruit if you extract the juice and add some sugar. Most natural fruit juice, you'll soon discover, will start to ferment without adding any yeast.

Fruit wines and mead, of course, are OK . . . but for real down-home, traditional, frontier wine, there's only one place to start and that's with dandelions. The flavoring is free, the brew is easy to make, and it's supposed to be good for you. Here's the formula for making one gallon of the golden drink:

Early in the morning when dew is still on the flowers, pick one gallon of PERFECT, OPEN dandelion blossoms. Put the flowers in a two-gallon-size or larger open crock and cover them with boiling water. Spread cheesecloth over the container and let it sit at room temperature for three days. Then squeeze all the juice out of the flowers, throw them away, and save the liquid.

Put this liquid into a big enameled pot and add three pounds of brown sugar, three or four lemons—chopped up juice, skin, seeds and all—and three or four oranges chopped up the same way.

Put a lid on the pot and boil the mixture for thirty minutes. Then, let it cool to lukewarm and pour the solution into the crock. Add one and a half to two packages of yeast. Then cover the container with cheesecloth and let the wine ferment for two to three weeks, until the bubbling stops.

Filter your dandelion wine through a clean piece of cheesecloth and carefully pour it into some repurposed wine bottles. Use corks to seal those bottles and don't cap them too tightly. A small amount of gas may form in each one and you want to let it escape. The brew will be ready to drink immediately, but the pioneers traditionally held their dandelion wine for winter consumption. They called it "bottled summer sunshine" and claimed it tasted better with snow on the ground.

CORNSTARCH MAKES SALT RUN MORE FREELY

SALT WILL RUN MORE freely in damp weather if a teaspoon of cornstarch is mixed thoroughly into each cup of the seasoning.

FOOD FOR THE TAKING

A LOT OF FOOD does go to waste in this country all the time . . . unless you know how to save it. For instance, we collect a big box of lettuce (the outer leaves peeled off the heads so that those same heads will appear more attractive to shoppers) every week from just one grocer. We don't eat these discards—although we could, there's nothing wrong with them—but our rabbits and chickens sure do.

I once had a very good deal with a big bakery in a large midwestern city. Every fortnight, that establishment let me have a whole truckload (piled right to the top of the cattle rack) of bread and rolls that hadn't been sold. Of course, before they'd let me haul it off, I had to promise very solemnly that I would feed the stuff only to my hogs and poultry and not sell or give it away to hungry people.

Well, I kept the promise—mostly—but I did eat an awful lot of sweet rolls that year and so did everyone who stopped by the farm. So go talk to a baker (remember, even the big commercial outfits are starting to deal in real whole-grained products again) and make yourself a deal. Your hogs will love you for it . . . and so will your friends and neighbors.

And by the way: If you take a loaf of stale bread and plunge it into cold water for just a split-second and then lay the bread on a grill in a moderately warm oven for ten to fifteen minutes, you'll find it freshens right up. Biscuits and cakes respond to the same treatment.

TOOTHPASTE TUBE TIPS

An OLD-FASHIONED SLIP-ON CLOTHESPIN or a giant cotter pin makes an ideal "key" for rolling up a tube of glue, toothpaste, and other such contained items. Nothing fancy about the idea at all . . . but it sure does help you neatly and precisely squeeze every last bit of material out of the container.

MAKE YOUR LADDER MORE EFFECTIVE

IF YOU'LL CUT A board as large as the top of your stepladder and hinge the two together with a bolt installed through one corner, you'll have yourself a handy swing-out shelf that will almost double the area of the ladder's top. Then, by boring a few holes of various sizes in the original shelf so that it'll hold small tools instead of letting them constantly roll off onto the floor, you'll have made that ladder a lot more efficient and pleasureful to use.

THE WINDCHILL FACTOR

EVEN IF A THERMOMETER tells you the temperature right down to a fraction of a degree, the information still doesn't mean much until you learn to interpret it properly. And that takes some experience.

For instance: The instrument may register 60°F on a winter day, but if that thermometer is in the sun and out of the wind, it's not telling you the true state of affairs. On the unprotected shady side of the house on the same day, it may be cold enough to freeze a scared dog fast to the sidewalk.

Even when you're sure a thermometer is accurate, you must make allowances for the velocity of the wind. If the temperature is 20°F and there's a twenty-mile-per-hour breeze blowing, for example, the "chill factor" of that air movement is equivalent to minus 10°F under calm conditions.

Likewise, if the indicated temperature is 5°F and the wind is twenty miles per hour, the true comfort (or *dis*comfort) index on the seat of a tractor as you drive out to feed the cattle their hay, is a minus 30°F. Repeat, 30°F below zero. And if you've ever been there, you know it. That's why lots of ranchers grow beards in the winter. At 30°F below zero, an unprotected face can freeze in two minutes.

HOW TO UNSTICK A CAKE

BEGINNING BAKERS ARE USUALLY baffled when their first cake sticks to the pan. Old hands in the kitchen, however, solve the problem by simply dampening a cloth in hot water and wrapping it around the baking container. The steam that soon forms releases the cake with no further difficulty.

A COLD-WEATHER CLOTHESLINE TIP

WHENEVER YOU HANG A wash outside in cold weather, it's a good idea to heat your wooden clothes pins beforehand. The warmed pins will be more pleasant to handle and will not split nearly so easily.

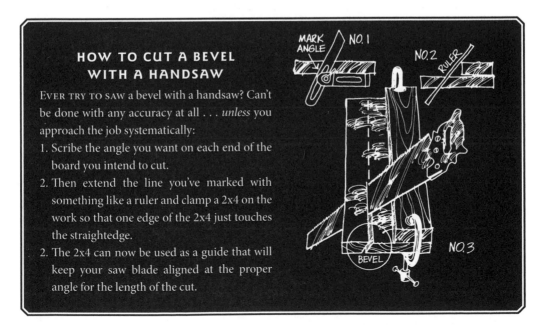

HOW TO CUT A BEVEL WITH A HANDSAW

EVER TRY TO SAW a bevel with a handsaw? Can't be done with any accuracy at all . . . *unless* you approach the job systematically:

1. Scribe the angle you want on each end of the board you intend to cut.
2. Then extend the line you've marked with something like a ruler and clamp a 2x4 on the work so that one edge of the 2x4 just touches the straightedge.
2. The 2x4 can now be used as a guide that will keep your saw blade aligned at the proper angle for the length of the cut.

IS RECYCLING WORTH IT?

WHEN DONALD SANDERSON, a former city councilman in Woodbury, NJ, led the effort to make recycling mandatory in the late 1970s, he was called names at city council meetings and criticized by the local press. Irate citizens dumped trash on his lawn. He persisted, however, and the law helped Woodbury save thousands of dollars in landfill costs, preventing the city from having to raise taxes or cut services.

Since then, the public's perception of the value of giving waste a second life has itself transformed, and recycling has diverted dramatic amounts of garbage from landfills.

So, is recycling worth it? In short, yes. But, to keep it effective, the way we think about waste must shift away from mindless consumption. Even as we're recycling more, we're creating more garbage—4.38 pounds per person per day in 2012, up 63 percent from 2.68 pounds in 1960.

To cut back on most materials, adopt a BYOC mentality: Bring Your Own Containers, such as cloth sacks or glass jars, to grocery stores for transporting produce, bulk foods, and meats and cheeses from the deli counter. Take containers to restaurants for carting home leftovers. Purchase reusable drink canisters. Try your hand at making your own condiments, body care concoctions, and cleaning products. Read on to find extra reduction tips for when you can't cut consumption.

When you do recycle, keep in mind that some substances are more worthwhile to recycle than others, depending on the energy required to extract the raw material, and the environmental footprint the substance leaves behind. Following is a list of materials, information about the worth of recycling each one, and tips for how to follow the three Rs in the right order: reduce, reuse, and, finally, recycle.

Is recycling glass worth it? Absolutely. Glass is made from all-natural materials and can be recycled endlessly into new glass. **Reduce:** Use bottle-deposit systems, such as those offered at some grocery stores for milk. Also, many breweries and some wineries allow customers to refill beverage bottles as opposed to buying new bottles when purchasing from a liquor store. **Reuse:** Glass jars can become all manner of useful household items, such as vases or stackable storage containers. And, of course, glass jars are some of the best vessels for delivering drinks from spout to mouth, and for storing your leftovers. **Recycle:** Don't toss non-container glass, such as light bulbs, window glass, ovenware, or crystal, into the bin, as it can cause problems for processors of used glass containers. Instead, if it's still intact, seek out local recycling alternatives, use it in a DIY project, or donate it to a secondhand store.

Is recycling metal worth it? Definitely. Most scrap aluminum cans are used to make new cans. Producing aluminum from raw materials is energy-intensive, and making products from recycled aluminum uses a whopping 90 percent less. Steel can also be recycled infinitely without any loss of quality. **Reduce:** Can your own foods in reusable glass canning jars, and cook dry beans purchased in bulk instead of buying their canned counterparts. Replace canned carbonated beverages with a home soda-making machine. You can also buy recycled aluminum foil. **Reuse:** You can wash and reuse aluminum foil and aluminum dishes and trays. **Recycle:** Recycling aluminum is efficient, so salvage as much as you can. In some states, you can redeem aluminum cans for money, usually

5 to 10 cents apiece. For other metals, locate a local scrap yard that will take your scrap metal. You may receive cash for your efforts, and some metals, such as copper, are especially valuable.

Is recycling paper worth it? Yes. Recycled paper supplies about one-third of the materials used to make other US paper products, and paper can be recycled five to seven times before its fibers become too short. **Reduce:** In lieu of paper towels, use washable rags to clean surfaces. Rather than buying new books, borrow them from the library or peruse a used-book store. **Reuse:** Projects for reclaimed paper range from practical to ornamental. Used paper can become a pot for seedlings or packing to place around delicate items you ship. You can even turn it into brand new paper. **Recycle:** You don't need to remove staples. Keep paper with food residue out of your bin (compost it instead). Follow local guidelines, because you may need to sort different kinds of paper into different bins.

Is recycling plastics worth it? Barely. As pervasive as plastic is, the setup to recycle it is dismal, and plastic can only be recycled a finite number of times. Because there are seven different types of plastic (indicated by the number, ranging from 1 to 7, stamped onto each product), sorting them properly is important. Mis-sorted plastics can contaminate the recycling stream and cause damage to recycling equipment. Perhaps most dismaying of all, plastic never "goes away." It breaks down into pieces too small to be seen by the naked eye. These particles find their way into our oceans, our food supply, and our bodies. Even most so-called "biodegradable" plastics are environmentally harmful and only break down when subjected to heat in commercial facilities, where very few biodegradable plastics actually end up. **Reduce:** Instead of bottled water, purchase a water filter and learn to love your tap water. Buy milk in returnable glass bottles. Replace plastic baggies with cloth alternatives. Bypass plastic shopping bags. Beth Terry, author of *Plastic-Free,* has many more tips for getting plastic out of your life on her blog, *My Plastic-Free Life.* **Reuse:** If you do use plastic baggies, wash and reuse them. **Recycle:** While reducing plastic is especially vital, recycling it is still better than throwing it away. Follow local guidelines to learn which types of plastic your recycling facility will accept, and pay attention to the numbers on the containers and their corresponding receptacles.

Follow Five Rs—Refuse, Reduce, Reuse, Recycle, Rot: The total annual household garbage for zero-waste zealot Bea Johnson fits into a quart jar, and she's reduced her family's recycling to a bare minimum too. "We don't buy food in packaging, we don't use plastic, and we buy secondhand," she says. "We found ourselves to be healthier, with more time and money," living lives "based on experience rather than stuff." Johnson, author of *Zero Waste Home: The Ultimate Guide to Simplifying Your Life by Reducing Your Waste*, and her family follow the five Rs (instead of the usual three) in order: Refuse what they don't need, reduce what they do need, reuse by avoiding disposables and buying secondhand, recycle what they can't refuse, and rot (compost) what's left. While she hasn't totally achieved her goal of producing absolutely no waste, Johnson says she's elated by the power she has over her decisions. Her family lives in a 1,400-square-foot house in Marin County, across the Golden Gate Bridge from San Francisco, a city with a goal to go zero-waste by 2020.

HOW TO POUR PAINT THINNER

IT'S HARD TO ESTIMATE the quarts of paint thinner and other liquids that are spilled in this country every year, merely because not one person in ten knows the simple trick of "starting" those flat, gallon cans with the off-center, screw-on lids.

The secret is to hold the container's opening UP as you pour off the first quarter or so of the can's contents. This allows air to enter as the fluid comes out, thereby eliminating all the messy "glugging" and dribbling.

SEPARATE EGGS WITH A SMALL FUNNEL

EVERY GOOD COOK KNOWS that a single speck of yolk left in the white of an egg will prevent the white from whipping. The trick is to separate the egg properly in the first place. The next time you face the problem, try breaking your hen fruit into a small funnel. The white should run right through while the yolk (all of it) stays behind.

THE 1899 REFUSE ACT

MOST OF US SEEM to approach pollution about the same way we handle sin. That is, we're all *against* it, in theory, but we all want in on the action when it's to our advantage. Well, I guess we little folks come by this two-faced attitude honestly, because corrupted enforcement of pollution-control seems to begin right at the top and filter down.

Take water pollution, for example. Way back in 1899 one single law was passed that—if properly enforced—could have ended, and could *still* end, all major water pollution in this country for all time.

This is the famous 1899 Refuse Act, and Section 13 of the law clearly prohibits ANYONE, including any individual, corporation, municipality, or group from discharging any refuse of any kind from a vessel or from the shore into this nation's rivers, lakes, streams, or tributaries. Furthermore, the act prohibits anyone from even placing any material on the banks of such watercourses so that high waters, storms, or floods can in any way wash that material into the water.

The 1899 Refuse Act—in other words—is as airtight as a law can be, and the penalty for violating the act is a fine that can range in the hundreds of dollars to the thousands of dollars or imprisonment for not less than thirty days nor more than one year or *both* the fine *and* imprisonment *for each day or instance of violation.*

Now that's pretty tough penalties for a pretty tough law, and it should have guaranteed that the waters of the United States would run clear forever—*except* our federal government never enforced it. And so the waterways in this country became open sewers.

Then—on March 18, 1970—prodded by the grass-roots interest in the environment, the US House of Representatives issued its report No. 91-917 that called attention to the fact that any citizen who furnished information to a US attorney and aided in the prosecution of Refuse Act violators is entitled to half of all fines collected.

THERE SEEMS TO BE about a thousand ways to pick up splinters, so it's good to know that there's more than one way to get them out. Here's a less painful alternative to digging at your skin with a needle or point of a knife (which is never much fun, even if there's a friend around to admire your Great Surgeon act).

For clean, easy extraction of slivers—according to at least one old-time source—fill a widemouthed bottle almost to the top with boiling water, place the injured spot over the mouth of the container, and press down tightly. The pushing should force the flesh back from that troublesome bit of wood, and—with luck—the heat will draw it out.

Well, that was more like it and, when John M. Burns then became an assistant to the US Attorney for the Southern District in New York State, he began to enforce the 1899 Refuse Act to the letter of the law for the first time in its seventy-two-year history. During his tenure, Mr. Burns won two noteworthy decisions against large polluters. (Unfortunately, he was shortly thereafter fired by the Department of Justice.)

Attorney Burns opened up the proverbial floodgates for ordinary people to champion the law and demand that our waterways get cleaned up. And, because of the fine-sharing aspect, people were able to collect more than a few dollars in the process. For example, a mother and her son collected $12,500 for reporting a concrete company that had been dumping waste into New York's East River. A sportsmans' club shared in a $200,000 fine levied against the Anaconda Wire and Cable Company. In a Wisconsin case, a congressman was awarded $1,750 for notifying authorities about evidence of pollution that was already on file. Other equally successful judgments have been rendered.

There's nothing to stop you from doing a good deed for the waterways of this country while adding a substantial sum to your bank account.

GROW CRYSTAL GARDENS

"Blacker than the inside of a cow and colder than a well digger's destination."

THAT'S THE WAY Uncle Jed Cauldwell used to describe the howling cold dead-of-winter nights on his Midwest homestead. Then, like as not, he'd throw another chunk of anthracite into the front parlor Acme Sunburst Base Burner (which was already jumping up and down from the roaring fire it contained) and settle back to watch his children outdo each other growing crystal gardens.

It's just as much fun for your youngsters (and adults!) to while away long, wintry evenings with a crystal garden today as it was for Jed's family then. Almost as inexpensive too.

Get yourself a brick, cover with a cloth—so the fragments won't fly up—and use a hammer to wallop the brick into walnut-size pieces. Then arrange the more artistic of the shards in the center of a 6-inch-wide dish or shallow bowl.

After that, mix—in the following order—four tablespoons of plain (*not* iodized) salt, four tablespoons liquid bluing, four tablespoons water, and one tablespoon of ammonia. *CAUTION: Ammonia can be harmful and children should use it only with adult supervision.*

Stir the mixture until the salt dissolves and pour it over the pieces of brick. Then, with an eyedropper, drip spots of food coloring onto the damp lumps.

That's it. In a few hours your garden of wispy, coral-like crystals will spring up in tints and shades of the coloring you used. Handle the dish gently and the fragile growths will delight you for weeks.

KEEP YOUR TEAKETTLE FROM LIMING UP

TEAKETTLES USED IN AREAS of hard water soon lime up and become worthless. A weak solution of cider vinegar, however, will cut such deposits loose when boiled for a few minutes in such a kettle. If a marble is then dropped into the pot and left there, it will roll around and help prevent the lime deposits from building up again.

BACK THAT PIG WHERE YOU WANT HIM

PIGS, JUST LIKE PEOPLE, often have ideas of their own—especially when you're trying to load one onto a truck or into a trailer. Beating and/or attempting to reason with a stubborn porker under those conditions usually does little good, but if you put a bushel basket over his head, you'll be able to back the pig wherever you want him to go.

BORAX REMOVES STAINS FROM DISHES

WHEN DISHES BECOME BROWN from baking, a soak in strong borax and water will remove the stain.

HOW TO BUY FARMLAND, EVEN IF YOU THINK YOU CAN'T

FOR THOSE OF US who were born to farm but, alas, not born on a farm, the ache to have your own land can be so intense you feel it in your belly. I thought it could never happen for me.

But now, after 20 years of farming and 15 years of interviewing farmers, I'm pretty sure that almost anyone can find and buy farmland by doing four things:

1. Be clear and realistic about the budget you'll need to support yourself and your farm, and about how you'll get the income you need.
2. Do your homework on the neighborhood and the land you're looking at to make sure it suits you and the type of farming you want to do.
3. Think outside the box: Be open to different options and timetables for buying land.
4. If you apply for a loan, find out what mortgage lenders require from borrowers and get those requirements in order.

If your plan includes off-farm income that requires commuting to a job, finding the job first and looking for the land second may be the best plan.

Next, if you plan to sell some of what you raise, you'll need to figure out where there are enough potential customers (usually in a city) and how you might sell to them—farmers markets, community supported agriculture (CSA) programs, etc.

You'll need to narrow your search area by considering which counties have off-farm employment options, markets for your farm products, and necessary farm support services. It's helpful to get an old-fashioned paper road map and draw two circles: one with the off-farm job in the center and a radius as long as the distance you are willing to commute, the other with your customer base in the middle and a radius as long as the distance you're willing to travel to market. Where the circles overlap is where you should look for land.

continued on next page

A good marketing plan is a cornerstone of any successful farm enterprise. Two solid resources on this topic are *Growing for Market*, a trade publication for local food producers, and the book *Market Farming Success* by Lynn Byczynski. The amazing National Sustainable Agriculture Information Service (NSAIS) offers a wealth of information to help you decide what to raise and how to sell it.

You'll need to seek other sources to find out whether necessary support services, such as veterinarians or organic feed suppliers, are available in your search area. Find these by talking with other farmers—start with the vendors at the local farmers market—and by picking up a copy of the local Yellow Pages at the phone company.

Now that you know where you're looking, it's time to start checking out property listings. Contact a local realtor and do some asking around at local cafes or farm-oriented businesses to find out who might be thinking of selling.

When you start walking properties, be sure to ask these questions—and don't rely solely on answers from realtors or the sellers:

- Is the water clean and sufficient for the needs of both the family and the farm?
- Is the soil farmable?
- Are the buildings, fences and utilities in working condition? If not, how much time and money will infrastructure improvements require?

Water. To learn about water quality as well as standards for the correct construction and siting of water delivery systems (whether a well, spring, pond, or cistern), contact your state's Department of Health or Department of Natural Resources (whichever handles private drinking water matters).

They can give you information on how to take a water sample, what you should get it tested for, and where to send it for testing. If the water source is a well, then also get the well driller's report from the county clerk, which will tell you the type, depth, and age of the well, and how many gallons per minute it delivered when first put in.

If you have any doubts about the quality, quantity, or reliability of the water supply, consult with a well driller or other professional. If you don't have enough clean water, you can't farm.

Lastly, if you're in a state where water and mineral rights are separate from property ownership—generally west of the Mississippi River—you need to get local, qualified legal advice to ensure that you'll be able to purchase enough water rights with the property.

Soil. Whether land can be farmed is determined primarily by soil type, as described in the USDA and Natural Resources Conservation Service's (NRCS) National Cooperative Soil Survey. You can get a map of the soil types on any property from the county extension agent's office.

Read the descriptions of the soil types, because these will tell you the depth of topsoil and subsoil, drainage, degree of slope, and which crops and farming activities that soil is suitable for.

If everything looks good so far, locate a local soil-testing lab (ask an extension agent), follow the lab's instructions for taking a soil sample, and have it tested for the basic nutrients. If the test reveals some major deficiencies, talk with a soil fertility specialist—such as an extension soil expert—about what bringing the soil to its full potential may cost.

Buildings, Utilities, Support Services. If you're uncomfortable with your ability to judge the soundness of buildings and the condition of plumbing, wiring, the furnace, fences, and the septic system, find someone who can inspect them for you. You may have a knowledgeable friend or relative, your realtor or banker may know someone locally, or you can find inspectors in the area.

Neighborhood. Before making an offer on a property, check out the neighborhood. Vacation there for a week if it's not local to you, subscribe to the local papers, talk to people, and drive around. Be sure to ask potential neighbors of any recent or pending land use changes.

Second, call your county offices for information on land use ordinances (including zoning) and current land uses. Land use ordinances at both the township and county levels may either limit or protect the types of farming and marketing you can do, and they will certainly impact the types and pace of future development. Landowner maps (sometimes called "plat maps")—also available at the county offices—show the property lines and identify the owner of every parcel of land in the county (except for small residential lots). They are well worth the purchase price if you're serious about buying land in that county.

There are four traditional options to investigate for borrowing money: your relatives, a landowner willing to self-finance all or part of the mortgage through a "contract for deed," the government, or a commercial lender (such as a bank). Often, as it did for us, it takes a couple different lenders to make a deal work. Several grant and loan programs assist new farmers with buying land. Most are administered through three agencies: the Farm Credit Administration, the Farm Service Agency, and USDA Rural Development.

What if you have no money, no experience, no off-farm employment, and so no appeal for a potential lender? Get a farm internship. World Wide Opportunities on Organic Farms offers paid and unpaid apprenticeships on farms around the world.

Enroll in classes on sustainable farming, including the business aspects. These may be available through nonprofit regional or local sustainable agriculture organizations, through state extension and universities, or through private colleges. The USDA maintains a list of colleges with sustainable agriculture programs.

Review the listings of foreclosed properties at county offices or local banks. If you go this route, do your homework on how these sales work to avoid the many potential pitfalls.

In many areas, land is too expensive for ownership to be possible for a beginning farmer. Instead, look into leasing or renting land. Contact landowners directly—a landowner map is extremely useful for this.

What about a group purchase? What one beginning farmer can't afford to buy, perhaps a group of them could.

Last but not least, don't give up. Somewhere, there's a farm waiting for you to find it.

GROW A GARDEN IN A BOTTLE

Most small, moisture-loving plants are best grown indoors in a sealed or semitransparent container. Such a miniature greenhouse—called a terrarium—easily maintains the dampish microclimate needed by the tiny garden inside, no matter how dry the air becomes in the heated house around it.

Almost any clear glass or plastic bottle, case, or jar can be transformed into a terrarium . . . but the small opening in something like a jug does make planting difficult. The soil that supports the vegetation in the glassed enclosure is usually placed right in the bottom of the tabletop greenhouse itself, although some people do prefer to create miniature landscapes with pre-potted plants in something like an old aquarium.

Bottle or jug gardens may be corked, fitted with an ordinary screw cap, or even left open. Any container with an extra-large opening, however—aquarium, glass case, widemouthed jar—should have a transparent (to admit light) glass or plastic cover. It can be used to seal the container—slid partially to one side for limited air circulation—or removed entirely.

To transform a large glass bottle into a terrarium, first wash the jug inside and out with hot, soapy water; rinse it several times and allow the container to dry thoroughly.

Next cover the bottle's bottom with a layer of pebbles and bits of charcoal (the latter will help prevent mold and will keep the soil in the garden "sweet"). Then fill the jar one-quarter full with a mixture of equal parts (1) sand, (2) loam, and (3) peat moss or leaf mold. Pour this potting soil through a funnel of rolled-up newspaper and place sphagnum moss around its edges if you don't want the dirt to show.

Add visual interest to your minigarden by burying a rock or two in the earth and/or shaping the dirt's surface into gentle hills and valleys. If the terrarium is to be viewed from one side only, you may even want to slope the soil upward all the way from front to back. Remember, however, that plants grow toward the light and your bottled

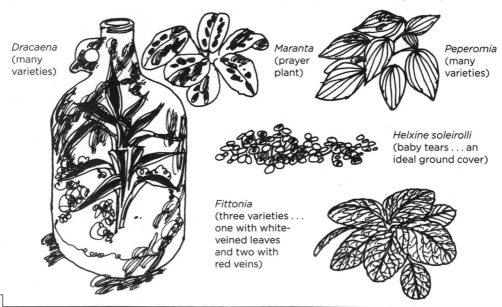

Dracaena (many varieties)

Maranta (prayer plant)

Peperomia (many varieties)

Helxine soleirolli (baby tears . . . an ideal ground cover)

Fittonia (three varieties . . . one with white-veined leaves and two with red veins)

landscape should be turned regularly if it receives its illumination from only one direction. It's a better idea to plant the glassed enclosure "in the round."

When the terrain of the vest-pocket greenhouse is to your liking, use two wooden planting sticks (about 2 feet 6 inches by ¾ inch by ¼ inch) to make holes in the earth, pass the plants through the neck of the container, and press the dirt around their roots. Dust off the greenery with a soft artist's brush, and funnel water (not too much!) gently down the jar's side so as not to disturb the landscape. The soil should be moist but not soggy.

Consider the light and temperature conditions of the area of your house where the minigreenhouse will be located when you choose plants for the bottle garden. A cool, shady spot is fine for partridge berries and other leafy green things from deep in the forest, but something less than ideal for plants—such as most flowering varieties—that need low night temperatures and lots of sunshine during the day.

For the conditions found in most homes—average room temperatures and good light but little direct sun—a terrarium should do well planted with any combination of the following:

Ivies, ferns, mosses, African violets (don't crowd them or sprinkle the leaves), and miniature begonias also generally do well in terrariums. Try cacti and succulents in a completely uncovered container if a very warm, sunny window is the only place you have for a bottle garden. Any good florist or plant supplier should be able to provide other suggestions as you select "inhabitants" for your enclosed landscape.

Experiment with the tabletop garden by placing it in different locations and by covering, uncovering and watering the terrarium until you find "just the right" balance. The little greenhouse probably can then be sealed altogether for days and even months at a time, giving you an enchanting view—through the glass—of a completely self-contained world of growing things.

TIRE STEM AND CIRCLE OF INNER TUBE

TIRE PUMP

A HEROIC DRAIN UNPLUGGER

A GOOD, OLD-FASHIONED plumber's helper will generally unplug minor drain stoppages. However, ever so often a really heroic jam-up proves too much for the plunger on a stick. What to do? Call in a professional for several ten spots? Maybe. But before you do, try moving that congestion out of the pipes with the homemade rig shown here.

Cut the valve stem (centered on a 6-inch-diameter circle of rubber) from an old inner tube. Attach a hand pump, wet the rubber, and press the assembly firmly over the troublesome drain while someone else operates the pump. A few solid strokes should clear all but the most tightly wedged stoppages.

CHEESE-POTATO SOUP

WORKING OUTSIDE ALL DAY in windy, near-zero weather can leave a person chilled through and through. A deep bath, hot enough to relax cold-clenched muscles, will help cure an individual of this condition. However, only a properly heroic prescription will fill that big, icy, gap where his or her stomach should be. The following midwestern farm recipe for Cheese-Potato Soup is one such formulation that does the latter job admirably.

For two moderately congealed people, peel and boil two slightly-larger-than-medium potatoes. Drain the tubers when they're done and save the liquid in which they were cooked. Then mash the potatoes well, add the water they were boiled in (and more liquid if necessary), and salt and pepper to taste.

Next, brown two to two and a half tablespoons of flour in two and a half tablespoons of butter (by stirring the flour and butter constantly, you can turn them a rich, golden color without burning them at all). Add the browned mixture to the potatoes and water and stir the whole savory solution as you boil it together for two or three minutes.

Finally, cut a good-size chunk of longhorn or mild cheddar cheese into enough small pieces to fill a big soup bowl one-third full. Cover the cheese with the thick, bubbling potato-butter-flour ambrosia, dice a quarter slice of onion on top of each serving and sprinkle a few drops of vinegar over all. Break out the spoons and crackers and eat it hot! This simple but robust one-dish meal is guaranteed to warm you from the inside out.

SPROUT GRAPEFRUIT SEEDS FOR WINTER GREENERY

FOR SOME COLD WEATHER greenery that will brighten the house and last all winter, try filling a flat pan with rich dirt and thickly planting the container in grapefruit seeds buried ½ inch deep. Keep the earth well watered. The seeds will be slow to sprout but are worth waiting for.

DRIED SOAP PROTECTS HANDS

IF YOU LATHER YOUR hands well with soap and allow them to dry that way before beginning any greasy or oily job, you'll find that washing up later will be an absolute breeze. The soap fills the pores of the skin and prevents the grime from entering.

LEMON JUICE PERKS UP FRUIT DRINKS

THE ADDITION OF A little lemon juice will improve the flavor of almost any fruit drink. It will also snap up the taste of banana, mince, apple, blackberry, pineapple, raspberry, and other pie fillings.

A "WAITING" GAME

IF IT LOOKS LIKE a long wait at the emergency room, or you just missed a bus that comes once an hour, there's a harmless amusement that can be enjoyed—in silence, if need be—by any two people with one free hand apiece: "Rock, Paper, Scissors."

To play, each person hides the aforesaid free hand behind his or her back and—on a signal—displays one of three signs: "rock" (clenched fist), "paper" (the hand held flat), or "scissors" (two fingers outstretched). For obvious reasons scissors outranks paper; paper beats rock because a rock can be wrapped up; and rock, which can't be cut, defeats scissors. The player who brings out the higher-ranking symbol wins that round (or gets a point if you keep score). Two signs alike mean a draw.

This old game—which is best played rather fast, rhythmically, and without thought—is oddly absorbing in a simple-minded way and can go on for a long time. Of course, passersby may get the idea that you and your friend are afflicted with dumbness and are having a violent argument in your own language —or they may end up learning the amusement from you and enjoying it themselves next time they get stranded somewhere.

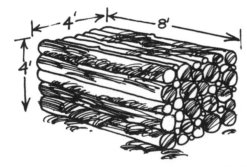

A CORD IS A CORD...OR IS IT?

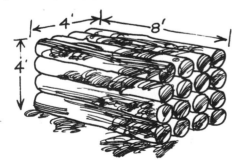

ALTHOUGH A CORD OF wood is supposed to be a fixed measure of 128 cubic feet (a stack 8 feet long by 4 feet wide by 4 feet high), this "precise" specification leaves much to be desired. Due to the open spaces between a few, large round logs—for instance—the buyer of a cord of wood made up of such timbers will receive somewhat less for his money than the purchaser of a cord composed of carefully selected and closely stacked random-size logs. It stands to reason, then, that you'll get more for your money if you always specify that some small kindling sticks be mixed with the larger-diameter timbers in any cord of wood you buy. You should also keep in mind the fact that a cord of softwood usually weighs out to slightly more than a ton while the same measure of hardwood tips the scales in the neighborhood of one and three-quarter tons. Hardwood, obviously, is the better bargain.

HOW TO REFRIGERATE CANTALOUPES

IF YOU'RE STORING CANTALOUPES in the refrigerator, it's a good idea to wrap or cover them so the melon flavor will stay inside the fruit where it's appreciated instead of penetrating every other food within range.

AN OLD COLD REMEDY

A TRADITIONAL REMEDY FOR colds or flu is a tea made from equal parts of cinnamon, sage, and bay leaves with a little lemon juice added before drinking.

HOW TO CUT IRON WITH A SAW

IRON BROUGHT TO A red heat and then placed in a vice may be cut with an old saw without difficulty.

PREVENTIVE FOLK MEDICINE

FORAGING CAN PUT SOME tasty victuals on the table, and what you find in nature just might cure what ails you too. The forager's method—an idea that came from the Native Americans of our eastern states—is a fine example of preventive folk medicine, a body of wisdom that needs more investigating.

We know, for example, a fellow—Al the Health Freak to his friends—who has his own treatment for scratches or small cuts (and he picks up quite a few because he's always burrowing into

blackberry thickets or crashing around in the woods on foraging trips). What Al does is, he licks the wound and then puts honey on it.

Of course, the idea of putting one's tongue to an open cut is enough to make most first-aid instructors faint dead away, but Al's explanation makes sense. His intention is to pick up whatever bacteria are in that wound and get them straight into his system so he can start forming antibodies that will guard against infection. And how about the germs in his mouth that get into the cut? No problem—he says that they're his own personal germs and he's resistant to them anyhow.

And why the honey? Because, says the Health Freak, it's antiseptic and contains enzymes that promote healing. (He uses *raw* honey, of course. The processed kind from the supermarket doesn't have any enzymes—they all got killed when the honey was heated before packing.) Other "nature doctors" of our acquaintance like to rub a wound with a cut clove of garlic when they can't get raw honey (it stings, but so do many other excellent disinfectants).

There are quite a number of health-saving tricks that work—like Al's wound-licking trick—by getting small amounts of a potential troublemaker into the system so the body can prepare its defenses before the full-scale attack begins. Some hay fever sufferers, for instance, desensitize themselves to local allergens before the sneezing season gets under way, with the help of "cappings" they buy from nearby beekeepers.

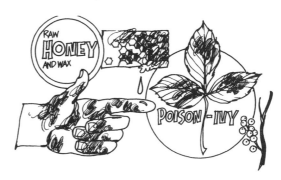

The theory is that cappings—the wax that's trimmed from honeycombs—contain pollen from the area's common plants. Therefore, when the allergy victim chews the wax like gum, his body absorbs traces of the irritating substances and gets to work on building immunity. After all, that's just what the allergist does with his long, costly series of desensitizing injections.

DELICIOUS FRIED MUSH

Don't let anyone tell you different. Cold winter weekends are the time for sleeping late and then getting up to a stick-to-the-ribs breakfast of old-timey fried mush. There's a trick to making this seemingly simple dish, though, so pay attention:

Mix together well one and one-half cups of yellow cornmeal, one and a half teaspoons of salt, and three tablespoons of white flour. Then stir one and one-half cups of cold water into the dry ingredients, mix until the thin batter is uniformly blended, and IMMEDIATELY stir the mixture into four and a half cups of boiling water.

You've just learned the trick. If you try to mix the cold water into the dry ingredients and then let the batter stand while you heat the boiling water, the cornmeal blend will solidify into a shapeless blob. If, on the other hand, you pour the dry cornmeal directly into the boiling water, the meal will lump. Heat the four and a half cups of water to boiling first, hold it on standby while you quickly stir the cold water into the dry ingredients, and then dump the cold batter into the boiling liquid—you should have no trouble.

At that point, bring the whole blended mixture to boiling and cook it until the mush thickens. Put a lid on the pan, lower the heat to simmer, and let the batch cook ten more minutes. Turn the firming glob into a buttered bread pan (about 9x5x2½ inches deep), loosely cover with a piece of wax paper (so that excess moisture can escape), and let it cool overnight on the back porch or in the refrigerator.

Slice the chunk as thin as possible in the morning, flour each slab on both sides (so it'll brown more quickly and fry crisper), and drop the pieces into a skillet of vegetable shortening or lard. Eat 'em smoking hot, either plain or smothered in butter and maple syrup. You should figure on about twelve slabs apiece all around the table!

AN EMERGENCY THIMBLE

If you're ever stuck with a tent, tarp, or piece of leatherwork to repair and you don't have a thimble on hand, tape a coin to your finger to help you push that heavy needle through the heavy fabric or leather.

COLD WATER PROTECTS FLOOR FROM GREASE SPILLS

When lard or other cooking grease is spilled on the floor, throw cold water on it immediately to keep it from spreading and from soaking into wood.

HOME WIND POWER: YES, IN MY BACKYARD!

SO MAYBE YOU'RE THINKING you want to generate your own electricity, and home wind power has crossed your mind. After all, who really enjoys paying a utility bill? Small wind energy is renewable, non-polluting, and, in the right circumstances, can save you money.

But is home wind power a good choice for you? The answer may surprise you, because living in a windy area is not necessarily the most important factor. In fact, many properties are not a good fit for installing a wind turbine even if they have a lot of wind (for reasons we'll get into). On the other hand, if you want to go off-grid and produce your own electricity, you almost certainly want to consider installing a home wind turbine, even if your location is not notably windy.

Here's the deal: For a home wind turbine to be worth your investment, you really need to live on an acre or more. That's the guideline from the US Department of Energy's Guide to Small Wind Electric Systems, a free publication for homeowners. Living in a rural area helps, because if you're in a residential neighborhood, you're likely to run into conflicts with zoning and local homeowners associations. Additionally, you're more likely to find a high average wind speed in wide open spaces far from windbreaks such as buildings and trees. Altogether, while installing a small wind turbine in a city or suburb is certainly possible, you're much more likely to have the right conditions for home wind power if you live well outside city limits.

That's the case for Cam and Michelle Mather, who live on 150 forested acres in rural Ontario. The Mathers live in an off-grid home powered by solar panels and their micro wind turbine, a 1-kilowatt (kw) Bergey Excel 1. On such a large property, they're nowhere near their closest neighbors, so there's no one who might be upset about the noticeable—but not unpleasant—wind turbine noise or the very visible 100-foot tower in the couple's yard.

What's surprising about the Mathers's situation is that their local wind speeds are not ideal, yet home wind power works beautifully for them. The biggest issue with the Mathers' property is that they have too many trees, and even though their small wind turbine is easily 40 feet above the tree line, the landscape slows down the wind. Wind still makes sense for them, though, because they're off the grid, so their only electricity is what they produce and then store in batteries. They started with solar panels, but adding a wind turbine to the mix made the whole system much more stable and efficient—a major benefit when you're solely responsible for generating your own electricity.

Renewable energy experts often recommend installing hybrid wind and solar energy systems for off-grid living. These systems work well because wind and solar energy tend to be most available at different times.

As a result of installing a small wind turbine, the Mathers are less dependent on a fossil fuel-powered generator to produce electricity when their batteries run low, which, as Cam points out, not only reduces their carbon footprint, but also helps insulate them from future energy insecurity. "We look at it from the standpoint of resilience," he says.

If your main goal is energy self-sufficiency, you may want to be off the grid. But if you're simply interested in producing your own residential wind power, a grid-connected system can

continued on next page

make a lot of sense. With this setup, anytime your wind turbine produces more power than your home needs, that power goes onto the local utility grid. When you need more power than you're generating, you draw power from the grid. Grid-connected systems are often cheaper, because without the responsibility of producing all of your own electricity, you can install a smaller, less expensive system. You can also opt to skip the battery pack and backup generator. Finally, if you consistently generate more electricity than you need, you may actually get cash back from the utility.

Putting in a wind turbine or any other renewable energy system is indeed an investment. The Mathers estimate the total cost of their 1-kw wind turbine was about $9,000, excluding batteries. They were able to save some money by installing the turbine themselves, and they do all of their own maintenance. And keep in mind that theirs is a small system. Even with a solid average wind speed of 9 mph, the estimated annual output is about 1,800 kwh. For a system large enough to provide all of your own energy—nearly 960 kwh per month for the average US home—the costs can be significantly higher.

Another couple, John Ivanko and Lisa Kivirist, estimate that the total installed cost of their 10-kw wind turbine was about $39,500, but their out-of-pocket costs were less than half of that, thanks to a state grant and other creative financing. For example, they reduced their labor costs by teaming up with wind energy educators to host a workshop on their property.

The Mathers chose off-grid living for environmental reasons, but the decision to go off-grid can sometimes make sense purely in financial terms. To begin with, if you live in a truly remote area and want to go off-grid, installing renewable energy systems will often be less expensive than paying the utility company to extend a power line to your property. In fact, some states require that the utility provide information on renewable energy alternatives whenever a customer requests a power line extension. The American Wind Energy Association gives a wide range of expected payback periods for a home wind turbine—between 6 and 30 years. Your savings will depend on a lot of individual factors.

One of the easiest factors to calculate is individual renewable energy incentives. In the United States, small wind turbines currently qualify for a federal tax credit of 30 percent, which is scheduled to continue through 2016. Other financial incentives may be available through your state or through individual utilities.

Another key factor in calculating how quickly your wind turbine will pay for itself is knowing how gusty your property actually is. The Department of Energy's wind guide recommends 10 miles per hour as a minimum average wind speed if you want to consider installing a grid-connected turbine. You can find out rough information about wind conditions where you live by asking a nearby airport for data on average wind speeds. In some wind-rich regions, you may also be able to find inde-

PUT A CRUTCH TIP ON YOUR BROOM HANDLE

FIT A RUBBER CRUTCH tip or cap from a chair leg over the end of your broom handle. Then, when you lean the broom against a wall or door, it will not slide, fall down, nor leave marks on anything.

pendent site assessors at a reasonable cost. The Midwest Renewable Energy Association, for example, maintains a list of site assessors. In other locations, you'll need to read up on suggestions for DIY wind site assessments, or go with the recommendation of local wind turbine dealers.

WHAT ELSE DO YOU really need to know if you're considering wind energy?

Tower Height. First, yes, you really do need that tall tower, because average wind speeds increase substantially with height. You'll see wind turbines mounted on shorter towers, and they may be producing some electricity—just likely not as much electricity as you'd want, and making the financial side of wind work out is difficult if you're not producing enough power.

Roof Mounting. Never install a turbine on the roof. The turbine has to be significantly above the roofline to be able to generate much electricity, which you wouldn't get unless you were mounting a tall tower on your roof—not the safest place to install a large machine.

Certification. Avoid being seduced by a new wind turbine design that sounds wonderful but doesn't have the test data to back it up. Look for established manufacturers with a proven track record and certified test results that show how much electricity you will be able to produce.

Safety. "Make sure that the turbine can be safely serviced and operated," wind turbine expert Paul Gipe says. "Based on available technology, that means making sure that the tower can be safely lowered to the ground." In other words, consider a tilt-down tower rather than one that requires you to work on the wind turbine 100 feet in the air.

Ivanko and Kivirist have a few additional words of wisdom: Get insurance. They didn't have to do anything special to get liability insurance—it was just one more item listed on their homeowners insurance policy, Ivanko explains. However, they also insured their wind turbine against damages and were grateful they had done so when the blades cracked during a severe storm last year. With climate change, extreme weather events are becoming more and more common, the couple warns, so good insurance is more necessary than ever. Buy from established manufacturers to be sure turbines are certified and warranty policies are reliable.

And some final words from Cam and Michelle Mather: don't be intimidated—you can do it! When the Mathers went off the grid 15 years ago, they had to learn everything themselves. But they made it work, and say they have found many benefits to this hands-on approach. "If I had to, I could bring the tower down in 20 minutes with a cordless drill," Cam says. "I'm comfortable with it because I've done it." Generating power from renewable energy and figuring out how to make their wind turbine work has been exciting for Cam. "I absolutely love it. In a big windstorm, I can stand there and look at it all day."

SOY SAUCE ADDS FLAVOR TO BROILED MEAT

FISH AND MEAT SEEM to broil especially well if you brush them with a mixture of oil and soy sauce before you pop them under the flame. This treatment apparently helps seal the surface of the food so the juices stay inside. The finished product is pleasantly brown and a little salty, and, oddly enough, doesn't taste like soy sauce at all.

CHARTS
& TABLES

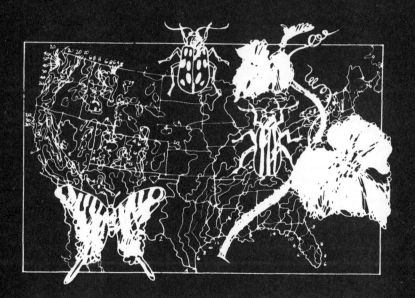

A HANDY COMPENDIUM of useful information, weights, measures, conversions, unusual facts, fancies, rules of thumb, tips, pointers, instructions, advice, suggestions, counsels, notices, hints, wisdom, lore, enlightenment, and diverse knowledge on various subjects too numerous to catalogue.

SOME INTERESTING FACTS ABOUT THE EARTH

SIZE, MASS, AND DENSITY

Equatorial diameter . . . 7,926 miles

Polar diameter . . . 7,900 miles

Volume . . . 260,000,000,000 cubic miles

Mass . . . 5,973,600,000,000 000,000,000 tons

Density . . . 5.52 times that of water

Acceleration of gravity . . . 32 feet per second per second

Velocity of escape . . . 6.96 miles per second

ORBIT

Perihelion (nearest) distance from sun . . . 91,400,000 miles

Aphelion (farthest) distance from sun . . . 94,500,000 miles

Mean (average) distance from sun . . . 92,960,000 miles

Mean orbital velocity . . . 18.52 miles per second

or 66,690 miles per hour

Orbital period (perihelion to perihelion) . . . 365 days, 6 hours, 13 minutes, 53 seconds

ROTATION

Rotational period (solar) . . . 24 hours

Rotational period (sidereal) . . . 23 hours, 56 minutes, 4.09 seconds

AREA

Total area . . . 196,951,000 square miles

Land area . . . 57,268,900 square miles

Water area . . . 139,668,500 square miles

TEMPERATURES

Highest recorded surface temperature . . . 134°F (Death Valley, California, 1913)

Lowest recorded surface temperature . . . -128.6°F (Vostok, Antarctica, 1983)

ELEVATIONS

Highest land (Mount Everest) . . . 29,035 feet above sea level

Lowest land (Dead Sea) . . . 1,349 feet below sea level

Average land elevation . . . 2,700 feet above sea level

Deepest ocean trench (Mariana) . . . 36,070 feet below sea level

Average ocean depth . . . 12,100 feet below sea level

STANDARD TIME DIFFERENCES

When it is noon, eastern standard time, the time in United States and Canadian cities is as follows:

Akron, OH . . . noon	Miami, FL . . . noon
Albuquerque, NM . . . 10:00 a.m.	Milwaukee, WS . . . 11:00 a.m.
Atlanta, GA . . . noon	Minneapolis, MN . . . 11:00 a.m.
Baltimore, MD . . . noon	Montreal, QC . . . noon
Birmingham, AL . . . 11:00 a.m.	Newark, NJ . . . noon
Bismarck, ND . . . 11:00 a.m.	New Orleans, LA . . . 11:00 a.m.
Boise, ID . . . 10:00 a.m.	New York, NY . . . noon
Boston, MA . . . noon	Norfolk, VA . . . noon
Buffalo, NY . . . noon	Oklahoma City, OK . . . 11:00 a.m.
Butte, MT . . . 10:00 a.m.	Omaha, NE . . . 11:00 a.m.
Calgary, AB . . . 10:00 a.m.	Ottawa, ON . . . noon
Charleston, SC . . . noon	Philadelphia, PA . . . noon
Charleston, WV . . . noon	Phoenix, AZ . . . 10:00 a.m.
Cheyenne, WY . . . 10:00 a.m.	Pierre, SD . . . 11:00 a.m.
Chicago, IL . . . 11:00 a.m.	Pittsburgh, PA . . . noon
Cincinnati, OH . . . noon	Portland, ME . . . noon
Cleveland, OH . . . noon	Portland, OR . . . 9:00 a.m.
Columbus, OH . . . noon	Providence, RI . . . noon
Dallas, TX . . . 11:00 a.m.	Quebec, QC . . . noon
Dawson, YT . . . 8:00 a.m.	Regina, SK . . . 10:00 a.m.
Denver, CO . . . 10:00 a.m.	Reno, NV . . . 9:00 a.m.
Des Moines, IA . . . 11:00 a.m.	Richmond, VA . . . noon
Detroit, MI . . . noon	Rochester, NY . . . noon
Duluth, MN . . . 11:00 a.m.	Saint John, NB . . . 1:00 p.m.
Edmonton, AB . . . 10:00 a.m.	St. John's, NL . . . 1:30 p.m.
Ft. Worth, TX . . . 11:00 a.m.	St. Louis, MO . . . 11:00 a.m.
Galveston, TX . . . 11:00 a.m.	St. Paul, MN . . . 11:00 a.m.
Gander, NL . . . 1:30 p.m.	Salt Lake City, UT . . . 10:00 a.m.
Goose Bay, NL . . . 1:30 p.m.	San Francisco, CA . . . 9:00 a.m.
Grand Rapids, MI . . . noon	Sante Fe, NM . . . 10:00 a.m.
Halifax, NS . . . 1:00 p.m.	Saskatoon, SK . . . 10:00 a.m.
Hartford, CT . . . noon	Savannah, GA . . . noon
Helena, MT . . . 10:00 a.m.	Seattle, WA . . . 9:00 a.m.
Honolulu, HI . . . 7:00 a.m.	Sioux Falls, SD . . . 10:00 a.m.
Houston, TX . . . 11:00 a.m.	Spokane, WA . . . 9:00 a.m.
Hull, QC . . . noon	Tacoma, WA . . . 9:00 a.m.
Indianapolis, IN . . . 11:00 a.m.	Tampa, FL . . . noon
Jacksonville, FL . . . noon	Toledo, OH . . . noon
Juneau, AK . . . 9:00 a.m.	Topeka, KS . . . 11:00 a.m.
Kansas City, MO . . . 11:00 a.m.	Toronto, ON . . . noon
Kingston, ON . . . noon	Tulsa, OK . . . 11:00 a.m.
Knoxville, TN . . . 11:00 a.m.	Vancouver, BC . . . 9:00 a.m.
Lincoln, NE . . . 11:00 a.m.	Victoria, BC . . . 9:00 a.m.
Little Rock, AR . . . 11:00 a.m.	Washington, DC . . . noon
London, ON . . . noon	Wichita, KS . . . 11:00 a.m.
Los Angeles, CA . . . 9:00 a.m.	Wilmington, DE . . . noon
Louisville, KY . . . 11:00 a.m.	Windsor, ON . . . noon
Memphis, TN . . . 11:00 a.m.	Winnipeg, MB . . . 11:00 a.m.

Note: Canadian abbreviations are: AB—Alberta; BC—British Columbia; MB—Manitoba;

NB—New Brunswick; NL—Newfoundland; NS—Nova Scotia; ON—Ontario; QC—Quebec; SK—Saskatchewan

THE RELATIONSHIP BETWEEN THE maximum amount of moisture that the air can hold and the amount of moisture that it actually does contain is called relative humidity. And we all know—or should know—that the moisture in the atmosphere during the summer makes us swelter quite as much as the heat in the air, just as lack of humidity during the winter can make a room feel much colder than it actually is.

To measure relative humidity, obtain two identical thermometers and completely wrap the bulb on one with a small square of wet lightweight cotton cloth. Tie the soaked fabric on with thread and place both thermometers in the breeze from a fan. Check the instruments after one to two minutes; note the reading of each (the wet-bulb thermometer will register somewhat lower than the dry), and compute the relative humidity on the chart below.

DRY-BULB TEMP. °F	DEPRESSION OF THE WET BULB, °F									
	2	4	6	8	10	12	14	16	20	24
	RELATIVE HUMIDITY (%)									
60	89	78	68	58	48	39	30	21	5	
62	89	79	69	59	50	41	32	24	8	
64	90	79	70	60	51	43	34	26	11	
66	90	80	71	61	53	44	36	29	14	
68	90	80	71	62	54	46	38	31	16	3
70	90	81	72	64	55	48	40	33	19	6
72	91	82	73	65	57	49	42	43	21	9
74	91	82	74	65	58	50	43	36	23	11
76	91	82	74	66	59	51	44	38	25	13
78	91	83	75	67	60	53	46	39	27	16
80	91	83	75	68	61	54	47	41	29	18
82	92	84	76	69	61	55	48	42	30	20
84	92	84	76	69	62	56	49	43	32	21
86	92	84	77	70	63	57	50	44	33	23
88	92	85	77	70	64	57	51	46	35	25
90	92	85	78	71	65	58	52	47	36	26
92	92	85	78	72	65	59	53	48	37	28
94	93	85	79	72	66	60	54	49	38	29
96	93	86	79	73	66	61	55	50	39	30
98	93	86	79	73	67	61	56	50	40	32
100	93	86	80	73	68	62	56	51	41	33

HOW TO CONVERT ALMOST ANYTHING INTO ALMOST ANYTHING

To convert, find the unit you'd like to convert from in bold, find the unit you want to convert to, then multiply the quantity by the number on the left.

Acres

square feet	43,560
square yards	4,840
square miles	0.00156
square meters	4,046.856
hectares	0.40468

Barrels

gallons	31.5
(not petroleum)	
gallons (petroleum)	42

Bushels

dry pints	64
dry quarts	32
pecks	4
cubic feet	1.24445
liters	35.239
cubic yards	0.04609

Centimeters

inches	0.3937
feet	0.0328

Chains (surveyor's)

feet	66
rods	4

Cubic centimeters

cubic inches	0.06102

Cubic feet

cubic inches	1,728
cubic meters	0.028317
cubic yards	0.037037
gallons	7.48
liters	28.32

Cubic feet of water

pounds at 60°F	62.37
gallons	7.481

Cubic inches

fluid ounces	0.554113
quarts	0.017316

Cubic inches

gallons	0.004329
milliliters	16.387064

Cubic meters

cubic feet	35.3145
cubic yards	1.30795

Cubic yards

cubic feet	27
cubic meters	0.76456

Cups

teaspoons	48
tablespoons	16
ounces	8

Drams (troy or apothecary)

grains	60
drams	2.194286
(avoirdupois)	
ounces	0.13714
(avoirdupois)	
ounces	0.125 or ⅛
(troy or apothecary)	
grams	3.88794

Drams (U.S. fluid)

minims	60
fluid ounces	0.125 or ⅛
cubic inches	0.22559
milliliters	3.6966

Fathoms

feet	6

Feet

centimeters	30.48
fathoms	0.16667
hands	3
miles	0.00019
kilometers	0.0003

Feet of water

pounds per sq. ft.	62.42
pounds per sq. in.	0.4335
inches of mercury	0.88265
at 0°C	

Feet per minute

feet per second	0.01667

Feet per second

miles per hour	0.68182

Gallons

milliliters	3,785
cubic inches	231
cubic feet	0.1337
cubic yards	0.00495
cubic meters	0.00379

fluid ounces	128

Gallons

quarts	4
liters	3.7853
British gallons	0.8327

Gallons of water

pounds of water	8.3453
at 60°F	

Gallons (British)

pounds of water	10
at 62°F	
US gallons	1.201

Grains

ounces	0.00229
ounces	0.00208
(troy or apothecary)	
grams	0.0648

Grains per gallon

parts per million	17.118
(ppm)	
grams per liter	0.01714

Grams

grains	15.432
drams	0.56438
drams	0.25721
(troy or apothecary)	
ounces	0.03527
ounces	0.03215
(troy or apothecary)	
pounds	0.0022
pounds	0.00268
(troy or apothecary)	

Grams per liter

grains per gallon	58.418

Hectares

square meters	10,000
acres	2.471

Horsepower

foot-pounds	33,000
per minute	
Btu per minute	42.42
Btu per hour	2,546
metric horsepower	1.014
kilowatts	0.7457

Inches

feet	0.08333
yards	0.02778
centimeters	2.54
meters	0.0254

Kilograms

grains	15,432.36
drams	564.3834
drams	257.21
(troy or apothecary)	
ounces	32.15075
(troy or apothecary)	
pounds	2.20462
pounds	2.67923
(troy or apothecary)	
short tons	0.0011
long tons	0.00098
metric tons	0.001

Kilometers

feet	3,280.8
miles	0.62137

Kilowatts

Btu per minute	56.90
horsepower	1.341
metric horsepower	1.397

Kilowatt-hours

Btu	3,413

Knots

nautical miles per hour	1
miles per hour	1.1508

Leagues

miles	3

Links (surveyor's)

feet	0.66
inches	7.92
chain	0.01
rod	0.04

Liters

fluid ounces	33.814
quarts	1.05669
gallons	0.2642
British gallons	0.21998
cubic inches	61.02374
cubic feet	0.03531
cubic meters	0.001
cubic yards	0.00131

Meters

inches	39.37
feet	3.2808
yards	1.094

Miles

nautical miles	0.869
feet	5,280
yards	1,760
meters	1,609.344

Miles (nautical)

statute miles	1.1508

Miles per hour

knots	0.8684
miles per minute	0.016667
feet per second	1.467

Miles per minute

knots	52.104
feet per second	88

Milliliters

minims	16.231
fluid drams	0.2705
fluid ounces	0.0338
cubic inches	0.061
inches	0.03937

Minims

fluid drams	0.01667
fluid ounces	0.002
milliliters	0.0616

Ounces

grains	437.5
drams	16
drams	7.292
(troy or apothecary)	
ounces	0.9146
(troy or apothecary)	
pounds	0.0625
pounds	0.07595
(troy or apothecary)	
grams	28.34952
kilograms	0.02835

Ounces (troy or apothecary)

grains	480
drams	17.55429
drams	8
(troy or apothecary)	
ounces	1.09714
(avoirdupois)	
pounds	0.08333
(troy or apothecary)	
pounds	0.06857
grams	31.1035
kilograms	0.0311

Ounces (fluid)

minims	480
pints	0.0625
quarts	0.03125
gallons	0.00781
cubic inches	1.80469
cubic feet	0.00104
milliliters	29.57353
liters	0.02957
teaspoons	6
tablespoons	2

Ounces (fluid, British)

ounces	0.96
(fluid, United States)	

Ounces per square inch

pounds per sq. in.	0.0625

Ounces per square inch

inches of water	1.73
inches of mercury	0.127

Pecks

bushels	0.25 or ¼

Pints (dry)

pecks	0.0625
bushels	0.01562
cubic inches	33.60031
cubic feet	0.01944
liters	0.55061

Pints (fluid)

fluid ounces	16
fluid quarts	0.5 or ½
gallons	0.125 or ⅛
cubic inches	28.875
cubic feet	0.01671
cups	2
milliliters	473.17647
liters	0.47318

Pounds

grains	7,000
drams	256
drams	116.6667
(troy or apothecary)	
ounces	16
ounces	14.58333
(troy or apothecary)	
pounds	1.21528
(troy or apothecary)	
grams	453.59237
kilograms	0.453592
short tons	0.0005
long tons	0.000446
metric tons	0.0004536

continued on next page

Pounds (troy or apothecary)

grains	5,760
drams (avoirdupois)	210.6514
drams (troy or apothecary)	96
ounces (avoirdupois)	13.16571
ounces (troy or apothecary)	12
pounds (avoirdupois)	0.82286
grams	373.24172
kilograms	0.45359

Pounds of water

gallons	0.1198

Quarts (dry)

pecks	0.125 or ⅛
bushels	0.03125

Quarts (dry)

cubic inches	67.2006

Quarts (fluid)

fluid ounces	32
cubic inches	57.749
cubic feet	0.033421
milliliters	946,358
liters	0.946333

Rods

chains	0.25 or ¼

Square centimeters

square inches	0.115
square feet	0.00108

Square feet

square inches	144
square yards	0.111111
square centimeters	929
square meters	0.0929

Square inches

square centimeters	6.452

Square meters

square feet	10.765
square yards	1.196

Square miles

acres	640
sq. kilometers	2.589998

Square yards

square meters	0.836

Tons (long)

pounds	2,240
kilograms	1,016.0470
short tons	1.12
metric tons	1.016

Tons (short)

pounds	2,000
kilograms	907.185
long tons	0.89286
metric tons	0.907185

Tons (metric)

pounds	2,204.62
kilograms	1,000
long tons	0.984206
short tons	1.10231

Watts

horsepower	0.00134

Yards

centimeters	91.44
meters	0.9144

GESTATION TABLE

DATE OF SERVICE	DATE ANIMAL DUE TO GIVE BIRTH			
	MARE	COW	EWE	SOW
January 1	December 6	October 10	May 30	April 22
February 1	January 6	November 10	June 30	May 23
March 1	February 3	December 8	July 30	June 22
April 1	March 6	January 8	August 28	July 21
May 1	April 5	February 7	September 27	August 20
June 1	May 6	March 10	October 28	September 20
July 1	June 5	April 9	November 27	October 20
August 1	July 6	May 10	December 27	November 20
September 1	August 6	June 10	January 26	December 21
October 1	September 5	July 10	February 25	January 20
November 1	October 6	August 10	March 27	February 20
December 1	November 5	September 9	April 26	March 22

SCIENTIFIC NAMES OF COMMON HOUSEHOLD CHEMICALS

Alcohol, Grain . . . Ethyl Alcohol

Alcohol, Wood . . . Methyl Alcohol

Alum, Common . . . Potassium Aluminum Sulfate

Aqua Regia . . . Nitric and Hydrochloric Acids, Mixed

Baking Soda . . . Sodium Bicarbonate

Baryta Water . . . Barium Hydroxide Solution

Bleaching Powder . . . Calcium Hypochlorite

Bluestone . . . Copper Sulfate

Blue Vitriol . . . Copper Sulfate

Boracic Acid . . . Boric Acid

Borax . . . Sodium Borate

Brimstone . . . Sulfur, Molded in Sticks

Calomel . . . Mercurous Chloride

Caoutchouc . . . Rubber

Carbolic Acid . . . Phenol

Carbonic Acid Gas . . . Carbon Dioxide

Caustic Potash . . . Potassium Hydroxide

Caustic Soda . . . Sodium Hydroxide

Chalk . . . Calcium Carbonate

Copperas . . . Ferrous Sulfate

Corrosive Sublimate . . . Mercuric Chloride (Bichloride of Mercury)

Cream of Tartar . . . Potassium Bitartrate

Epsom Salt . . . Magnesium Sulfate

Flowers of Sulfur . . . Sulfur Crystals (also Powdered Sulfur)

Glauber's Salt . . . Sodium Sulfate

Green Vitriol . . . Ferrous Sulfate

Hartshorn . . . Ammonium Carbonate

Hypo . . . Sodium Thiosulfate

Laughing Gas . . . Nitrous Oxide

Limewater . . . Calcium Hydroxide Solution

Litharge . . . Lead Oxide, PbO

Liver of Sulfur . . . Potassium Sulfide (also Sulfurated Potash)

Lunar Caustic . . . Silver Nitrate, Cast in Thin Sticks

Lye . . . Sodium or Potassium Hydroxide

Meerschaum . . . Magnesium Silicate

Muriatic Acid . . . Hydrochloric Acid

Oil of Vitriol . . . Sulfuric Acid

Oleum . . . Fuming Sulfuric Acid

Orpiment . . . Arsenic Trisulfide, As_2S_3

Oxone . . . Sodium Peroxide

Plumbago . . . Graphite

Potash Alum . . . Potassium Aluminum Sulfate

Quicklime . . . Calcium Oxide

Quicksilver . . . Mercury

Realgar . . . Arsenic Sulfide, As_2S_2

Red Lead . . . Lead Oxide, Pb_3O_4

Red Prussiate . . . Potassium Ferricyanide of Potash

Rochelle Salt . . . Potassium Sodium Tartrate

Sal Ammoniac . . . Ammonium Chloride

Sal Soda . . . Sodium Carbonate

Sal Volatile . . . Ammonium Carbonate and Ammonium Bicarbonate

Saleratus . . . Sodium (or Sometimes Potassium) Bicarbonate

Salt (Common) . . . Sodium Chloride

Salt (Rock) . . . Sodium Chloride

Saltpeter (Bengal) . . . Potassium Nitrate

Saltpeter (Chile) . . . Sodium Nitrate

Salts of Sorrel . . . Potassium Acid Oxalate

Slaked Lime . . . Calcium Hydroxide

Soda Ash . . . Sodium Carbonate

Spirits of Hartshorn . . . Ammonium Hydroxide (Ammonia Water)

Spirits of Salt . . . Hydrochloric Acid

Sugar of Lead . . . Lead Acetate

Tartar Emetic . . . Antimony Potassium Tartrate

Yellow Prussiate . . . Potassium Ferrocyanide of Potash

Washing Soda . . . Sodium Carbonate

Water-Glass . . . Sodium Silicate (or sometimes) Potassium Silicate

White Vitriol . . . Zinc Sulfate

COMMON GARDEN PESTS AND THEIR NATURAL CONTROLS

A GROWING NUMBER OF gardeners—tired of drenching their vegetable patches with chemical fertilizers and wide-spectrum, persistent pesticides—are turning to more organic methods of raising food. Elsewhere in this book you'll find instructions for making compost . . . and here are a few insect controls recommended by organic gardeners.

SPECIAL NOTE: Pyrethrum, rotenone, and ryania are *not* chlorinated hydrocarbon, persistent pesticides. All three are derived from plants and none of the three presents the cumulative dangers to plants, animals, and people inherent in the broad-spectrum chemical insect controls.

INSECT	NAME and DESCRIPTION	ATTACKED
	Aphids or plant lice: Small, soft, pear-shaped, various colors, work in massed groups.	All
	Asparagus beetle: Blue or orange, ¼" long.	Asparagus
	Twelve-spotted asparagus beetle: Larger than asparagus beetle and with 12 spots on wing covers.	Asparagus
	Bean weevil: Small, chunky snouted beetle, rather square across the back and tapering into a wedge shape toward the front. Brownish-gray or olive.	Bean
	Blister beetle: Slender, cylindrical insects ½ to 1" long, gray, black, or yellow with black stripes. Moves in colonies or swarms late in season.	Beet, chard, potato, bean, cabbage, corn, tomato, and others.
	Cabbage maggot: Yellow-white, up to ⅓" long. Adult fly resembles housefly but is smaller and rests on ground until disturbed.	Cabbage, radish, cauliflower, turnip, cruciferous crops.
	Imported cabbage worm: Smooth, leaf-green, up to 1½" long. Larvae of white cabbage butterfly.	Cabbage, cauliflower, and other cruciferous crops.
	Cabbage looper: Same size as above but lighter green with white stripes. Humps its back as it crawls.	Same as above plus lettuce, beet, celery, and others.

HALF-BURIED BOTTLE CONTAINING STALE BEER ATTRACTS AND DROWNS DESTRUCTIVE SLUGS.

BEER

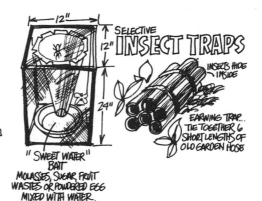

SELECTIVE INSECT TRAPS

12"
12"
24"

INSECTS HIDE INSIDE

EARWIG TRAP... TIE TOGETHER 6 SHORT LENGTHS OF OLD GARDEN HOSE

"SWEET WATER" BAIT MOLASSES, SUGAR, FRUIT WASTES OR POWDERED EGG MIXED WITH WATER.

INJURY	TREATMENT
Suck juices, causing plants to wither and sometimes become blotched. Leaves may curl badly, yellow, and thicken.	Ladybugs are a very effective natural control . . . or spray the aphids with a strong stream of water, soapy water, rotenone, or pyrethrum. Crush by hand. Prevent attacks by planting nasturtiums between rows of plants to be protected. Treatment is most effective if started at first signs of attack.
Feeds on foliage, attacks tender shoots and later gnaws the stalks.	Pick stalks daily in season. Dust with rotenone to kill larvae in April and May. In fall, clean the garden and plow, with poultry following behind to eat larvae. Let hens have run of asparagus beds.
Feeds almost exclusively on the berries.	Same as above.
Attacks mature seeds in storage. Chews holes in pod and eats out interior of seeds.	The easiest way to avoid this pest is by planting early or late so that adult beetles miss the plants' blossoms. Cure seeds properly by pulling up plants with pods on them and placing them off the ground on stakes for six weeks or more. Obtain seed from a reputable dealer. If seed floats in water, don't use it.
Eat leaves.	Handpick . . . but wear gloves because these little devils really will give you blisters. Believe it or not, swarms can be driven out with the sweeping motion of a branch or stick.
Tunnels into roots and stems, causing plant to wither and die.	All season long. Find where maggots are working, pull dirt away, put heaping tablespoon of wood ashes around stem, replace dirt, firm plant and water. Put 4" circle or square of tar paper around stem of plant to repel adult female fly and keep her from laying eggs.
Eats leaves full of holes, often delaying growth and heading for several weeks.	Handpick worms from undersides of leaves. Dust cabbage in the early morning with rye flour or powdered lime. Spray with a mixture of two teaspoons of table salt in one gallon of water or use rotenone or pyrethrum. Try companion plantings of tansy, tomatoes, sage, catnip, mint, hemp, rosemary, or nasturtium.
Same as above.	Same control as above.

INSECT	NAME and DESCRIPTION	ATTACKED
	Larvae of the diamondback moth: Small, green worm.	Cabbage and other cruciferous crops.
	Celery leaf tier: Greenish caterpillar up to ¾" long. Moths are brown with wings crossed by dark wavy lines.	Celery
	Colorado potato beetle (potato bug): Larvae is brick-red, soft, humped. Adult is chunky, yellow with 10 black stripes on back. About ⅜" long.	Potato, eggplant, tomato.
	Corn earworm: Brown, green, or pink larvae, up to 2" long and striped.	Corn, tomato, pepper, potato, squash, bean, cucumber, asparagus, and other crops.
	Cutworm: Plump, soft-bodied, dull-colored light to black, scantily covered with coarse bristles or hairs, 1 to 1½" long. Feed at night, curl when exposed.	All.
	Earwig: Reddish-brown, up to ¾" long with forceps on tail end.	All.
	Flea and leaf beetle: Many species, ⅟₁₆" long, black, brown, or striped. Leap like fleas.	Vegetables including beets, peppers, potatoes, tomatoes. Transplants, brassicas.
	Grasshopper: Dull brown, gray, green, black, yellow, up to 2" or more in length. Jump and have wings.	All crops.
	Harlequin cabbage bug: One of the stink bugs. Black or dark blue with red or yellow spots. Shield shaped, up to ⅜" long.	Cabbage, cauliflower, and other cruciferous crops.
	Japanese beetle: About ½" long, oval, metallic green and brown. Larvae is 1" long, white with brown head.	Bean, okra, corn, most plants.

INJURY	TREATMENT
Usually known to feed on undersides of leaves and not until the pests are numerous are the holes eaten clear through.	Same as above.
Eat holes in leaves, and often fasten leaves together with webbing.	Handpick the worms and discard leaves that appear damaged. Dust with ground tobacco, lime, pyrethrum, or sulfur and repeat after 30 minutes.
Both larvae and adults eat foliage.	Handpick beetle or larvae. Use ladybugs, mulch, dust with rotenone, or spray with extracts from common or sweet basil. Companion plant with bush beans.
Eat leaves and buds. On corn, feed on silk and kernels near the tip of an ear.	Electric insect traps. For corn, after silks go limp and tips start to turn brown, apply five or six drops of mineral oil to the end of each ear. Or handpick. For other vegetables, use a dusts of rotenone or ryania.
Cut off plants even with the ground. Some cutworms burrow into the stalks or through heads and roots of vegetables.	When you put out plant seedlings in the spring, place paper or tin can (with both ends cut out) collars around each little plan. Set the collars 2" deep in the soil. Spread and cover crushed eggshell between and around plants. Handpick the worms and cultivate lightly. Encourage your garden's toad population. Allow no grass to grow in the vegetable patch. Plow in spring and fall and let hogs and chickens root and pick through the freshly turned soil.
Eat plant parts (and some aphids and other sucking insects . . . making then partially—but only partially—beneficial). Feed at night.	Trap earwigs under boards or in newspaper that has been rolled up and left in the garden overnight. Be sure burn the paper daily.
Leaves first become blotched with minute white dots, then look like they've been shot full of holes.	Keep weeds down. Dust with mix of fine ashes and tobacco dust, pyrethrum, or rotenone.
Eat vegetation and sometimes completely devour whole plants.	Handpick and destroy, use as fish bait, or—like the Native Americans—fry or roast the pests and eat them. Spray rotenone on nonedible (such as potato) leaves. Till in the fall at least 5" deep.
Suck sap from leaves causing wilt.	Look for and destroy eggs (capsules with black stripes) on early blooming plants. Plant a trap crop of turnip, mustard, radish, or rape and destroy the cabbage bugs that gather. If early arrivals are destroyed, later ones will not follow. Dust with sabadilla or pyrethrum when your cruciferous crop leaves look brown and scalded. Keep garden weeded.
Eat foliage. Larvae eat roots.	Handpick or trap beetles. Spray them with rotenone. Treat soil once with milky spore disease to eliminate larvae. Interplant crops to be protected with garlic.

INSECT	NAME and DESCRIPTION	ATTACKED
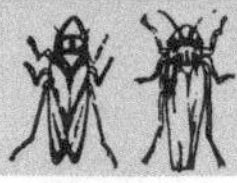	**Leaf hopper:** Wedge shaped, ⅛" long, greenish or brown, active.	Bean, lettuce, celery, eggplant, tomato, potato, other plants.
	**Lygus bug or tarnished plant bug:** Oval, flat, almost ¼" long, brownish, marked with yellow and black. When disturbed hides behind stems.	Beets and nearly all crops.
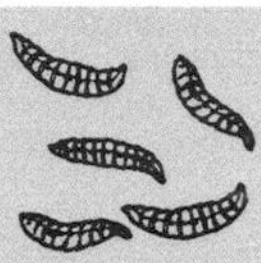	**Maggot:** Several species look like ¼" long grubs without legs.	Onion, bean, pea, corn, beet, radish, potato, cabbage, and other brassicas.
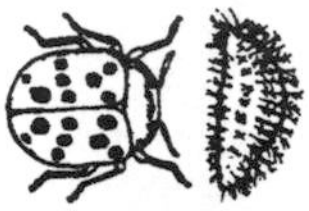	**Mexican bean beetle:** Copperish brown, oval, with 16 spots on back. Larvae are orange to yellow, furry or spiny, up to ⅓" long. Eggs are orange in clusters on leaves' undersides.	Bean.
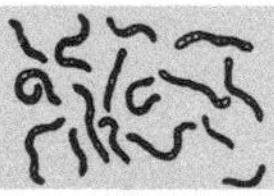	**Nematode or eelworm:** Tiny worms, from 1⁄25" long, white or colorless. Not an insect.	Many.
	**Onion thrip:** Not over 1⁄20" long, active insects, brownish or yellowish with fringed wings. Jump like fleas.	Onions and nearly all garden crops.
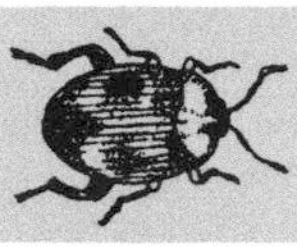	**Pea weevil:** Stout, chunky beetle about ⅕" long, dark brown with black and white marks. Larvae are white with small brown head and about ⅓" long.	Pea.
	**Pickleworm:** Yellowish-white with brownish head, dark spots on young, up to ¾" long.	Pumpkin, cantaloupe, cucumber, and squash, late in season.
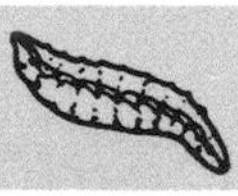	**Seed-corn maggot:** Small, yellowish-white, legless larvae, narrow at front with enlarged posterior.	Bean.
	**Spotted cucumber beetle:** Yellowish-green with 12 black spots on back, ¼" long.	Squash and other cucurbits and beans.
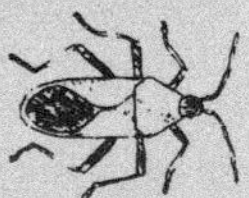	**Squash bug:** One of the stink bugs. Brownish-black, mottled yellowish underneath. Flat and ½–¾" long. Oval brown eggs, laid in clusters.	Squash and cucurbits.
	**Squash vine borer:** White grubs about 1" long. Brown to black head and small brownish legs on forepart.	Pumpkin and squash.

INJURY	TREATMENT
Suck the undersides of leaves and spread the virus disease *yellows*.	Spray with pyrethrum or rotenone. Dust with sulfur. Plant lettuce in sheltered places near hedges or buildings.
Suck juices causing plants to wither and carries diseases from plant to plant.	Hides in trash and weeds, so eliminate these from the garden in fall or spring. Dust with sabadilla or spray with pryrethrum.
Flies deposit eggs on plants or in soil, maggots hatch and kill young plants by tunneling into seeds, roots, and stems. Cause decay of onion bulbs.	Surround young plants with tar-paper squares. Dust earth with ashes. Don't plant onions in rows, scatter them throughout garden.
Feed on pods and underside of leaves, skeletonizing them.	Interplant beans with potatoes and marigolds. Plant early. Remove vines immediately after harvest and eliminate debris and dead plants. Spray under leaves with rotenone or pyrethrum.
Damage roots and suck juices. Cause knots and swellings.	Interplant with marigolds. Change location of garden, rotate crops. Plant resistant varieties, keep weeds down, add humus to the soil.
Suck juices from plant, causing white splotches and brown tips on leaves, both upper and lower sides. Plants then wilt and bulbs rot.	Destroy hibernating insects by plowing under or burning all grass and weeds near onion field in the spring. Plant White Persian, Sweet Spanish, and other resistant varieties. Drench plants with hose. Spray or dust with rotenone, pyrethrum, or nicotine.
Adults feed on blossoms of peas and lay eggs on young pods. Larvae burrow into the green seed.	Heat seed for 5–6 hours at 120–130°F. Put livestock or poultry in the pea patch after harvesting. Plow deeply and remove any possible shelter. Dust with rotenone. Plant early.
Feeds on flowers and leaf buds, often tunnels into flowers, terminal buds, vines, and fruit.	Handpick worms before they reach fruits, dust with rotenone or sabadilla. Plant earlier trap crops, like squash.
Bores into seeds, sprouts, and stems underground, causing bean plants to wither and die.	Regulate plant growth by planting in warm weather, not wet. If loss is great, replant. Handpick maggots by lifting plants from ground, removing maggots, and resetting plant.
Eats blossoms of cucurbits and leaves and pods of beans.	Plant with radishes. Handpick. Trap under boards. Protect young plants with screen cages. Spray upper and lower sides of leaves with a handful of wood ashes and a handful of hydrated lime dissolved in two gallons of water.
Suck juices causing wilt and death of plant. May transmit diseases.	Crush eggs. Handpick using gloves. Trap under boards. Dust with mixed wood ashes and hydrated lime or with sabadilla. Dust or spray with tyania. Destroy old vines after harvest. Plant earlier hills of squash for traps. Grow radishes, nasturtiums, and marigolds nearby.
Bore into squash and pumpkin vines, eat holes in stems near base of runner. Can get into the fruits.	Look for piles of yellow sawdust-like excrement that falls from holes in infested stems. Slit such stems open, remove or stab grubs, heap moist soil over vine to protect it and induce rooting. Plant summer squash trap crop as early as possible between rows of later, main crop . . . when trap plants are well infested, pull and burn them. Sprinkle black pepper around vines of main crop.

INSECT	NAME and DESCRIPTION	ATTACKED
	Striped cucumber beetle: Yellowish-green with three black stripes on back and about ¼" long. Larvae are white, slender, brownish at ends, and ⅓" long.	Squash, cucumber, cucurbits of all kinds.
	Tomato hornworm: Smooth, green, diagonal lines on sides and prominent horn on the rear. Up to 4" long.	Tomato, potato, eggplant, and pepper.
	White grub: Soft-bodied worm with brown head, curved, ½–1" long. Often June bug larvae.	All crops.
	Wireworm: The larvae of the click beetle. Up to 1½" long, light to dark brown or yellow with dark head and tail. Slender, clumsy, looks like a jointed wire.	Beet, bean, corn, lettuce, onion, potato, carrot, turnip, cabbage, and most crops on poorly drained soil.

SIMPLE INTEREST

AMOUNT AND TIME		4%	5%	6%	7%	8%
$1.00	1 month	$ .003	$ .004	$ .005	$ .005	$ .006
$1.00	2 months	.007	.008	.010	.011	.013
$1.00	3 months	.011	.013	.015	.017	.020
$1.00	6 months	.020	.025	.030	.035	.040
$1.00	12 months	.040	.050	.060	.070	.080
$100.00	1 day	.011	.013	.016	.019	.022
$100.00	2 days	.022	.027	.032	.038	.044
$100.00	3 days	.034	.041	.050	.058	.067
$100.00	4 days	.045	.053	.066	.077	.089
$100.00	5 days	.056	.069	.082	.097	.111
$100.00	6 days	.067	.083	.100	.116	.133
$100.00	1 month	.334	.416	.500	.583	.667
$100.00	2 months	.667	.832	1.000	1.166	1.333
$100.00	3 months	1.000	1.250	1.500	1.750	2.000
$100.00	6 months	2.000	2.500	3.000	3.500	4.000
$100.00	12 months	4.000	5.000	6.000	7.000	8.000

TO FIND THE INTEREST ON ANY SUM FOR ANY TIME

Count off two places from the right of the principal and multiply it by the number of months. One-half the result is the interest at 6 percent. Deduct one-sixth for 5 percent; one-third for 4 percent; add one-sixth for 7 percent; one-third for 8 percent, etc.

INJURY	TREATMENT
Adults feed on leaves and spread bacterial wilt. Larvae bore into roots and feed on stems causing plants to wilt and die.	Mulch heavily. Interplant with marigolds. Dust with soot or charcoal or spray upper and lower sides of leaves with a mixture of one handful of wood ashes, one handful of hydrated lime, and two gallons of water.
Feed on foliage, eat all but skeletons of leaves and damages fruit.	Handpick and destroy unless worms are covered with small white bodies (which are parasites that will kill the worms and move on to others).
Feed on roots and tubers, causing plants to wilt and die. Reduces yields and quality.	Try to avoid planting in newly turned sod. Plow in both fall and spring. Keep garden free of grass and weeds. Kill exposed grubs.
Attack germinating seeds, roots, and tubers.	Avoid planting in infested soil. Develop good drainage. Plow sod once a week for 4–6 weeks before planting. Enrich earth with humus and compost. Companion plant vegetables with alfalfa and Mexican marigolds. Treat infested plants with tobacco dust. Bury half a potato 4" deep, dig up in a week, and destroy worms.

CIRCLES

DIAMETER (INCHES)	CIRCUMFERENCE (INCHES)
1/16	13/64
1/8	25/64
3/16	19/32
1/4	25/32
5/16	63/64
3/8	1 11/64
7/16	1 3/8
1/2	1 37/64

DIAMETER (INCHES)	CIRCUMFERENCE (INCHES)
9/16	1 49/64
5/8	1 31/32
11/16	2 5/32
3/4	2 23/64
13/16	2 35/64
7/8	2 3/4
15/16	2 15/16

TO FIND THE CIRCUMFERENCE OF A CIRCLE

Multiply the diameter by 3.1416 (π) or 3 ½.

$$
\begin{array}{r}
3.1416\ (\pi) \\
\times\ 2''\ \text{diameter} \\
\hline
6.2832''\ \text{or}\ 6\ \tfrac{1}{4}''\ \text{circumference}
\end{array}
$$

BIRDHOUSES

DIMENSIONS FOR BIRDHOUSES*

KIND OF BIRD	A SIZE OF FLOOR (INCHES)	B DEPTH OF BIRD BOX (INCHES)	C HEIGHT OF ENTRANCE ABOVE FLOOR (INCHES)	D DIAMETER OF ENTRANCE HOLE (INCHES)	HEIGHT TO FASTEN ABOVE GROUND (FEET)
Bluebird	5x5	8	6	1 ½	5-10
Chickadee	4x4	8-10	6-8	1 ⅛	6-15
Titmouse	4x4	8-10	6-8	1 ¼	6-15
Nuthatch	4x4	8-10	6-8	1 ¼	12-20
House wren and Bewick's wren	4x4	6-8	4-6	1 ¼	6-10
Carolina wren	4x4	6-8	4-6	1 ½	6-10
Violet-green swallow and Tree swallow	5x5	6	1-5	1 ½	10-15
Purple martin**	6x6**	6**	1**	2 ½	15-20
House finch	6x6	6	4	2	8-12
Starling	6x6	16-18	14-16	2	10-25
Crested flycatcher	6x6	8-10	6-8	2	8-20
Flicker	7x7	16-18	14-16	2 ½	6-20
Golden-fronted woodpecker and red-headed woodpecker	6x6	12-15	9-12	2	12-20
Downy woodpecker	4x4	8-10	6-8	1 ¼	6-20
Hairy woodpecker	6x6	12-15	9-12	1 ½	12-20
Screech owl	8x8	12-15	9-12	3	10-30
Saw-whet owl	6x6	10-12	8-10	2 ½	12-20
Sparrow hawk	8x8	12-15	9-12	3	10-30
Wood duck	10x18	10-24	12-16	4	10-20

*This and the next table are from *Homes For Birds*, Conservation Bulletin 14, US Department of the Interior, Washington, DC.

**These are dimensions for one compartment, or a martin house for one pair of birds. It is customary to build martin houses eight compartments at a time, which constitutes a section.

DIMENSIONS FOR NESTING SHELVES WITH ONE OR MORE SIDES OPEN

KIND OF BIRD	SIZE OF FLOOR (INCHES)	DEPTH OF BIRD BOX (INCHES)	HEIGHT TO FASTEN ABOVE GROUND (FEET)
Robin	6x8	8	6–15
Barn swallow	6x6	6	8–12
Song sparrow	6x6	6	1–3
Phoebe	6x6	6	8–12

NESTING MATERIALS

Once your new birdhouses are properly spaced and secured, the next springtime chore is providing some suitable nest-building materials. While most of our feathered friends are very resourceful, feathers, bits of rag, hair, and pieces of string always help. Here are some suggestions:

- *Feathers* help house wrens, phoebes, titmice, bluebirds, chickadees, and others.
- *Rags*, *twine*, and *string* are used by mockingbirds, robins, and Baltimore orioles.
- *Mud* is needed by robins, phoebes, barn swallows, wood thrushes, grackles, and chimney swifts to build nests.

And as a final complement to your yard, add a birdbath and keep it filled with fresh, clean water.

WEIGHT TABLE

(Per Cubic Foot)

Pine, yellow . . . 34		Earth, loose . . . 94	
Pine, white . . . 34		Marble, Italian . . . 169	
Ash . . . 53		Marble, Vermont . . . 165	
Oak, white, dry . . . 54		Mortar . . . 110	
Poplar . . . 23		Mud . . . 102	
Poplar, white . . . 33		Water, salt . . . 64	
Walnut . . . 41		Water, rain . . . 62	
Walnut, black . . . 31		Ice . . . 57 ½	
Stone, com . . . 158		Hay, baled . . . 95	
Sand, wet . . . 128		Hay, pressed . . . 25	
Brick, com . . . 102		Coal, L'y'a . . . 50	
Clay . . . 120		Coal, Lehigh . . . 56	

MORE THAN YOU WANT TO KNOW ABOUT LATH

• A standard lath (the thin, narrow strip of wood nailed to studding as a support for plaster or tile) is four feet long and 1½ inches wide.

• A standard bundle of laths will cover three square yards.

• One thousand laths are enough to cover about 20 square yards of surface.

• The application of 1,000 laths requires about 11 pounds of lath nails.

DISTANCE TO PLANT TREES

Apples . . . 30 to 40 feet each way	Currants . . . 3 to 4 feet each way
Apples, dwarf . . . 10 to 15 feet each way	Gooseberries . . . 3 to 4 feet each way
Pears . . . 20 to 30 feet each way	Raspberries . . . 3 to 5 feet each way
Pears, dwarf . . . 10 to 15 feet each way	Blackberries . . . 6 to 7 feet each way
Plums . . . 16 to 20 feet each way	Grapes . . . 8 to 12 feet each way
Peaches . . . 16 to 20 feet each way	Kumquat . . . *10 to 12 feet
Cherries . . . 16 to 25 feet each way	Orange . . . *15 to 20 feet
Apricots . . . 16 to 20 feet each way	Lemon . . . *20 to 25 feet
Nectarines . . . 16 to 20 feet each way	Grapefruit . . . *25 to 30 feet
Quinces . . . 8 to 14 feet each way	Lime . . . *15 to 20 feet

* Distance must be gauged from richness of soil.

FREEZING POINTS, RECOMMENDED STORAGE CONDITIONS, AND LENGTH OF STORAGE PERIOD OF VEGETABLES AND FRUITS

COMMODITY	FREEZING POINT °F	PLACE TO STORE	STORAGE CONDITIONS		LENGTH OF STORAGE PERIOD
			TEMP. °F	HUMIDITY	
VEGETABLES					
Dry beans and peas	...	Any cool, dry place	32° to 40°	Dry	As long as desired
Late cabbage	30.4	Pit, trench, or outdoor cellar	Near 32° as possible	Moderately moist	Through late fall and winter
Cauliflower	30.3	Storage cellar	"	"	6 to 8 weeks
Late celery	31.6	Pit or trench; roots in soil in storage cellar	"	"	Through late fall and winter
Endive	31.9	Roots in soil in storage cellar	"	"	2 to 3 months
Onions	30.6	Any cool, dry place	"	Dry	Through fall and winter
Parsnips	30.4	Where they grew, or in storage cellar	"	Moist	"
Peppers	30.7	Unheated basement or room	45° to 50°	Moderately moist	2 to 3 weeks
Potatoes	30.9	Pit or in storage cellar	35° to 40°	"	Through fall and winter
Pumpkins and squashes	30.5	Home cellar or basement	55°	Moderately dry	"
Root crops (miscellaneous)	...	Pit or in storage cellar	Near 32° as possible	Moist	"
Sweet potatoes	29.7	Home cellar or basement	55° to 60°	Moderately dry	"
Tomatoes (mature green)	31.0	"	55° to 70°	"	4 to 6 weeks
FRUITS					
Apples	29.0	Fruit storage cellar	Near 32° as possible	Moderately moist	Through fall and winter
Grapefruit	29.8	"	"	"	4 to 6 weeks
Grapes	28.1	"	"	"	1 to 2 months
Oranges	30.5	"	"	"	4 to 6 weeks
Pears	29.2	"	"	"	...

CAPACITY OF A SILO

DIAMETER	DEPTH	CAPACITY IN TONS	ACRES TO FILL 15 TONS TO ACRE	COWS IT WILL KEEP 6 MONTHS, 40 POUNDS PER DAY
10	20	31	2⅓	8
12	20	45	3	12
12	24	54	3⅗	15
12	28	63	4⅕	17
14	22	67	4½	18
14	24	74	5	20
14	28	87	5⅔	24
14	30	93	6	26
16	24	96	6⅖	27
16	26	104	7	29
16	30	120	8	33
18	30	152	10⅕	42
18	36	183	12⅓	50

A silo, properly filled—that is, if the contents are made compact throughout—contains one ton of silage for every 50 cubic feet of space.

Multiply the square of the diameter by 0.7854 and that will be the area of the circular floor. Multiply the area of the floor by the height and that will give the number of cubic feet. One cubic foot of silage weighs forty pounds. Multiply the cubic feet by 40, and the result is the number of pounds of silage the silo will contain. Divide that by 2,000 to find the number of tons.

BEST SIZES FOR SILOS

The average silo is about 12 feet in diameter and 32 feet high. A silo 12 feet by 32 feet will hold about 75 tons of silage; 34 feet high about 80 tons; 36 feet high about 87 tons; 38 feet high about 94 tons; and 40 feet high about 101 tons. It is better to build two small silos than one large one.

TO FIND THE NUMBER OF TONS OF HAY IN A MOW

Multiply the length by the width by the height (all in feet) and divide by 400 to 500, depending on the kind of hay and how long it has been in the mow.

TO FIND THE NUMBER OF TONS IN A HAYSTACK

Multiply the overthrow (the distance from the ground on one side over the top of the stack to the ground on the other side) by the length, by the width (all in feet); multiply by 3; divide by 10, and then divide by 500 to 600, depending upon the length of time the hay has been in the stack.

NUMBER OF POUNDS TO THE BUSHEL

Alfalfa Seed . . . 60
Apples (Dried) . . . 24
Apples (Green) . . . 48
Barley . . . 48
Beans (Castor) . . . 46
Beans (Soy) . . . 60
Beans (White) . . . 60
Bluegrass Seed . . . 14
Bran . . . 20
Brome Grass . . . 14
Buckwheat . . . 48
Cherries . . . 40
Clover (Burr) . . . 10
Clover Seed . . . 60
Corn (Shelled) . . . 56
Corn (In Ear) . . . 70
Corn (Pop, In Ear) . . . 70
Corn (Pop, Shelled) . . . 56

Cornmeal . . . 50
Cranberries . . . 32
Charcoal . . . 20
Coal, Hard . . . 80
Coke . . . 40
Crested Wheat Grass . . . 22
Fescue, Meadow . . . 22
Fescue (Other Varieties) . . . 14
Flax Seed . . . 56
Grapes . . . 40
Hair (Plastering) . . . 8
Hemp Seed . . . 44
Kafir Corn . . . 56
Lespedeza . . . 25
Lime . . . 80
Malt . . . 38
Millet (Hungarian) . . . 48
Millet Seed (Common) . . . 50
Oats . . . 32

Onions . . . 57
Orchard Grass Seed . . . 14
Peaches (Dried) . . . 33
Peaches (Fresh) . . . 48
Peanuts (Spanish,
   Unshelled) . . . 32
Peanuts (Virginia or
   Whites, Unshelled) . . . 23
Peas (Dried) . . . 60
Potatoes . . . 60
Potatoes (Sweet) . . . 50
Red Top Seed . . . 14
Rice (In Rough) . . . 45
Rye . . . 56
Timothy Seed . . . 45
Tomatoes . . . 50
Turnips . . . 55
Wheat . . . 60

Approximate. Legal weights may vary in different states.

ONE MONTH TO SAME DAY IN ANOTHER

From to	Jan.	Feb.	Mar.	Apr.	May	June	July	Aug.	Sept.	Oct.	Nov.	Dec.
Jan.	365	31	59	90	120	151	181	212	243	273	304	334
Feb.	334	365	28	59	89	120	150	181	212	242	273	303
Mar.	306	337	365	31	61	92	122	153	184	214	245	275
Apr.	275	306	334	365	30	61	91	122	153	183	214	244
May	245	276	304	335	365	31	61	92	123	153	184	214
June	214	245	273	304	334	365	30	61	92	123	153	183
July	184	215	243	274	304	335	365	31	62	92	123	153
Aug.	153	184	212	243	273	304	334	365	31	61	92	122
Sept.	122	153	181	212	242	273	303	334	365	30	61	91
Oct.	92	123	151	182	212	243	273	304	335	365	31	61
Nov.	61	92	120	151	181	212	242	273	304	334	365	30
Dec.	31	62	90	121	151	182	212	243	274	304	335	365

EXPLANATION: To find the number of days from January 20th to December 20th, follow the horizontal line opposite January until you reach the column headed by December, where you will find 334, representing the required number of days, and so on, with the other months. During leap year, if February enters into the calculation, add one day to result.

CAPACITY OF CORN IN CRIBS (DRY CORN)

In Bushels *(Height: 10 feet)*

LENGTH in feet

WIDTH in feet	½	1	12	14	16	18	20	22	24	28	32	36	48	64
6	12	24	288	336	384	432	480	528	576	672	768	864	1,152	1,536
6¼	12	25	300	350	400	450	500	550	600	700	800	900	1,200	1,599
6½	13	26	312	364	416	468	520	572	624	728	832	936	1,248	1,664
6¾	13	27	324	378	432	486	540	594	648	756	864	972	1,296	1,728
7	14	28	336	392	448	504	560	616	672	784	896	1,008	1,344	1,792
7¼	14	29	348	406	464	522	580	638	696	812	928	1,044	1,392	1,856
7½	15	30	360	420	480	540	600	660	720	840	960	1,080	1,440	1,920
7¾	15	31	372	434	496	558	620	682	744	868	992	1,116	1,488	1,984
8	16	32	384	448	512	576	640	704	768	896	1,024	1,152	1,536	2,048
8½	17	34	408	476	544	612	680	748	816	952	1,088	1,224	1,632	2,176
9	18	36	432	504	576	648	720	792	864	1,008	1,152	1,296	1,728	2,304
10	20	40	480	560	640	720	800	880	960	1,120	1,280	1,440	1,920	2,560

EXAMPLE: A crib 24 feet long, 7½ feet wide and 10 feet high will hold 720 bushels of ear corn, reckoning 2½ cubic feet to hold a bushel. (A "bushel" of ear corn is the average amount that will yield a bushel—1¼ cubic feet—of shelled corn.)

If the crib is not 10 feet high, use the table anyway, but multiply the result by ¹⁄₁₀ the actual height. Example: If the above crib were only 8¾ feet high, it would hold 720 x .875 equals 630 bushels.

When using this table for bins of grain or shelled corn, multiply result by 2. To find the number of bushels of grain or shelled corn in a small bin or wagon box, find the volume in cubic feet and multiply by 0.8.

Ear corn of good quality, measured when settled, will hold out at 2½ cubic feet to the bushel. Allowance should be made for snapped corn, corn that is poorly husked, or otherwise inferior in quality, which will hold out at more than 2½ cubic feet per bushel.

Rule: At 2½ cubic feet to the bushel, divide the cubic feet in crib by 2½ or multiply by 2 and divide by 5.

TO MEASURE CORN IN BINS

To find the number of bushels of grain in a bin, multiply length by the width by the height, thus ascertaining the number of cubic feet and deduct one-fifth. For instance, a bin containing 10 cubic feet will hold 8 bushels of grain, 8 being four-fifths of 10.

TO MEASURE EAR CORN IN CRIB

Determine the number of cubic feet and multiply by 4; then divide by 10. Most corn in cribs is figured by this rule. However, if the cribs are well filled and the corn is sound and dry, divide by 9. If cribs are not well filled or if corn is damp, divide by 11.

JOHN DEERE HANDY ACREAGE GUIDE

Copyright John Deere and Company

DIRECTIONS: In the left-hand column, find the line that represents the working width of your equipment. Follow the line to the right until it touches the diagonal line representing the speed of travel. Follow vertical line to the bottom of chart and estimate hourly acreage from nearest figure. In figuring acreage for implements wider than 100 inches, figure as above for half the width and multiply the result by two.

EXAMPLE: (Using a three-bottom, 16-inch tractor plow cutting 48 inches, traveling at 3¼ mph.) Follow the line numbered 48 to a point midway between the diagonal lines marked 3 mph and 3½ mph, which represents the speed at which you are traveling. From this point, drop down to the bottom of the chart. Acreage covered is just a trifle less than 1⅝ acres per hour.

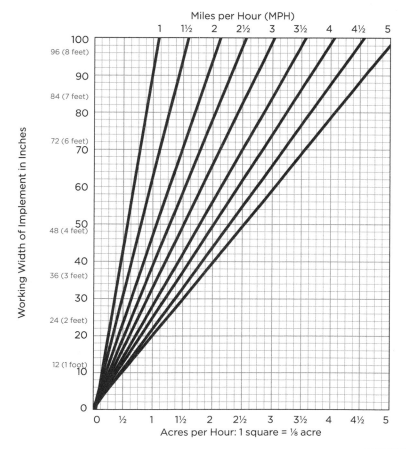

COMMODITY WEIGHTS AND MEASURES

• A pint's a pound—or very nearly—of the following: water, wheat, butter, sugar, and blackberries.

• A gallon of milk weighs 8.6 pounds; cream, 8.4 pounds; 46½ quarts of milk weigh 100 pounds.

• A keg of nails weighs 100 pounds. • A barrel of flour weighs 196 pounds; of salt, 280 pounds; of beef, fish, or pork, 200 pounds; cement (four bags) 376 pounds.

• Cotton in a standard bale weighs 480 pounds. • A bushel of coal weighs 80 pounds.

• A barrel of cement contains 3.8 cubic feet; of oil, 42 gallons.

• A barrel of dry commodities contains 7,056 cubic inches, or 105 dry quarts.

• A bushel leveled contains 2,150.42 cubic inches; a bushel heaped: 2,747.7 cubic inches. (Sometimes used to measure apples, potatoes, and shelled corn in bin.)

• A peck contains 537.605 cubic inches. • A dry quart contains 67.201 cubic inches.

• An acre contains 4,840 square yards, or 43,560 square feet.

• A square acre measures 208.71 feet on each side.

• A board foot equals 144 cubic inches; a cord contains 128 cubic feet.

• A barrel of rice (in rough) weighs 162 pounds. • A pocket of rice (clean) weighs 100 pounds.

• A bag of rice weighs 200 pounds.

TO FIND THE VALUE OF ARTICLES SOLD BY THE TON

Multiply the number of pounds by the price per ton, count off three places, and divide by 2.

US GOVERNMENT LAND MEASURE

A township: 36 sections . . . each 1 mile square

A section: 640 acres

A quarter section: ½ mile square . . . 160 acres

An eighth section: ½ mile long, north and south, and ¼ mile wide . . . 80 acres

A sixteenth section: ¼ mile square . . . 40 acres

The sections are all numbered 1 to 36, commencing at the northeast corner.

The sections are divided into quarters, which are named by the cardinal points.

TO ESTIMATE NUMBER OF TONS OF HAY

IN SQUARE OR OBLONG STACKS.

Multiply the length in feet by the width in feet, and multiply this figure by one-half the height. Divide the result by 300.

IN ROUND STACKS.

Square the distance around the stack in yards. Multiply this by 4 times the height in yards. Count off two places from the right and divide the remainder by 20.

AMOUNT OF PAINT REQUIRED FOR A GIVEN SURFACE

It is impossible to give a rule that will apply in all cases, as the amount varies with the kind and the thickness of the paint, the kind of wood or other material to which it is applied, the age of the surface, among others. The following is an approximate rule: Divide the number of square feet of surface by 200. The result will be the number of gallons of liquid required to give two coats.

CAPACITY OF BOXES AND BINS

A box 4 feet 8 inches long by 2 feet 4 inches wide and 2 feet 4 inches deep will hold 20 bushels.

A box 24 inches long by 16 inches wide and 28 inches deep will contain a barrel.

A box 26 inches long by 15½ inches wide and 8 inches deep will hold a bushel.

A box 12 inches long by 11½ inches wide and 9 inches deep will contain a half bushel.

LONG MEASURE

1 mile = 80 chains
= 320 rods
= 5,280 feet

1 chain = 4 rods
= 66 feet
= 100 links

1 rod = 5½ yards
= 16½ feet
= 25 links

1 link = 0.66 feet
= 7⅞ inches

1 pole = 16½ feet

SQUARE MEASURE

1 sq. mile = regular section
= 640 acres

1 acre = 10 sq. chains
= 160 sq. rods
= 43,560 sq. feet

An acre is about 208¼ feet qu.
An acre is about 8 rods wide, 20 rods long, or any area the product of whose length by its width (in rods) is 160 or in chains is 10.

1 sq. rod = 30¼ sq. yds.
= 272¼ sq. ft.

1 sq. ft. = 144 sq. inches

1 furlong = 220 yards

FIELD MEASUREMENT

EXAMPLE (taken from last entry on chart): 100 rows planted on 36" centers will have to be 146 feet long to equal an acre, whereas —if the same 100 rows are spaced 42" on center—they'll only have to be 125 feet in length to cover the acre.

ROWS/ ACRE	LENGTH OF ROWS IN FEET				ROWS/ ACRE	LENGTH OF ROWS IN FEET			
	36"	38"	40"	42"		36"	38"	40"	42"
1.0	14,559	13,794	13,104	12,479	4.0	3,640	3,449	3,276	3,120
1.1	13,235	12,540	11,913	11,345	4.2	3,466	3,284	3,120	2,971
1.2	12,133	11,495	10,920	10,399	4.4	3,309	3,135	2,978	2,836
1.3	11,199	10,611	10,080	9,599	4.6	3,165	2,999	2,849	2,713
1.4	10,399	9,853	9,360	8,914	4.8	3,033	2,874	2,730	2,600
1.5	9,706	9,196	8,736	8,319	5.0	2,912	2,759	2,621	2,496
1.6	9,099	8,621	8,190	7,799	5.2	2,800	2,653	2,520	2,400
1.7	8,564	8,114	7,708	7,341	5.4	2,696	2,554	2,427	2,311
1.8	8,088	7,663	7,280	6,933	5.6	2,600	2,463	2,340	2,228
1.9	7,663	7,260	6,897	6,568	5.8	2,510	2,378	2,259	2,152
2.0	7,280	6,897	6,552	6,240	6.0	2,427	2,299	2,184	2,080
2.1	6,933	6,569	6,240	5,942	6.2	2,348	2,225	2,114	2,013
2.2	6,618	6,270	5,956	5,672	6.4	2,275	2,155	2,048	1,950
2.3	6,330	5,997	5,697	5,426	6.6	2,206	2,090	1,985	1,891
2.4	6,066	5,748	5,460	5,200	6.8	2,141	2,029	1,927	1,835
2.5	5,824	5,518	5,242	4,992	7.0	2,080	1,971	1,872	1,783
2.6	5,600	5,305	5,040	4,800	7.2	2,022	1,916	1,820	1,733
2.7	5,392	5,109	4,853	4,622	7.4	1,967	1,864	1,771	1,686
2.8	5,200	4,926	4,680	4,457	7.6	1,916	1,815	1,724	1,642
2.9	5,020	4,757	4,519	4,303	7.8	1,867	1,768	1,680	1,600
3.0	4,853	4,598	4,368	4,160	8.0	1,820	1,724	1,638	1,560
3.1	4,696	4,450	4,227	4,025	8.2	1,775	1,682	1,598	1,522
3.2	4,550	4,311	4,095	3,900	8.4	1,733	1,642	1,560	1,486
3.3	4,412	4,180	3,971	3,782	8.6	1,693	1,604	1,524	1,451
3.4	4,282	4,057	3,854	3,670	8.6	1,693	1,604	1,524	1,451
3.5	4,160	3,941	3,744	3,565	8.8	1,654	1,568	1,489	1,418
3.6	4,044	3,832	3,640	3,466	9.0	1,618	1,533	1,456	1,387
3.7	3,935	3,728	3,542	3,373	9.2	1,583	1,499	1,424	1,356
3.8	3,831	3,630	3,448	3,284	9.4	1,549	1,467	1,394	1,328
3.9	3,733	3,537	3,360	3,200	9.6	1,517	1,437	1,365	1,300

ROWS/ ACRE	LENGTH OF ROWS IN FEET				ROWS/ ACRE	LENGTH OF ROWS IN FEET			
	36"	38"	40"	42"		36"	38"	40"	42"
9.8	1,486	1,408	1,337	1,273	25.0	582	552	524	499
10.0	1,456	1,379	1,310	1,248	26.0	560	531	504	480
10.5	1,387	1,314	1,248	1,188	27.0	539	511	485	462
11.0	1,324	1,254	1,191	1,134	28.0	520	493	468	446
11.5	1,266	1,199	1,139	1,085	29.0	502	476	452	430
12.0	1,213	1,150	1,092	1,040	30.0	485	460	437	416
12.5	1,165	1,104	1,048	998	31.0	470	445	423	403
13.0	1,120	1,061	1,008	960	32.0	455	431	410	390
13.5	1,078	1,022	971	924	33.0	441	418	397	378
14.0	1,040	985	936	891	34.0	428	406	385	367
14.5	1,004	951	904	861	35.0	416	394	374	357
15.0	971	920	874	832	36.0	404	383	364	347
15.5	939	890	845	805	38.0	383	363	345	328
16.0	910	862	819	780	40.0	364	345	328	312
16.5	882	836	794	756	42.0	347	328	312	297
17.0	856	811	771	734	46.0	317	300	285	271
17.5	832	788	749	713	50.0	291	276	262	250
18.0	809	766	728	693	55.0	265	251	238	227
18.5	787	746	708	675	60.0	243	230	218	208
19.0	766	726	690	657	65.0	224	212	202	192
19.5	747	707	672	640	70.0	208	197	197	178
20.0	728	690	655	624	80.0	182	172	164	156
20.5	710	673	639	609	90.0	162	153	146	139
21.0	693	657	624	594	100.0	146	138	131	125
21.5	677	642	609	580					
22.0	662	627	596	567					
22.5	647	613	582	555					
23.0	633	600	570	543					
23.5	620	587	558	531					
24.0	607	575	546	520					
24.5	594	563	535	509					

FRUITS AND VEGETABLES

THEIR LATIN NAMES, ORIGINS, AND DATES OF FIRST CULTIVATION

Apple	*Malus pumila*	Southwestern Asia	400 BC
Apricot	*Prunus armeniaca*	Western Asia	unknown
Artichoke	*Cynara scolymus*	Western Mediterranean	500 BC
Asparagus	*Asparagus officinalis*	Eastern Mediterranean	200 BC
Avocado	*Persea americana*	Central America	AD 1000
Banana	*Musa sapientum*	Tropical Asia	100 BC–AD 100
Beet	*Beta vulgaris*	Mediterranean	200 BC
Broccoli	*Brassica oleracea*	Mediterranean	AD 100
Brussels Sprouts	*Brassica oleracea*	Northern Europe	AD 1100
Cabbage	*Brassica oleracea*	Europe	500 BC
Cantaloupe	*Cucumis melo*	Western Asia, Africa	2000 BC
Carrot	*Daucus carota*	Afghanistan	500 BC
Cauliflower	*Brassica oleracea*	Eastern Mediterranean	500 BC
Celery	*Apium graveolens*	Western Asia	850 BC
Cherry	*Prunus avium*	Europe, Asia	300 BC
Chives	*Allium schoenoprasum*	Eastern Mediterranean	100 BC
Corn	*Zea mays*	Central and South America	2000 BC
Cucumber	*Cucumis sativus*	India	200 BC
Date	*Phoenix dactylifera*	Southwestern Asia, Africa	unknown
Garlic	*Allium sativum*	Western Asia	3000 BC
Grape	*Vitus vinifera*	Eastern Mediterranean	4000 BC
Grapefruit	*Citrus paridisi*	West Indies	AD 1600–1750
Green Pea	*Pisum sativum*	Central Asia	2500 BC
Lemon	*Citrus limon*	Southeast Asia	100 BC–AD 100
Lettuce	*Lactuca sativa*	Mediterranean, Asia Minor	500 BC
Lime	*Citrus aurantifolia*	Southeast Asia	100 BC–AD 100
Onion	*Allium cepa*	Western Asia	4000 BC
Orange	*Citrus sinensis*	Indochinese Peninsula	2000 BC
Parsnip	*Pastinaca sativa*	Eastern Europe	100 BC
Peach	*Prunus persica*	China, Western Asia	2000 BC
Peanut	*Arachis hypogaea*	South America	AD 750
Pear	*Pyrus communis*	Western Asia	1000 BC
Pepper	*Capsicium frutescens*	South America	AD 500
Plum	*Prunus domestica*	Western Asia	2000 BC
Potato	*Solanum tuberosum*	Andes of South America	AD 100
Radish	*Raphan us sativus*	China	2000 BC
Rhubarb	*Rheum rhaponticum*	Asia Minor	3000 BC
Soybean	*Soja max* or *Glycine soja*	China	2000 BC
Spinach	*Spinacia oleracea*	Iran	AD 600
Snap Beans	*Phaseolus vulgaris*	The Americas	AD 750
Sweet Potato	*Ipomoea batatas*	Central America	AD 850
Tomato	*Lycopersicum esculentum*	South and Central America	AD 700
Turnip	*Brassica rapa*	Western Asia	500 BC
Watermelon	*Citrullus vulgaris*	Central Africa	2000 BC
Yams	*Dioscorea*	Africa	AD 800

PLANTING TABLE FOR CROPS GROWN IN THE UNITED STATES

Check with your local farm agency for more recent and specific recommendations.

Compiled from USDA Reports

NEW ENGLAND

KIND OF CROP	DATE OF PLANTING	BEST SOIL	AMOUNT MANURE PER ACRE	AMOUNT SEED PER ACRE	WEEKS TO MATURITY
Corn	May 10–30	Sandy or clay loam	8–12 tons	8–12 quarts	14–17
Wheat	Fall or Spring	Clay loam	18 tons	2 bushels	20
Oats	April–May	Strong loam	6–8 tons	2–3 bushels	11–15
Barley	April–June 20	Strong loam	7–8 tons	2–3 bushels	10–15
Rye	April–May, September	Medium loam	7–8 tons	5–6 pecks	40
Buckwheat	June 1–20	Light loam	4–6 tons	1–1¼ bushels	10–15
White Beans	May–June	Sandy loam	7–8 tons	8–16 quarts	8–14
Potatoes	April 15–May 1	Rich loam	15–20 tons	8–20 bushels	12–20
Turnips	July 1–August 3	Sandy loam	10 tons	1 pound	10
Mangels	April 15–May 5	Strong heavy loam	8–15 tons	4–6 pounds	17–22
Tobacco	Seed bed April	Sandy loam	8–12 tons	…	9–12
Hay	…	…	…	…	…

CENTRAL AND WESTERN STATES

KIND OF CROP	DATE OF PLANTING	BEST SOIL	AMOUNT MANURE PER ACRE	AMOUNT SEED PER ACRE	WEEKS TO MATURITY
Corn	April 1–June 1	Black or sandy loam	5–10 tons	6 quarts	16–20
Wheat	Fall–Spring	Strong loam	8 tons	2 bushels	40–42
Oats	April 1–May 1	Clay loam	8 tons	2–3 bushels	12–14
Barley	Fall or Spring	Clay loam	8 tons	2 bushels	11–13
Rye	September 1–30	Light loam	8 tons	1–2 bushels	35–40
Buckwheat	June	Clay loam	5 tons	1–2 bushels	10–12
White Beans	May 10–June 10	Clay loam	8 tons	1½ bushels	12
Potatoes	March 15–June 1	Sandy loam	5–10 tons	5–10 bushels	10–20
Mangels	April–May 15	Sandy loam	8–12 tons	6–8 pounds	22–24
Flax	March 15–May 15	Loam	10–15 tons	2–3 pecks	15–20
Tobacco	Seed bed, March	Sandy loam	8–10 tons	ounce–6 sq. rd.	15–18
Hay	April–May	Clay loam	10 tons	8–15 pounds	…

PLANTING TABLE FOR CROPS GROWN IN THE UNITED STATES

Check with your local farm agency for more recent and specific recommendations.

Compiled from USDA Reports

SOUTHERN STATES

KIND OF CROP	DATE OF PLANTING	BEST SOIL	AMOUNT MANURE PER ACRE	AMOUNT SEED PER ACRE	WEEKS TO MATURITY
Cotton	February–May 15	Sandy loam	...	1–3 bushels	20–30
Corn	February–June	Rich loam	8–10 tons	8 quarts	18–20
Wheat	September–November	Clay loam	8 tons	2 bushels	43
Oats	February–May, September	Clay loam	8–10 tons	2½ bushels	17
Barley	April–May	Clay loam	8–10 tons	2½ bushels	17
Rye	September–October	Clay loam	10 tons	½ bushels	43
White Beans	March–May	Light loam	8 tons	1–2 bushels	7–8
Cabbage	October, March–May	Light loam	6–10 tons	¼–½ pound	14
Watermelon	March 1–May 10	Rich, light loam	5 tons	2–7 pounds	16–20
Onions	February 1–April 10	Loam or muck	...	...	16–24
Potatoes	Janary, February–April	Light loose loam	8–12 tons	8–10 bushels	11–15
Sweet Potatoes	May–June	Sandy loam	...	10–12 bushels	12–15
Pumpkins	April 1–May 1	Rich, light loam	...	4–7 pounds	17–20
Tomatoes	January 1–February 19	Rich, sandy loam	...	4–9 ounces	14–20
Tobacco	Seed bed, March	Sandy loam	8–15 tons	ounce–sq. rd.	18—20
Cow peas	May 1–July 15	Sandy loam	200–300 pounds phosphorus	2–5 pecks	...

MIDDLE STATES

KIND OF CROP	DATE OF PLANTING	BEST SOIL	AMOUNT MANURE PER ACRE	AMOUNT SEED PER ACRE	WEEKS TO MATURITY
Corn	April 20–May 30	Medium loam	8–12 tons	6–8 quarts	16–18
Wheat	September 20–October 20	Loam	8 tons	2 bushels	41–43
Oats	March–May	Moist clay loam	8 tons	2–2½ bushels	16–17
Barley	March–May	Clay loam	8 tons	2–2½ bushels	13–16
Rye	September 1–October 1	Sand or gravel loam	8 tons	1½ bushels	40–43
Buckwheat	June–July	Loam	5 tons	½–1 ½ bushels	8–10
White Beans	May–June	Sandy loam	8 tons	1 ½ bushels	13–14
Potatoes	March–May	Loam	10–18 tons	8–15 bushels	14–22
Sweet Potatoes	May–June	Sandy loam	...	10–12 bushels	10–15
Cabbage	March–July	Clay or sandy loam	...	4–8 ounces	8–15
Turnips	July	Loam	...	2–5 pounds	10–12
Mangels	May	Loam	10–20 tons	10–15 bushels	15–18
Flax	May	Limestone loam	...	20 quarts	8–10
Tobacco	Seed bed, March	Sandy loam	Commercial fertilizer	...	15–20
Hay, timothy	August–October	Clay loam	...	6–8 quarts	...
Hay, clover	February–April	Clay loam	...	6 quarts	...

PLANTING TABLE FOR FAMILY GARDENING

NAME	WHEN TO PLANT	SEED NEEDED for 100 feet	PLANTING DEPTH	DISTANCE APART	COMMENTS
Asparagus	Early spring	75 roots	10 inches	18 inches	Needs rich, well-drained soil and fall mulch.
Beans, green or wax	Early spring to sixty days before frost	1 pound	½ to 1 inch	4 inches	Mulch or cultivate shallowly.
Beans, lima	Midspring to early summer	1 pound	1 inch	10 inches	Make successive plantings.
Beans, pole	Early spring	10 ounces	2 inches	3 to 4 feet	Sow six seeds to a hill and thin to three plants.
Beets	Very early spring to midsummer	1 ounce	½ inch	3 inches	Will need thinning; use pulled plants in salads.
Broccoli	Early spring to early summer	Small packet	¼ inch	18 inches	Start seed in flats and transplant after last spring frost.
Cabbage	Early spring to midsummer	¼ ounce	½ inch	18 to 24 inches	Sow seed in flats and transplant. Late varieties need more space between plants.
Cantaloupe	After danger of spring frost	½ ounce	½ inch	5 feet	Sow six seeds to a hill and thin to the three strongest plants.
Carrots	Early spring to midsummer	½ ounce	½ inch	2 inches	May be mixed with radishes which are harvested much sooner. Carrots will then require less thinning.
Cauliflower	Early spring to early summer	Small packet	¼ inch	18 inches	Sow seed in cold frame and transplant after six weeks. Needs good soil and moisture.
Corn, sweet	Early spring to midsummer	4 ounces	1 inch	15 inches	Make successive plantings for fresh corn over a longer period.
Cucumbers	After danger of spring frost	½ ounce	½ inch	5 feet between hills	Sow six seeds to a hill and thin to three plants.
Lettuce	Very early spring through midsummer	Small packet	¼ inch	16 inches	Thin plants and transplant to another row. Make successive plantings.
Onions	Very early spring	½ ounce seed or 2 pounds sets	½ inch	2 inches seeds; 4 inch sets	When onions are pulled, dry them completely in the sun (approximately two days) before storing.

NAME	WHEN TO PLANT	SEED NEEDED for 100 feet	PLANTING DEPTH	DISTANCE APART	COMMENTS
Parsnips	Early	½ ounce	½ inch	3 inches	Soak seed in tepid water for twenty-four hours before planting. Roots may be left in ground all winter.
Peas	Very early spring	1 pound	2 inches	1 to 2 inches	Soak seeds until they sprout to give them a head start.
Peppers	Start in flats or cold frame about six weeks before last spring frost	Small packet	½ inch	24 inches	Transplant to garden after all danger of frost is past.
Potatoes, sweet	Two weeks after last spring frost	80 plants	slightly below previous level	30 inches	A good crop for poor soil. Cure in the sun for a week before storing.
Potatoes, white	Early spring	½ peck cut seed potatoes	4 inches	12 inches	Let cut seed potatoes dry for twenty-four hours before planting to heal cut edges.
Pumpkins	Spring to midsummer	½ ounce	1 inch	5 feet between hills	Thin to two or three plants per hill. Save space by planting in corn rows.
Radishes	Early spring to late summer	½ ounce	½ inch	1 to 2 inches	Make successive plantings for continuous supply.
Rhubarb	Very early spring	25 roots	2 inches	3 feet	Plant rhubarb where it will not be disturbed and it will keep sprouting for years. Leaves are poisonous.
Spinach	Very early spring to early fall	½ ounce	½ inch	2 to 4 inches	Keep sowing at two-week intervals for continuous supply.
Squash	Early spring to early summer	1 ounce	½ inch	6 feet between hills	Thin to one or two plants per hill.
Tomatoes	Start in flats in February or March	Small packet	½ inch	3 feet	Transplant after danger of frost; set plants 1 to 3 inches deeper than previous level.
Turnips	Spring to early fall	¼ ounce	⅛ inch	2 to 3 inches	Cover seed lightly; may be broadcast when planting large area. Very hardy. Good storage crop to feed livestock.
Watermelon	Early spring	½ ounce	1 inch	8 feet between hills	Thin to one or two plants per hill.

ANNUAL PRECIPITATION
Average Annual Precipitation (Inches)

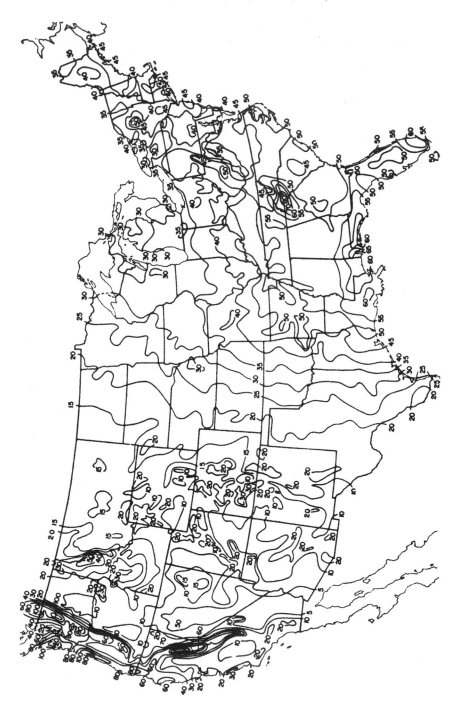

LAST FROST

Average Dates of Last Killing Frost in Spring

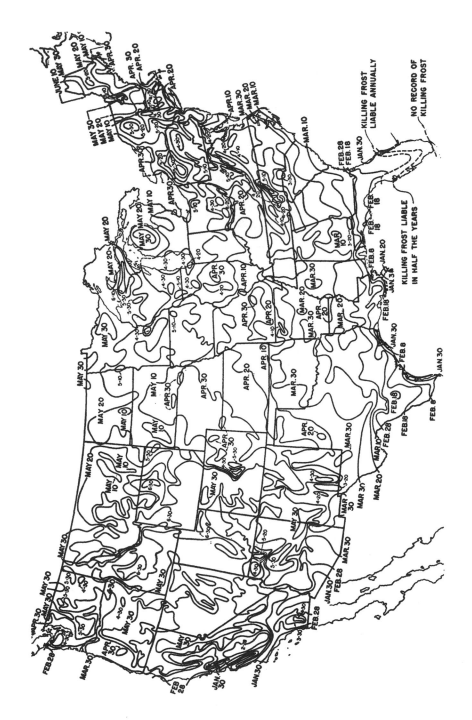

FIRST FROST

Average Dates of First Killing Frost in Fall

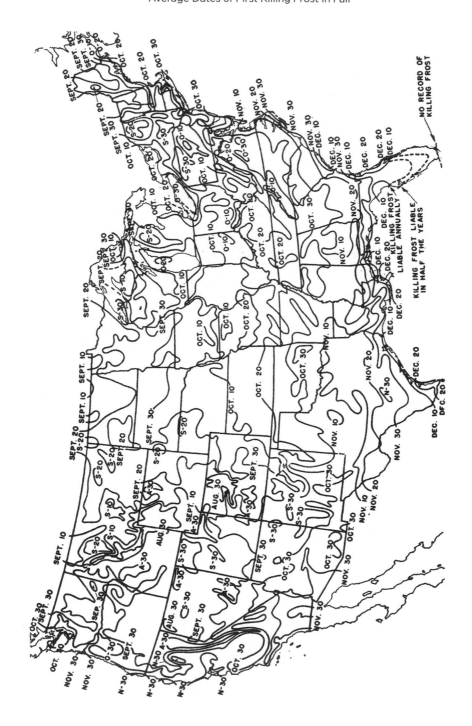

FROST PENETRATION

Average Depth of Frost Penetration (Inches)

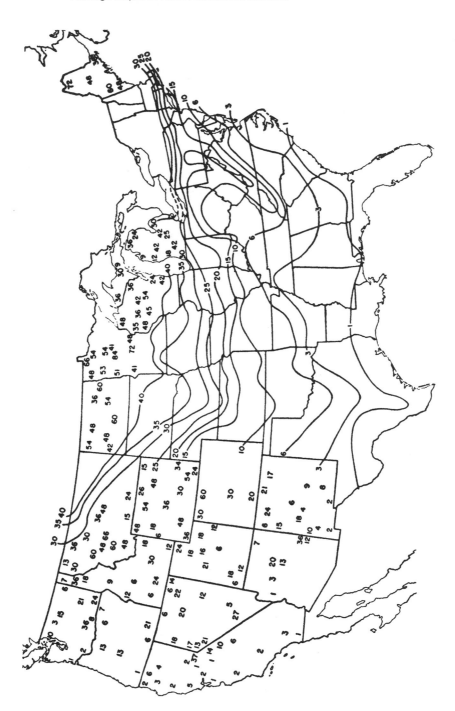

INDEX

fried mush, 188

front-end loaders, 35

frost

first, 228

last, 227

penetration of, 229

frozen food, rescuing, 161

fruit trees

birds and, 92

judging, 116

keeping birds from, 79

money from, 138

planting distance for, 210

supports for, 46

See also individual fruits

fruits

facts on, 220

measuring, 213

planting tables for, 224–225

storing, 211

See also individual fruits

funnels

separating eggs with, 176

shut-off for, 21

for string, 27

furniture

cleaning with newspaper, 155

cleaning with salt, 122

G

garbage can

extending life of, 143

protecting with spring, 62

garden in a bottle, 182–183

garden pests, 200–207

garlic

facts on, 28

for small cuts, 187

gates, 89

germination temperatures, 19

gestation table, 198

ghost towns, 106

gingerbread, 162

glass

cleaning with newspaper, 123, 155

fogging and, 32

glass slivers, cotton and, 90

glasses, unsticking, 129

glassware, 86

gloves, as tool holster, 127

glycerin, 32

gourds, growing, 117–118

grain, sprouting, 48–50

grain sacks, patching, 33

granola, recipe for, 14

grape, as cosmetic, 41

grapefruit seeds, sprouting, 184

grapevines, 29

gravel, under outdoor faucet, 60

grease

protecting floor from, 188

wallpaper and, 116

grindstones, cleaning, 38

grumps, wild violets and, 163

H

half hitch, 74

hammer, increasing leverage of, 169

hand trucks, path for, 32

handles, for buckets, 35

hands

cold and, 129

dry and chapped, 101

moisturizer for, 159

protecting with soap, 184

hanging scale, doubling capacity of, 84

hardtack, 123

hay

making, 59–60

measuring, 212

hay fever, 187

headaches, 39

headlights, reflecting with mirror, 67

hens

feeding eggshells, 103

health of, 41